From Ancient Egypt

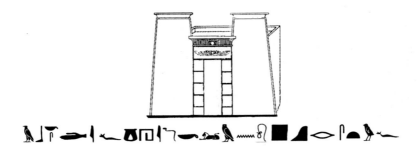

To

GREECE

ΑΒΧΔΕΦΓΗΙϑΚΛΜΝΟΠΘΡΣΤΥςΩ#ΨΖ

THIRD EDITION - EXPANDED

Black and Nobel Books
Retail and Wholesale
215-965-1559
1409 W Erie Ave
Philadelphia PA 19140
Email BlackNobel1@yahoo.com
Monday-Sunday 7am-7pm
www.weshiptoprisons.com

Cruzian Mystic Books

P.O.Box 570459
Miami, Florida, 33257
(305) 378-6253 Fax: (305) 378-6253

First U.S. edition © 1998 By Reginald Muata Ashby

Second edition © 2002 By Reginald Muata Ashby

Third edition © 2005 By Reginald Muata Ashby

The author is available for group lectures and individual counseling. For further information contact the publisher.

Ashby, Muata
African Dionysus: The Ancient Egyptian Origins of Ancient Greek Myth, Culture, Religion and Philosophy, and Modern Masonry, Greek Fraternities, Sororities, ISBN: 1-884564-47-X

Library of Congress Cataloging in Publication Data

1 Egyptian Mythology 2 Spirituality 3 Religion 4 Yoga 5 Self Help.

Also by Muata Ashby

Egyptian Yoga: The Philosophy of Enlightenment
Initiation Into Egyptian Yoga: The Secrets of Sheti
Egyptian Proverbs: Tempt Tchaas,
Mystical Wisdom Teachings and Meditations
The Egyptian Yoga Exercise Workout Book
Mysticism of Ushet Rekhat: Worship of the Divine Mother
See back section for more listings

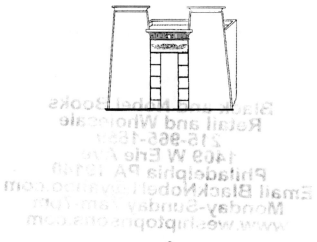

THE SEMA INSTITUTE

The term "Sma" (Sema, the term "Smai Tawi" Higher and lower Self, Sema Institute of Yoga, founded by Dr. Muata ("Seba" is a Kamitan spiritual preceptor and abbreviation of the word sublime goal the Ancient Kamitan upliftment of humanity and attainment of Smai primary goals are: Firstly to ancient spiritual teachings in forms of communication. instruction and training in the including Kamitan (Ancient Egyptian)

Sama) is a derivative of meaning union of the i.e. Yoga. Thus, The Temple of Aset, Ashby, Seba Maa term that means "Maa" is an "Maat") has as its dissemination of the Teachings for the through the practice Taui (Divine Union). Its provide the wisdom of books, courses and other Secondly, to provide expert various yogic disciplines Religion and Mystical Philosophy,

Christian Gnosticism, Indian Mysticism which are outgrowths of Kamitan Religion. Thirdly, to promote world peace and Universal Love. As Kamitan culture, from Africa, brought forth civilization, religion and mystical philosophy to the world, a primary focus of our tradition is to identify and acknowledge the Kamitan principles within all religions and to relate them to each other in order to promote their deeper understanding and show the essential unity. In our view, Kamitan Philosophy can be the foundation for the rebuilding of African culture and bridge the gap between religious differences, which will promote harmony and peace among peoples of differing creeds and ethnic backgrounds. The Institute is open to all that believe in the principles of peace, non-violence and spiritual emancipation regardless of sex, race, or creed. The Sema Institute is an organization, which recognizes the unifying principles in all spiritual and traditions throughout the world.

"Per Aset" means Temple of Aset. In Ancient times the Temple of Aset was a mecca for all mystics, saints and sages. It was a place where the disciplines of Smai Tawi was disseminated and practiced and its influence touched Ancient Greek culture and Ancient Roman culture as well as early Christianity. The Per Aset, now based in Miami, Florida, USA, follows the rediscovered disciplines of Kamitan Smai Tawi (Yoga) and teaches these through classes, worship services and publications.

Priest, Author, lecturer, poet, philosopher, musician, publisher, counselor and spiritual preceptor and founder of the Sema Institute-Temple of Aset, Muata Ashby was born in Brooklyn, New York City, and grew up in the Caribbean. His family is from Puerto Rico and Barbados. Displaying an interest in ancient civilizations and the Humanities, Seba Maa began studies in the area of religion and philosophy and achieved doctorates in these areas while at the same time he began to collect his research into what would later become several books on the subject of the origins of Yoga Philosophy and practice in ancient Africa (Ancient Egypt) and also the origins of Christian Mysticism in Ancient Egypt.

Seba Maa (Muata Abhaya Ashby) holds a Doctor of Philosophy Degree in Religion, and a Doctor of Divinity Degree in Holistic Health. He is also a Pastoral Counselor and Teacher of Yoga Philosophy and Discipline. Dr. Ashby received his Doctor of Divinity Degree from and is an adjunct faculty member of the American Institute of Holistic Theology. Dr. Ashby is a certified as a PREP Relationship Counselor. Dr. Ashby has been an independent researcher and practitioner of Egyptian Yoga, Indian Yoga, Chinese Yoga, Buddhism and mystical psychology as well as Christian Mysticism. Dr. Ashby has engaged in Post Graduate research in advanced Jnana, Bhakti and Kundalini Yogas at the Yoga Research Foundation. He has extensively studied mystical religious traditions from around the world and is an accomplished lecturer, musician, artist, poet, screenwriter, playwright and author of over 25 books on Kamitan yoga and spiritual philosophy. He is an Ordained Minister and Spiritual Counselor and also the founder the Sema Institute, a non-profit organization dedicated to spreading the wisdom of Yoga and the Ancient Egyptian mystical traditions. Further, he is the spiritual leader and head priest of the Per Aset or Temple of Aset, based in Miami, Florida. Thus, as a scholar, Dr. Muata Ashby is a teacher, lecturer and researcher. However, as a spiritual leader, his title is *Seba,* which means Spiritual Preceptor.

Seba Dr. Ashby began his research into the spiritual philosophy of Ancient Africa (Egypt) and India and noticed correlations in the culture and arts of the two countries. This was the catalyst for a successful book series on the subject called "Egyptian Yoga". Now he has created a series of musical compositions which explore this unique area of music from ancient Egypt and its connection to world music.

TABLE OF CONTENTS

Cicero, Marcus Tullius (106-43 BC)

There is no more important knowledge to a people than their history and culture. If they do not know this they are lost in the world.

—Cicero, Roman Philosopher (106-43 BC)

INTRODUCTION

FROM
EGYPT TO GREECE

How to Compare Cultures and Determine Their Similarities and Differences?

This insightful manual is a quick reference to Ancient Egyptian mythology and philosophy and its correlation to what later became known as Greek and Rome mythology and philosophy. It outlines the basic tenets of the mythologies and shows the ancient origins of Greek culture in Ancient Egypt.

In order to commence this study it is necessary to have a basic understanding of the parameters that will be used to compare the Ancient Egyptian/Nubian culture with the ancient Greek culture. Therefore, the following section outlines the cultural comparison method that will be used. Then the basic aspects of Ancient Egyptian/Nubian culture and ancient Greek culture will be determined and compared using the cultural comparison method outlined in the following section. The proper evidences will be presented and categorized so that the reader may have the opportunity to review them directly.

Cultural Interactions, Their Effect on the Emergence of New Religions and The Adoption of Myths, Symbols and Traditions from one Culture to Another

How Do Cultures Interact?

How do people from different cultures interact? How do religions borrow and or adopt myths, symbols, philosophies or traditions from each other? Several examples from history will be used here to show how spirituality, as an aspect of one culture, was influenced by other cultures. The following essays relate documented historical accounts of cultural interactions of the past between two or more civilizations. They are included to illustrate how the process of cultural interaction leads to cultural exchanges, adoptions, inculturations, etc., as well as the emergence of new religions and philosophies out of teachings received from other cultures. They will also serve to provide insight into the manner in which ancient African history has diffused into present day cultures by introducing various basic principles of cultural interaction and how these interactions are to be recognized and studied.

Principles of Cultural Expression

What is Culture?

The concept of culture will be an extremely important if not the most important aspect of humanity to our study and so it will be a developing theme throughout our study. The following principles are offered as a standard for understanding what culture is, how it manifests in the world, and how that manifestation affects other cultures.

> **cul·ture** (kŭl′chər) *n.* **1.a.** The totality of socially transmitted behavior patterns, arts, beliefs, institutions, and all other products of human work and thought.
>
> -American Heritage Dictionary

Purpose of Culture:

- **Culture is a people's window on whatever they perceive as reality (to understand the world around them) and their concept of self.**

- Culture is a conditioning process, necessary for the early development of a human being.

- Culture defines the agenda of a society (government, economics, religion). Religion is the most powerful force driving culture.

The Study of Culture

Cultural Anthropology is the study concerned with depicting the character of various cultures, and the similarities and differences between them. This branch of anthropology is concerned with all cultures whether simple or complex and its methodology entails a holistic view, field work, comparative analysis (both within the society and cross-culturally), and a tendency to base theoretical models on empirical data rather than vice versa.[1]

Ethnology, is the comparative study of cultures. Using ethnographic material from two or more societies, ethnology can attempt to cover their whole cultural range or concentrate on a single cultural trait. Ethnology was originally a term covering the whole of anthropology, toward the end of the 19th century historical ethnology was developed in an attempt to trace cultural diffusion. Now ethnologists concentrate on cross-cultural studies, using statistical methods of analysis.[2]

---

[1] Random House Encyclopedia Copyright (C) 1983,1990
[2] ibid.

While this work may be considered as a form of cultural anthropology and ethnology, it will also serve as an overview of the theological principles espoused by the cultures in question. The techniques used in this book to compare cultures will lay heavy emphasis on iconographical and philosophical factors as well as historical evidences, as opposed to statistical methods of analysis. It is possible to focus on the apparent differences between cultures and religious philosophies. This has been the predominant form of philosophical discourse and study of Western scholarship. The seeming differences between religions have led to innumerable conflicts between the groups throughout history, all because of the outer expression of religion. However, throughout this work I will attempt to focus on the synchretic aspects of the philosophies and religions in question because it is in the similarities wherein harmony is to be found; harmony in the form of concurrence in ideas and meaning. In light of this idea of harmony, it is possible to look at the folklore of cultural traditions throughout the world and see the same psycho-mythological message being espoused through the various cultural masks. They are all referring to the same Supreme Being. While giving commentary and adding notes, which I feel will be helpful to the understanding of the texts which I will compare, I have endeavored to use the actual texts wherever possible so that you, the reader, may see for yourself and make your own judgment.

Culture is everything a human being learns from living in a society including language, history, values and religion, etc. However, the outer learning masks an inner experience. Spirituality is that movement to transcend culture and discover the essence of humanity. This Ultimate Truth, known by many names, such as God, Goddess, Supreme Being, and their varied names in all of the world's cultures, is revered by all peoples, though culture and folk differences color the expression of that reverence. This is what is called the *folk expression of religion based on culture and local traditions.* For example, the same Ultimate Reality is expressed by Christians based on European culture and traditions, as God. The same Ultimate Reality is expressed by Muslims based on Arab culture and traditions as Allah. The same Ultimate and Transcendental Reality is worshipped by Jews based on Hebrew culture and traditions. The same Ultimate and Transcendental Reality is worshipped by the Chinese based on Chinese culture and traditions, etc. If people who practice religion stay at the outer levels (basing their religious practice and wisdom on their culture, myths and traditions), they will always see differences between faiths. Religion has three aspects, myth, ritual and mysticism. Myth and ritual relate to the folk expression of religion, whereas mysticism relates to that movement of self-discovery that transcends all worldly concepts. Mysticism allows any person in any religion to discover that the same Supreme Being is being worshipped by all under different names and forms, and by different means. It is the worship itself and the object of that worship that underlies the human movement. Therefore, the task of all true mystics (spiritual seekers) is to go beyond the veil of the outer forms of religion, including the symbols, but more importantly, the doctrines, rituals and traditions (see model below).

Below: The Culture-Myth Model, showing how the folk expression of religion is based on culture and local traditions.

Below: The Culture-Myth Models of two world spiritual systems, showing how the folk expression of each religion is based on culture and local traditions.

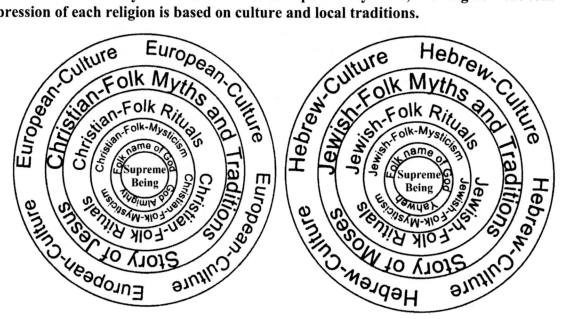

In studying and comparing diverse groups of peoples, we are essentially comparing their cultures. Culture includes all activities and manners of manifestation, which a group of peoples have developed over the period of their existence. Cultural expressions may fall under the following categories. An important theme to understand throughout this study is that the underlying principle purpose or function of culture in a given society may be equal to that of another culture, but the mode of manifestation will invariably be unique. The exception to this is when there is contact between the cultures. Some coincidental similarities may be found between two cultures that have never been in contact with each other, but the frequency and quality of those correlations belies the superficiality of the contact or random nature of the correlation. Similarities and commonalties pointing to a strong interrelationship between the cultures can be expected when comparing two apparently different cultures if the cultures in question have sustained some form of contact or emerged from a common origin. The degree of parallelism and harmony between varied cultures can be measured by the nature and frequency of synchronicity or concordance of the factors from each culture being compared.

In the study of the theology[3] of the varied religious traditions of the world (comparative religious studies), it is very possible to encounter similar general points of philosophical conceptualization in reference to the institutions for the worship of a spiritual being or divinities. In other words, religion itself is a point of commonality in all cultures and all historical periods. The basic common ideas manifested by cultures in and of themselves cannot be used as justification for concluding that there is a common origin or common cultural concept being expressed by two different religions. So just because two religions espouse the idea that there is a Supreme Being or that Supreme Being is one, a scholar cannot conclude that the religions have a common origin or that their concept in reference to the entity being worshipped is compatible. The factor of theology is there in both cultures, but the mode of expression may be different, and even if it is not different, it may have been arrived at by different means. That is, the myth-plot system of the religion may contain various episodes which are not synchronous, thus expressing a divergent theological idea even though it may ultimately lead to the same philosophical realization. The forms of iconography may show depictions of the divinities in different situations and engaged in different activities. The rituals and traditions related to the myths of the religions may be carried out in different ways and at different times. These deviating factors point to a different origin for the two cultures in question. On the other hand it is possible to have a common origin and later observe some divergence from the original expression while the theme and plot of myth within the religion stays essentially the same. This finding may not only point to a common origin, but also to a divergent practice in later times. If two traditions are shown to have been in contact, and they are found to have common elements in the basis of their espoused philosophy, as well as the manifestation of that philosophy through iconography, artifacts, rituals, traditions, myth-plots, etc., then this determination suggests a strong correlation in the origin, and or contact throughout the development of the cultures in question. In order to make such a judgment, it is necessary to identify and match several essential specific criteria or factors confirming the commonality or convergence indicating a communal[4] origin and or common cultural factor.

---

[3] **the·ol·o·gy** (thē-ŏl′ə-jē) *n., pl.* **the·ol·o·gies.** *Abbr.* **theol. 1.** The study of the nature of God and religious truth; rational inquiry into religious questions. (American Heritage Dictionary)

[4] **com·mu·nal** *(kə-myōō′nəl, kŏm′yə-) adj.* **1.** *Of or relating to a commune.* **2.** *Of or relating to a community.* **3.a.** *Of, belonging to, or shared by the people of a community; public.* **b.** *Marked by collective ownership and control of goods and property.* (American Heritage Dictionary)

Table of Categories of Cultural Expression and Factors of Cultural Expression

Categories of Cultural Expression

1. Art: design (lay out), composition-style, and pattern
2. Artifacts - tools
3. Customs and Traditions - secular
4. Ethnicity
5. Folklore - legend
6. Form –Architecture
7. Language
8. Music and Performing arts – Theater
9. Philosophy
   a. Social
      i. Economics
      ii. Legal system
      iii. Government

10. Religion-Spirituality
    a. Myth and Mythological motif
    b. Customs and Traditions - Ritual
    c. Mystical philosophy

These categories can be correlated by matches in the following features:

Factors of Cultural Expression

Myth and Religion Related Correlation Methods

1. Gender concordance[5]
2. Iconography
    a. Conventional
    b. Naturalistic
    c. Stylized
3. Myth-
    a. Plot
    b. Motif [6]
    c. Theme
4. Rituals and or Traditions
    a. Function
    b. Actions performed
5. Scriptural Synchronicity

General Correlation Methods

1. Evidence of Contact
    a. <u>Concurrent</u> – cultures develop at the same time - equal exchanges relationship
    b. <u>Dependent</u> – one culture depends on the other for technology, instruction - Donor – recipient relationship
    c. <u>Common Origins</u>- Cultures originate from the same point with the same primary categories and then branch off and develop independently.
    d. <u>Eye witness accounts</u>
    e. <u>Self descriptions</u> – Their own writings acknowledge the contact.
    f. <u>Pacts</u> – treaties, etc.
2. Form
    a. Architecture
    b. Artifacts
3. Function – usage -purpose
    a. Architecture
    b. Artifacts
4. Grammar
    a. Phonetics
    b. Linguistics
5. Historical Events
    c. Common origins of the Genesis of the Cultures
    d. Concurrent events throughout the history of the cultures
6. Genetics
7. Nationality

---

[5] Gender of characters in the myth
[6] Myth and Mythological motif (subject matter)

Definitions of the Categories of Cultural Expression and Factors of Cultural Expression system of Cultural Anthropology

The following are general designations to describe the dominand cultures or world views being expored in this volume. These do not include all the cultures of the world.

Definition: *Western Culture* = For the purpose of this study, "Western Culture" constitutes the traditions, beliefs and productions of those people who have developed societies in the western part of the continent of Asia (Europe), and who see this part of the world as their homeland or view the world from the perspective of the traditions (including religion) and norms of that region (Eurocentric). This includes the United States of America, Canada, as well as other countries which have societies that are descendants from the European colonial rulers, and which control the governments of the former colonies (including Australia, New Zealand, etc.). Also included are countries where the political order is supported or enforced (neocolonialism or capitalistic globalism) by the Western countries. In a broad sense, Western Culture is a way of thinking that has spread far a field and now includes all who adopt the philosophies, norms and customs of that region, including secularism and religions that are predominantly Christian, followed by the Jewish and Islamic.

Definition: *Arab Culture* = For the purpose of this study, "Arab Culture" constitutes the traditions, beliefs and productions of those people who have developed societies in the south-western part of the continent of Asia (Arabia, Mesopotamia and now also north Africa), and who see this part of the world as their homeland or view the world from the perspective of the traditions (including religion) and norms of that region. In a broad sense, Arab Culture is a way of thinking that has spread far a field and now includes all who adopt the philosophies, norms and customs of that region.

Definition: *Eastern Culture* = For the purpose of this study, "Eastern Culture" constitutes the traditions, beliefs and productions of those people who have developed societies in the Eastern part of the continent of Asia (India, China) and who see this part of the world as their homeland or view the world from the perspective of the traditions (including religion) and norms of that region (Indocentric). In a broad sense, Eastern Culture is a way of thinking that includes all who adopt the philosophies, norms and customs of that region.

Definition: *African Culture* = For the purpose of this study, "African Culture" or "Southern Culture" constitutes the traditions, beliefs and productions of those people who have developed societies in the continent of Africa (Sub-Saharan countries) and who see this part of the world as their homeland or view the world from the perspective of the native traditions (including religion) and norms of that region (Africentric {Afrocentric}). In a broad sense, African Culture is a way of thinking that includes all who adopt the philosophies, norms and customs of that region.

The following definitions are the two simple keys to understanding the Categories of Cultural Expression and Factors of Cultural Expression system of Cultural Anthropology.

Definition: *Categories of Cultural Expression* = Broad areas whereby a culture expresses itself in the world. Exp. Religion is a broad category of cultural expression. All cultures may have a religion, however, those religions are not necessarily the same. What are the differences? How can these differences be classified and compared?

Definition: *Factors of Cultural Expression* = methods or means by which a culture expresses its categories. Exp. Myth is a factor of religion by which a religion is expressed in a unique way by a particular culture. In determining the common elements of different religions, there are several factors which can be used as criteria to determine whether or not cultures had common origins. If cultures are related, they will use common stories or other common factors or patterns to express the main doctrines of the religion or spiritual path, social philosophy, etc. These are listed below. The following section introduces the categories of cultural expression as well as factors or aspects of the Categories which reflect the unique forms of manifestation within a given culture.

The Universal Vision of Comparative Mythology

In the book *Comparative Mythology,* the author, Jaan Puhvel, traces the term "myth" to the writings of Homer (900 B.C.E.), with the usage *épos kai muthos* 'word and speech.' In the writings of Homer and the ancient Greek writers of tragic plays, Jaan Puhvel also sees that the term can mean "tale, story, narrative," and that this story or tale can be without reference to truth content.[7] Truth content here implies a historical or real relationship to time and space events or realities. In the writings of the later Greek authors such as Herodotus, Puhvel sees a different meaning in the term Mûthos, that of fictive "narrative," "tall tale," and "legend." It is felt that Herodotus spoke of Mûthos as those items he himself found incredulous, and used the term *logos* for that information which he felt was more or less based on truth or facts. Further, with the writings of Plato, a new interpretation of the terms emerge, as Mûthos takes on a different character in relation to logos. Mûthos (myth) is more of a non-rational basis for understanding existence while logos is seen as the rational basis. In Western Culture, the term logos has come to be associated with absolute knowledge and logical thinking and analysis. In terms of mysticism, it is understood as the Divine intelligence, consciousness, which permeates and enlivens matter, time and space. In later times logos came to be known as 'the Word' or inner, esoteric spiritual knowledge, and in early Christianity, Jesus became 'the word (logos) made flesh.' From these origins and many deprecating arguments from the church and western scientists, through the middle and dark ages and into the renaissance period of Western Culture, the meaning of the word, myth, in modern times, has come to be understood primarily in Western Culture as a colloquialism to refer to anything devoid of a basis in truth or reality. Saying "it's a myth" has come to be understood by most people as a reference to something that does not contain even a fragment of truth. Myth has come to be thought of in terms of being neurotic expressions of ancient religions, movie ideas spinning out of Hollywood, governments telling myths (lies) or Madison Avenue advertising (the "myth-makers"), etc., in other words, something without any truth or factual basis. In ancient times, Plato referred to the term 'mythologia' as meaning "myth-telling," as opposed to storytelling. Modern scholars refer to this term as mythology (the study of myth), which, until recently, primarily meant Greek Mythology. The body of ancient Greek narratives relating to the legends and traditions connected to the gods and goddesses of Greece are referred to as the mythological narratives.

---

[7] *Comparative Mythology,* Jaan Puhvel

Mythology is the study of myths. Myths (mythos) are stories which relate human consciousness to the transcendental essence of reality. This work is essentially a study in comparative mythology. It seeks to discover the common elements in two or more systems of mythos in order to understand their deeper meaning and develop the larger picture as they are fitted into the overall patchwork of traditions throughout history. In effect, this work attempts to show a connection and continuity between traditions that will enable the comprehension of them as a flow of the one primordial and recurrent theme of self-discovery. In such a study, there are always some who object, maintaining that differences are the overriding defining factors in any aspect of life. But this way of thinking is incongruous in the face of all the scientific evidence pointing to a common origin for all humanity as well as of Creation itself. Therefore, it seems that the movement to understand our common bonds as human beings should as well move into to the arena of the mythology and psychology. In this manner we may discover that what binds us is greater than that which tears us apart, for when we examine the arguments and concepts used to separate, they are inevitably derived from emotion, politics, misconception or superficialities based on ignorance. These lead to major controversies, debates, refutations and egoistic opinions founded on nothing but faith in rumors, conjectures and speculation, and not on first hand examination of the traditions from the point of view of a practitioner. Joseph Campbell summed up this issue as follows.

> "Perhaps it will be objected that in bringing out the correspondences I have overlooked the differences between the various Oriental and Occidental, modern, ancient, and primitive traditions. The same objection might be brought, however, against any textbook or chart of anatomy, where the physiological variations of race are disregarded in the interest of a basic general understanding of the human physique. There are of course differences between the numerous mythologies and religions of mankind, but this is a book about the similarities; and once these are understood the differences will be found to be much less great than is popularly (and politically) supposed. My hope is that a comparative elucidation may contribute to the perhaps not-quite desperate cause of those forces that are working in the present world for unification, not in the name of some ecclesiastical or political empire, but in the sense of human mutual understanding. As we are told in the Vedas: "Truth is one, the sages speak of it by many names."
>
> -J.C. New York City June 10, 1948

In *Comparative Mythology*, Puhvel underscored the importance of myth and the operation of myth as an integral, organic component of human existence. It is a defining aspect of social order in which human existence is guided to discover the "sacred" and "timeless" nature of self and Creation. He also discusses how the "historical landscape" becomes "littered with the husks of desiccated myths" even as "societies pass and religious systems change," remaining submerged in the traditions and epics of modern times.

> "Myth in the technical sense is a serious object of study, because true myth is by definition deadly serious to its originating environment. In myth are expressed the thought patterns by which a group formulates self-cognition and self-realization, attains self-knowledge and self-confidence, explains its own source and being and that of its surroundings, and sometimes tries to chart its destinies. By myth man has lived, died, and-all too often-killed. Myth operates by bringing a sacred (and hence essentially and paradoxically "timeless") past to bear preemptively on the present and inferentially on the future ("as it was in the beginning, is now, and ever shall be"). Yet in the course of human events

societies pass and religious systems change; the historical landscape gets littered with the husks of desiccated myths. These are valuable nonmaterial fossils of mankind's recorded history, especially if still embedded in layers of embalmed religion, as part of a stratum of tradition complete with cult, liturgy, and ritual. Yet equally important is the next level of transmission, in which the sacred narrative has already been secularized, myth has been turned into saga, sacred time into heroic past, gods into heroes, and mythical action into "historical" plot. Many genuine "national epics" constitute repositories of tradition where the mythical underpinnings have been submerged via such literary transposition. Old chronicles can turn out to be "prose epics" where the probing modem mythologist can uncover otherwise lost mythical traditions. Such survival is quite apart from, or wholly incidental to, the conscious exploitative use of myth in literature, as raw material of fiction, something that Western civilization has practiced since artful verbal creativity began."[8]

The key element in myth is its metaphorical purpose in that its stories and characters are designed to provide a reference towards an etiological, moral or spiritual message that transcends the story itself. This means that there is an exoteric meaning which refers to the events and circumstances in the story, which may or may not have a basis in fact, and also an esoteric or mystical meaning which refers to a deeper teaching or message which transcends the boundaries of the events in the story. This message is spiritual in nature when the myth is religious. Through the myth many ideas which are not easily explained in rational, logical terms can be freely explored and elucidated in imaginative and colorful ways. Mystical myths are particularly important because their purpose is to point to where the answers to the most important questions of every individual may be found. Everyone is searching for answers to questions like "Who am I really?" "Is this all that I am?" "Where do I come from?" "What is death?" and "What is my purpose in life?" Through myths, the teachings of Sages and Saints can take full flight, free of the constraints of normal grammatical or thematic boundaries. Therefore, myths are an ideal way to impart spiritual truths which transcend ordinary human experiences and ordinary human concepts of rationality.

The question of the similarities between myths, rituals and traditions has been explored in the book *"The Mythic Image,"* where the late world renowned mythologist, Joseph Campbell explained the concepts surrounding the treatment of equivalent elements and symbols that can be seen in myths from apparently separate cultures.

One explanation that has been proposed to account for the appearance of homologous structures and often even identical motifs in the myths and rites of widely separate cultures is psychological: namely, to cite a formula of James G. Frazer in *The Golden Bough,* that such occurrences are most likely *"the effect of similar causes acting alike on the similar constitution of the human mind in different countries and under different skies."*

There are, however, instances that cannot be accounted for in this way, and then suggest the need for another interpretation: for example, in India the number of years assigned to an eon[9] is 4,320,000; whereas in the Icelandic *Poetic Edda* it is declared that in Othin's warrior hall, Valhall, there are 540 doors, through each of

---

[8] *Comparative Mythology,* Jaan Puhvel
[9] A "Great Cycle" *(Mahayuga)* of cosmic time.

which, on the "day of the war of the wolf,"[10] 800 battle-ready warriors will pass to engage the antigods in combat.' But 540 times 800 equals 432,000!

Moreover, a Chaldean[11] priest, Berossos, writing in Greek ca. 289 B.C., reported that according to Mesopotamian belief 432,000 years elapsed between the crowning of the first earthly king and the coming of the deluge.

No one, I should think, would wish to argue that these figures could have arisen independently in India, Iceland, and Babylon.[12]

Campbell explains that there is a view that the commonalties observed in myth, symbolism, etc., are a factor of psychological forces that are common to all human beings. One example of this concept is that every human being on earth feels the desire for happiness. Therefore, when we see people from different places (*"different countries and under different skies"*), who have never met each other, pursuing happiness in similar ways, we should not be surprised. However, Campbell makes the point that some coincidences go beyond the nature of conformity due to a primal urge. Those concurrences can only be explained by a closer relationship, because the uniformity of "structure" or configuration of the myths as well as the usage of the exact same symbols and rites could only occur when there is an intimate relationship between the cultures. In other words, the two pursuers of happiness can be explained by the theory of common urges, however, the pursuit of happiness using the same procedures (rites or rituals), the same way of defining happiness, the same philosophy of how to go about looking for happiness, idealizing happiness in the same way (myth), representing happiness the same way (symbolism), etc., are signs that the cultures have had a common origin, upbringing, socialization, indoctrination, contact, etc. This occurs when a culture "diffuses" some new technology, philosophy or cultural element to another culture. Campbell continues:

> A second approach to interpretation has therefore been proposed, based on the observation that at certain identifiable times, in identifiable places, epochal transformations of culture have occurred, the effects of which have been diffused to the quarters of the earth; and that along with these there have traveled constellations of associated mythological systems and motifs.[13]

Thus, Campbell introduces another way to understand the commonalties observed in separate cultures that cannot be explained by the theory of similar forces operating on the minds of separate individuals. There are milestones in history wherein major social events or advancements in culture affect humanity as if like a ripple of water caused by a stone being dropped into a calm lake. The resulting undulations of powerful concepts, and technologies move along the trade and communication routs, the arteries of human communication and interaction, spreading (diffusing) the advanced knowledge in waves across the cultural ocean of humanity throughout the world. Like a surfer, being carried along with the force of the wave, so too the concepts and symbols move across the human landscape being empowered by the innate human desire to achieve higher understanding and the intellectual capacity to recognize something better or a new way to express the same treasured truths. This important principle related to the transference of ideas and symbols between cultures was seminal to Campbell's groundbreaking work as a teacher of comparative mythology in the West.

---

[10] i.e., at the ending of the cosmic eon, Wagner's *Götterdämmerung.*

[11] According to the Egyptians, Diodorus reports, the Chaldaens were *"a colony of their priests that Belus had transported on the Euphrates and organized on the model of the mother-caste, and this colony continues to cultivate the knowledge of the stars, knowledge that it brought from the homeland."*

[12] *The Mythic Image*, Joseph Campbell

[13] *The Mythic Image*, Joseph Campbell

Psychomythology

Mystical teaching holds that the essence of Creation and therefore, of each individual human being, is transcendental; it transcends the ordinary bounds of mental perception and understanding. However, all human experiences occur in and through the mind. Therefore, the heart of all human experiences, be they painful or pleasurable, is rooted in the mind. The purpose of myth is to bridge the gap between the limited human mind and its conscious, worldly level and that which transcends all physicality as well as the mind and senses. Thus, religious myths, which will be our primary focus in this volume, must be understood in the light of their psychological and mystical (transcending body, mind and senses) implications. We will refer to this concept by a new term: *"Psycho-Mythology."*

So the term *"psycho,"* as it is used here, must be understood as far more than simply that which refers to the mind in the worldly sense. The term "psycho" must be understood to mean everything that constitutes human consciousness in all of its stages and states, but most importantly, the subconscious and unconscious levels of mind. *"Mythology"* here refers to the study of the codes, messages, ideas, directives, stories, culture, beliefs, etc., that affect the personality through the conscious, subconscious and unconscious aspects of the mind of an individual, specifically those effects which result in psycho-spiritual transformation, that is, a transpersonal or transcendental change in the personality of an individual which leads to the discovery of the transcendental reality behind all existence.

A myth should never be understood literally even though some of its origins may involve actual events or actions, otherwise one will miss the transcendental message being related through the metaphor. This would be like going to a theater to see a fictional movie or reading a fantasy novel, and believing it to be real. However, as a movie or novel may be based on unreal events and yet carry an important message which is imparted through the medium of actors, a plot and so on, mystical myths are not to be understood as being completely baseless nor as having been put together purely for entertainment or as "primitive mumbo-jumbo." Myths constitute a symbolic language that speaks to people in psycho-symbolic ways, satisfying their conscious need for entertainment, but also affecting the subconscious and unconscious mind and its need for spiritual evolution. This psychological language of myths can lead people to understand and experience the transcendental truths of existence, which cannot be easily expressed in words.

Myth is the first stage of religion and the reenactment of the myth constitutes the second level religion: Ritual.[14] Myths constitute the heart and soul of rituals. Myth is a mystical language for transmitting and teaching the principles of life and creation. Rituals are the medium through which the myths are practiced, lived and realized.

The study of religious mythical stories is important to gain insight into the *"Psycho-Mythology"* or psychological implications of myth for the spiritual transformation of the individual which leads to the attainment of Enlightenment. Enlightenment implies the attainment of an expanded state of consciousness, termed as *"awet ab,"* dilation (expansion) of the heart in Ancient Egyptian Mystical Philosophy, in which there is a full and perfect awareness of one's existence beyond the mind and body. Thus, when you delve into a myth, you must expect more than just entertainment. You should be equipped with the knowledge which will allow you to decipher the hidden meanings in the story so that you may also begin to experience and benefit from them on a personal level, i.e. live the myth and on a spiritual level, i.e. attain enlightenment. Only then

---

[14] *Resurrecting Osiris*, Muata Ashby, 1997

will a person be able to engender a real transformation in their life which will lead you to true fulfillment and happiness as well as contentment. This is the third level of religious practice, the mystical or metaphysical level.

The Keys to Reading and Understanding a Myth

Religion without myth not only fails to work, it also fails to offer man the promise of unity with the transpersonal and eternal.

—C. G. Jung (1875-1961)

Key #1: Myths (Religious/Mystical) are relevant to our lives in the present.

The first and most important key to understanding a myth is comprehending that the myth is not talking about some ancient personality or story which occurred a long time ago and which has no relevance to the present. In fact, the myth is speaking about you. It is a story about human life, its origins, its destiny, its plight and the correct action, in the present, which is based on the same principles of the past, for leading a truly successful life which paves the way to Enlightenment and true happiness.

Key #2: Myth is a journey of spiritual transformation.

The second key to understanding a myth is comprehending that it is usually written in the form of a journey in which the subject must learn about himself or herself and transcend the ordinary human consciousness, thereby discovering a greater essence of self. In this movement there are experiences of happiness, sorrow, struggle and learning. It is a movement from ignorance and darkness towards light, wisdom and ultimately, to spiritual Enlightenment.

Key #3: Myths are to be lived in order to understand their true meaning.

The third key to understanding a myth is that comprehension comes from living the myth. Living a myth does not mean simply reading a myth, being able to recount the events with perfect memory or simply practicing the rituals of a myth without a deeper understanding of their implications and purpose. It means making the essence of the teaching being conveyed through the myth an integral part of your life. If this practice is not implemented, the teachings remain at the intellectual level and the deeper truths of the myth are not revealed. One lives with dry intellectualism or blind faith, the former leading to a superficial and therefore frustrated spiritual life, and the latter leading to dogmatism and emotional frustration. Therefore, you must resolve to discover the myth in every facet of your life, and in so doing, you will be triumphant as the hero(ine) of the myth.

Key #4: Myth points the way to victory in life.

Myths show us our heritage as a culture as well as the legacy we are to receive. They give human beings a place in the scheme of things as well as a purpose in life and the means to achieve the fulfillment of that purpose. The ultimate purpose is to achieve victory in the battle of life, to defeat the forces of ignorance within oneself which lead to adversity and frustration and thereby become masters of life here and hereafter, discovering undifferentiated peace, love and joy...Enlightenment.

"God is a metaphor for a mystery that transcends all human categories of thought...It depends on how much you want to think about it, whether or not it's doing you any good, whether it's putting you in touch with the mystery which is the ground of your own being."

—Joseph Campbell

Thus, when comparing the myths of different cultures for the purpose of religious studies, it is necessary to understand their respective metaphorical aspects as well as their attendant underlying philosophies along with their apparent iconographical form and artistic intent (naturalistic[15] or stylized[16]).

Other Aspects of Myth

Plot refers to the plan of events or main story in a narrative or drama.[17] The synchronicity in the situations presented in myths can be used as a factor in discerning the communal nature of two myths. This congruence must be specific, involving characters of similar age group, gender and genealogy or provenance, experiencing similar situations in the same or similar ways.

In comparing myths, there are several important concerns. The purpose of myth, the language of myth and the levels of myth must be understood prior to making a comparison. *Myth is a language*[18] by which sages and saints transmit the basic elements of culture through a "common story" for all within the culture to believe in as well as draw answers to the basic questions of life such as, Where do I come from?, To which group do I belong? What is the purpose of life? and How do I fulfill that purpose? This is all conveyed through the story, plot and theme of the myth and their inherent teachings of social order as well as their spiritual morals.

Most religions and spiritual philosophies tend to be *deistic* at the elementary levels. **Deism**, as a religious belief or form of theism (belief in the existence of a Supreme Being or gods) holds that the Supreme Being's action was restricted to an initial act of creation, after which He/She retired (separated) to contemplate the majesty of His/Her work. Deists hold that the natural creation is regulated by laws put in place by the Supreme Being at the time of creation which are inscribed with perfect moral principles. Therefore, deism is closely related to the exoteric or personal but also outer (phenomenal) and dogmatic and conventional understanding of the Divinity.

> Two approaches to myth dominate the intellectual landscape during the first half of the twentieth century: the ritualistic and the psychoanalytic. The former, epitomized by the "myth and ritual" or Cambridge school beholden to the Oxonian E. B. Tylor's *Primitive Culture* (1871) and with James G. Frazer's *Golden Bough* as its central talisman, owes its theoretical underpinnings to Jane E. Harrison's *Prolegomena to the Study of Greek Religion* (1903) and *Themis* (1912). Harrison provided a strikingly simple and exclusionary definition of myth: myth is nothing but the verbalization of ritual, "the spoken correlative of the acted rite"

---

[15] Imitating or producing the effect or appearance of nature.

[16] To restrict or make conform to a particular style. **2.** To represent conventionally; conventionalize.

[17] American Heritage Dictionary

[18] *The Power of Myth,* Joseph Campbell

(*Themis,* P. 328), *ta legomena* 'what is said' accompanying *ta dromena* 'what is being done', myth and ritual being accordingly but two sides of the same religious coin; thus in principle there can be no myth without ritual, although time may have obliterated the act and left the narrative free to survive as myth or its debased subspecies (saga, legend, folktale, etc.). [19]

An assumption adopted by many comparative mythology scholars is the idea that myth is a means of explaining ritual. This idea is often predicated upon the concept that "primitive" cultures developed myth as a means of coping with the mysteries of life and Creation due to the lack of "scientific" knowledge. In the absence of science, ritual and superstition were substituted in order to allay the fears caused by the unknown. Further, this theory therefore holds that myth developed as an emanation of the actions of the practitioners of the rituals to justify those rituals. While this point of view is accurate with respect to certain cultures whose practitioners who are ignorant as to the reason behind the rituals of their religion, it is wholly incorrect when considering cultures possessing mystical philosophy. In those cultures the sacred writings of their religions present models of rituals as expressions of myth, and myth as expressions of philosophy or mysticism. Ritual is therefore a means to understand myth, and the realization of myth is a means to attain spiritual enlightenment. The erroneous concept is evident not only in modern scholarship, but also in ancient cultures which adopted symbols and myths from other cultures without fully understanding their purpose or the philosophy behind them. The following example given by Count Goblet D' Alviella provides an insight into the process called "iconological mythology."

> Sometimes, in similar cases, the new owners of the image will endeavor to explain it by a more or less ingenious interpretation, and in this manner they will restore to it a symbolical import, though applied to a new conception.
> The rising sun has often been compared to a new-born child. Amongst the Egyptians, this comparison led to Horus being represented as an infant sucking its finger. The Greeks imagined that he placed his finger on his lips to enjoin secrecy on the initiated, and they made him the image of Harpocrates, the god of silence. [20]
> This is what M. Clermont-Ganneau has very happily termed *iconological mythology*; it is here no longer the myth which gives rise to the image, but the image which gives rise to the myth.
> We may further quote, as an interpretation of the same kind, the legend related by Hygin, which made the Caduceus originate in Hermes throwing his wand between two serpents fighting. It is evident that, here also, this hypothesis, soon to be transformed into a myth by the popular imagination, was due to a desire, unconscious perhaps, to explain the Caduceus.
> Most frequently it is a conception pre-existent in the local traditions which we think we find amongst the products of foreign imagery. [21]

Another case in point is the relationship between Ancient Egypt and Greece. The Greeks adopted what they could understand of Ancient Egyptian philosophy, but did not adopt the culture or social philosophy. The Greeks made some changes in what they learned. Therefore,

---

[19] *Comparative Mythology,* Jaan Puhvel
[20] G. Lafaye. *Historie des divinités d'Alexandrie hors de l' Egypte.* Paris, 18984, p.259
[21] *The Migration of Symbols,* Count Goblet D' Alviella, 1894

Greek culture cannot be claimed as an African (Ancient Egyptian) heritage. The problem was so severe that the Sages of Ancient Egypt felt the need to reprimand and denounce the Greek distortions. They indicted Greek culture as the culprit leading to the way of speech (communication and relation) which was of a "loose," "disdainful" and "confusing" character.

> "The Greek tongue is a noise of words, a language of argument and confusion."

> "Keep this teaching from translation in order that such mighty Mysteries might not come to the Greeks and to the disdainful speech of Greece, with all its looseness and its surface beauty, taking all the strength out of the solemn and the strong - the energetic speech of Names."

> "Unto those who come across these words, their composition will seem most simple and clear; but on the contrary, as this is unclear, and has the true meaning of its words concealed, it will be still unclear, when, afterwards, the Greeks will want to turn our tongue into their own - for this will be a very great distorting and obscuring of even what has heretofore been written. Turned into our own native tongue, the teachings keepeth clear the meaning of the words. For that its very quality of sound, the very power of Kamitan names, have in themselves the bringing into act of what is said."

Cultural Category - Factor Correlation System: Application

Theoretical Methodology for the Comparison of Cultures

A myth in its pristine state is by definition specific to a given human environment. How it fares from then on (its "life;' "afterlife'" survival, transposition, revival, rediscovery, or whatever) is a matter of historical accident. It follows that the study of any specific past body of myth has to be mainly a historical discipline employing written sources, whereas contemporary myth can be pursued by the methods of field anthropology. [22]

In the book *Comparative Mythology*, (quoted above), the author introduces certain formats for the study of comparative mythology, beginning with the premise that a myth is "specific to a given human environment." If human environment is taken to mean culture, then it follows that the study of myth needs to be carried out within the context of the culture, using the parameters of the culture. In other words, the myth needs to be studied from the perspective of someone living in the culture and not as an outsider. That is, a student of myth needs to practice and live the myth, to be part of the myth. Only in this way will the myth be fully understood. Otherwise, there will be a superimposition of outside cultural bias from the researcher or student on the myth being studied. This is one of the most difficult problems for any scientist to overcome, how to fully understand the object of study. The usual logic in Western scientific methodology is to strive for "objectivity."

Modern science has now accepted that research examining or studying "physical reality" cannot exist outside of the person conducting the experiments. An older theory held that the person conducting the experiment could be considered separate and apart from the phenomena

---

[22] *Comparative Mythology,* Jaan Puhvel

being observed. Modern science now holds that nature and all phenomena occur because of an experimenter's ability to conceptualize the phenomena and to interpret it. Therefore, the observer is inevitably part of the phenomena being observed. Consequently, modern science now uses a new term for the experimenter. The new term is <u>Participant.</u> Thus, the experimenter is really a participant in the experiment because his or her consciousness conceives, determines, perceives, interprets and understands it. No experiment or observed phenomena in nature can occur without someone to conceive that something is happening, determine that something is happening, perceive that something is happening (through instruments or the senses), and finally to interpret what has happened and to understand that interpretation.

Since everything in the universe is connected at some underlying level and since human existence and human consciousness is dependent upon relationships in order to function, then it follows that objectivity is not a realistic attitude for most human beings, including scientists. The only way to achieve objectivity is to transcend "human" consciousness. That is, one must extricate one's egoistic vision of life, which based on the limitations of the mind and senses, by discovering one's "transcendental" nature. This grants one the experience of knowing the true, unchanging and unaffected nature and essence of existence beyond the limited capacities of the mind and senses. In this capacity one can temporarily identify with the object, any object of study, and achieve a complete knowledge of the subject. This capacity has been the legacy of science and the mystical disciplines, for concentration on any subject is the key to discovering the nature of that subject. However, the mystical disciplines go a step beyond in allowing the scientists to discover their essential nature as one with the object of study. Therefore, mystical training is indispensable in the study of any subject and the acquisition of the knowledge of the essential nature of a subject or object. This form of philosophy is antithetical to the orthodox practice of the "scientific method" but until the scientific method is adjusted to incorporate the training of the mystical disciplines, the knowledge gained from the sciences will be limited to the capacities of the logical mind and senses as well as the technological instruments that may be devised to extend the range of those limited, and therefore illusory, human abilities. So the historical and field anthropology[23] disciplines of study must be guided by the mystical experience.

When comparing two given cultures, we are not only concerned with the superficial aspects of their cultural expression, but also the underlying foundations of these. The fundamental core of any culture is its outlook or philosophy on life. This underlying philosophy gives rise to the varied forms of cultural expression just as the many leaves and branches of a tree arise from a seed (common origin). The mystical philosophy of a given culture is translated by the sages and saints of that culture into an easily understandable and transmittable myth using the cultural factors available to them within that particular culture. Therefore, a sage in Kamitan culture may espouse a teaching using metaphors particular to Kamitan culture while a Christian sage may espouse the same teaching while using a different cultural metaphor which is particular to Christian culture. The myth is supported and sustained by the plots and story-lines. Next, it is supported by the rituals and traditions associated with them. The rituals and traditions are supported by the combined factors of cultural expression including: architecture, iconography, artifacts and ritual objects (amulets, etc.), spiritual scriptures, language, form and function of objects produced by the culture, etc. Thus, when there is an overwhelming number and quality of synchronicities between the factors of expression in two cultures, a commonality in their underlying philosophies will also be discovered.

---

[23] The scientific study of the origin, the behavior, and the physical, social, and cultural development of human beings.

How the philosophy of a culture expresses through the cultural factors of that culture:

Architecture, iconography, artifacts and ritual objects (amulets, etc.)

↑

Form and function of objects produced by the culture

↑

Ritual and Tradition

↑

Plots and story-lines of the myth

↑

Spiritual scriptures

↑

Language (linguistics-phonetics)

↑

Myth

↑

Mystical Philosophy

Through studies based on the factors and parameters listed above, it has been possible to show that there are at least four main world religions that have a strong basis in a common origin which transcends the cursory or superficial levels of similarity. These traditions are the Kamitan, Ancient Greek, Hindu, and Judeo-Christian. I have already presented and in-depth exploration of the Kamitan/Greek connection in my book *From Egypt to Greece* and the Kamitan/Judeo-Christian connection in my book *The Mystical Journey From Jesus to Christ*. Through these kinds of study, it is possible to bring unity to disparaging and conflicting points of view which lead to dissent, disagreement and misunderstanding that are based on ignorance, adherence to dogma and cultural-theological pride[24] and orthodoxy, instead of the deeper nature and purpose of culture which is to lead human beings to spiritual enlightenment. By such studies it is possible to lead open-minded people to understand the purpose of religion and to discover the value of all traditions which are ultimately seeking to accomplish the same task, to bring harmony, peace and order to the world and to allow human beings of all cultures to discover the supreme and essential nature of existence.

The Standard for Determining Whether or Not a Correlation is Present

Determining an objective standard for any critical study is an enormously difficult task since the human mind is ultimately what must be satisfied in a particular judgment. That is, when we are trying to determine some kind of rule or guideline to follow which will lead to an unbiased conclusion, the mind of the observer, with his/her preconceived notions, desires, leanings, etc., comes into play, and what one person may consider reasonable, another may regard as groundless. For example, a person may think a color is especially suited for a particular room while another person may say that that color is exactly the opposite of what should be used. Who is right? Well, in this question there is an arbitrary, aesthetic factor which draws upon a person's particular upbringing, particular experiences, particular education, etc. Another example seen often in modern culture is a situation where one person sees a business opportunity as clear as day, while others do not. That person will later capitalize on that opportunity. Was the opportunity there all along or was it a coincidence? In addition, we recognize factors in life that cannot be objectively proven, and yet we "know" they exist. There is a transcendental reality about them that we recognize. When that businessperson, with their training and intuition, spots

---

[24] The belief that one's own culture is primary and superior to other cultures.

an opportunity, they perceive it and register it as a reality. In this manner, scientists using training, data collection and intuition in order to "discern" the underlying truth of myths, can discover the correlating factors between cultures. Nonetheless, in the study of science, one would expect the process to be more "objective," being "either right or wrong," but even in the sciences, the ego and its prejudices can impinge on reason. So what kind of standard can be used to discern between coincidences and synchronous correlations between cultures? Any standard to be used must be based on verifiable evidence and logical analysis, but also on reason. However, if unreasonable people review the evidence, no amount of evidence will suffice, because their minds are already prejudiced.

There is often much confusion and conflict in the world due to disagreements and misunderstandings. Many have cited the lack of reason as a primary cause of human conflict. But what is reason? The following dictionary and encyclopedic definitions may provide some guidance.

> **reason: 1** to think logically about; think out systematically; analyze **2** to argue, conclude, or infer: now usually with a clause introduced by *that* as the object **3** to support, justify, etc. with reasons **4** to persuade or bring by reasoning.

> **reasoning:** (-i) *n.* **1** the drawing of inferences or conclusions from known or assumed facts; use of reason **2** the proofs or reasons resulting from this.

> **in reason**. With good sense or justification; reasonably. **Within reason**: Within the bounds of good sense or practicality.

In the context of the definitions above, reason is that faculty in human consciousness wherein two minds can arrive at a conclusion that is within the bounds of practical reality based on known or assumed facts which justify or support the conclusions drawn. But how is it possible for people to apply those standards and draw rational or reasonable conclusions? Certainly, maturity in life and qualitative experience in human interactions, (i.e. based on honesty, truth, righteousness, justice and universal love) scholarship and balance in life are prerequisites for promoting soundness of the intellect and an understanding of reality within the sphere of human interactions and social intercommunications.

Methodology for the Comparisons Between Cultures in Order to Determine the Correlations Between Cultures

The methodology for understanding mythology and its purpose, which has been presented in the previous section as well as those which will follow, present myth and metaphor as abstract principles that manifest through cultural factors in the form of recurrent themes. While these are subject to some interpretation, the possibility for bias becomes reduced as the associated factors add up to support the original conjecture about the particular factor being compared. In other words, *single event proposed correlations* (correlations between cultural factors that are alleged but not yet proven or supported) between cultures can often be explained away as coincidences. However, when those correlations are supported by related factors or when those correlations are present in the framework of other correlations, then the position of bias or simple disbelief is less tenable. The basis for the objective standard will be set forth in the following logical principles which indicate congruence between the two cultures. In order to study and compare the Kamitan and Indian cultures, we will make use of the categories of cultural expression.

As explained earlier, in determining the common elements of different religions, there are several factors that can be used as criteria to determine whether or not cultures had common origins. If cultures are related, they will use common stories or other common factors or patterns to express the main doctrines of the religion or spiritual path, social philosophy, etc. These are listed below. Before proceeding to the items being compared, the criteria used to compare them must be understood. The following section introduces the categories of cultural expression factors and some subdivisions within them.

The Possible Standards for Use in Determining the Correlations Between Cultures

The Scientific Method for Studying Correlations Between Cultures

"Scientific Method, general logic and procedures common to all the physical and social sciences, which may be outlined as a series of steps: (1) stating a problem or question; (2) forming a hypothesis (possible solution to the problem) based on a theory or rationale; (3) experimentation (gathering empirical data bearing on the hypothesis); (4) interpretation of the data and drawing conclusions; and (5) revising the theory or deriving further hypotheses for testing. Putting the hypothesis in a form that can be empirically tested is one of the chief challenges to the scientist. In addition, all of the sciences try to express their theories and conclusions in some quantitative form and to use standardized testing procedures that other scientists could repeat."[25]

Many Western scholars adhere to the "Scientific Method" of research. This concept originated in Western Culture for the study of nature, to determine the criteria for what can be accepted as truth. The definition above provides the step by step procedures accepted in the Western conception of a scientific method. It is further defined and contrasted from philosophy by the Encarta Encyclopedia as *(highlighted portions by Dr. Ashby)*:

"Scientific Method, term denoting the principles that guide scientific research and experimentation, and also the philosophic bases of those principles. Whereas philosophy in general is concerned with the why as well as the how of things, science occupies itself with the latter question only. Definitions of scientific method use such concepts as objectivity of approach to and acceptability of the results of scientific study. Objectivity indicates the attempt to observe things as they are, without falsifying observations to accord with some preconceived worldview. Acceptability is judged in terms of the degree to which observations and experimentations can be reproduced. *Such agreement of a conclusion with an actual observation does not itself prove the correctness of the hypothesis from which the conclusion is derived.* It simply renders the premise that much more plausible. The ultimate test of the validity of a scientific hypothesis is its

---

[25] Random House Encyclopedia Copyright (C) 1983,1990

consistency with the totality of other aspects of the scientific framework. This inner consistency constitutes the basis for the concept of causality in science, according to which every effect is assumed to be linked with a cause."[26]

Refutation of Conclusions arrived at through the Scientific Method

Conversely, if one attempts to show that a scientific conclusion is wrong, it is necessary to:

(1) show a misconception or wrongly stated a problem or question;
(2) show that the hypothesis (possible solution to the problem) based on a theory or rationale is incorrect;
(3) show that the experimentation (gathering empirical data bearing on the hypothesis) is biased or being carried out in an incorrect way;
(4) show that the process for interpreting the data and drawing conclusions has not followed a logical procedure or is biased;
(5) show that the revising process of the theory or deriving further hypotheses for testing is needed.
(6) show that the experiment is not consistent with the totality of other aspects of the scientific framework.
(7) show evidences that contradict the conclusion.
(8) show more evidences to prove other conclusions than what have been presented to advance the other unreasonable conclusion.

The Limitations of the Scientific Method

The scientific method is an attempt to remove ambiguity from the body of human knowledge and the means by which knowledge is added to the storehouse of human learning. The problem with this method of gathering knowledge is that it necessarily receives information only from empirical evidence. However, as the great scientist Einstein and the modern day quantum physicists have proven, Creation is not absolute or empirical. Creation is composed of variables wherein some aspects operate in different ways under different circumstances. This is why the concept of cause and effect is also flawed. Ignorance of the mystical law of cause and effect known as the law of *Ari* in Kamitan philosophy and Karma in Indian philosophy, leads scientists to seek for causes or reasons for what they see in nature, somewhere within the confines of the time and space of the event in question. In reference to Yoga and mystical religion, as concerns people and their actions, mostly, what is occurring today could be a result of what happened in a previous lifetime (philosophy of reincarnation-already proven in parapsychology experiments).[27] As concerns nature, what occurs today is sustained by the Transcendental Essence, i.e. Supreme Being. Further, the observers, the scientists themselves, and the very perception of these experiments are factors in the experiments and are therefore, factors in the results. This is where the problem of skewing of the results and interpretations of results based on conscious or unconscious prejudices or misconceptions comes in, that is, the problem of "falsifying observations to accord with some preconceived worldview."

---

[26] "Scientific Method," Microsoft (R) Encarta. Copyright (c) 1994
[27] for evidences see the book *The Conscious Universe: The Scientific truth of Psychic Phenomena* By Dean Radin, Ph. D.

As the modern discipline of Quantum Physics has shown, nature itself is not what it appears. It is not solid and distinct but rather interrelated energies in varied forms of expression. Physics experiments have shown that matter is not solid as it appears but that it is rather, energy in different forms of manifestation. So the instruments used to discern reality, the logical conditioned mind, and the limited senses, are inadequate for discriminating between what is real and what is unreal. The fallacy of believing in the absolute authority of science is evident in the inability of science to discover anything that is absolute. Something absolute is unchangeable in the beginning, middle and end. Every decade medical science makes "new breakthroughs." This means that they are discovering something "new" which supersedes their previous knowledge. This necessarily means that the previous knowledge was conditional and imperfect and therefore, illusory. Thus, science has its value, but it is not to be considered a reliable source for truth or as a substitute for the disciplines of self-knowledge. So, only a mind that has been trained in transcendental thinking and intuitional realization can discover "truth." Yoga and mystical religion are spiritual sciences that promote the cultivation of the higher faculties of the mind. The mystics of Yoga the world over have for thousands of years proclaimed that the mystical reality which is to be discovered through the disciplines of Yoga and Mystical religion is the same Absolute essence which has always sustained Creation and all existence, including human consciousness. It is the same essence that was discovered by Imhotep and other Sages of Kamit, the Upanishadic Sages of India, Buddha, Jesus, etc., and it is the same absolute reality that can be discovered by anyone today or in the future, who applies the teachings of Yoga and Mystical religion.

So, the idea of the objective observer or that only experimental results which can bring forth repeatable results or parameters that show "consistency with the totality of other aspects of the scientific framework" are valid is sometimes contradictory with respect to nature and logic. Nature is not a machine and even if it were to be treated as such it is not a machine for which the parts are all known and understood. There is an aspect of nature that transcends empirical observation; it must be intuited. This aspect of nature is ignored by the scientific method, by its own bindings, and therefore, the ability to use science as a tool to discover truth, is limited. Since the world is variable (relative), then it follows that any "scientific" data obtained from experiments will also be relative and variable. It is useful within the framework of science, but not beyond that framework. In other words, it cannot be used to ascertain anything about realities outside of its framework. This is why philosophy is an important tool of science. It allows the intuitive faculty of the mind to be cultivated and directed towards discovering the aspects of nature that no physical testing equipment can penetrate.

The world is not to be discerned through the intellect because the intellect is also limited. It cannot comprehend the totality of Creation. However, by intuitional (knowing that transcends the thought process) reasoning through transcendence of the relativity of nature, it is possible to discover that absolute reality which is common, and therefore uniform in its *"consistency with the totality"* of human and spiritual experience. The problem is that this aspect of existence can only be approached through a scientific application of philosophical principles and disciplines that can provide results only in the mind of an individual. The Western scientific community shuns this approach, likening it to primitive and unscientific speculations. By ignoring the "why" of things, as the definition of the scientific method above suggests, the scientific method is cutting itself off from the source of knowledge, and looking only at its effect, the "what," and then accepting this as a basis to discern reality. It is like experimenting on the sunrays, neglecting to notice the sun, but extrapolating from the limited experiments and making assertions about what the sun is. In like manner, science looks at nature and notices the relativity, but does not allow itself to explore the mystical-spiritual dimensions of cause. Rather, it seeks to ascribe factors within the realm of the flawed relative field of Creation itself, as the reason behind existence. In fact, for all the knowledge that Western Culture has amassed, in reality there is perhaps no more important

31

knowledge than that which has been recently derived from Quantum Physics, because these clearly point to a transcendental essence of Creation.[28 / 29/30]

Western Culture's adherence to the "Scientific Method" has turned it away from the science of self-development (myth, religion and yoga mysticism) since it (spiritual evolution) cannot be proven empirically according to its current criteria as different people are at different stages of evolution and the process may require many lifetimes to complete. Here again, even the parameters set by Western Culture as the procedure of the "Scientific Method" are not being followed. The statement that there is no science beyond the existential aspect of Creation is in effect a violation of the "scientific" rule of objectivity to *observe things as they are, without falsifying observations to accord with some preconceived world view.* The predilection to discount the transcendent as "un-provable" is a worldview which typifies Western Culture. Thus, the objectivity in the scientific method has at least two built in flaws. First, is the insistence on determining scientific fact based on evidence that can be observable to the physical senses with or without assistance from technology, and therefore can only exist in time and space. Secondly, the necessity for human standards in determining *"conclusions"* based on the data, for it has been shown that the same data can lend itself to different interpretations based on conflicting views, even within the scientific community. A true scientific method should require an objective standard which cannot be violated by the whims of the observers or scientists. Its conclusions must be accepted and not refuted by opinions or desires to uphold particular worldviews. However, again, all of the best standards will be useless if the scientists are biased.

A further connotation, prevalent in Western Culture arising from adherence to the "scientific method" is that what is transcendent is imagined, superstition and unfounded illusion, and only what the "Scientific Method" deems as provable is correct and acceptable. Hence, since myth and mysticism are in the realm of the transcendent, then by this type of Western logic it follows that they are also un-provable and unreal. This is a very powerful argument that further develops into the most dangerous concept, that Western Culture is the determiner of what is truth and that the art, culture, science and religion, etc., of other cultures, past or present, are inferior due to their primitive and "unscientific" manner of approaching nature.

Applying the Scientific Principles and Procedures to study Mysticism

The application of scientific principles and procedures in mystical philosophy can and should be accomplished in the following manner. A theory that the Supreme Being exists, for instance, can be developed. Now the experiment is to practice certain myths, rituals and mystical exercises (technologies). Then the practitioner must insightfully look within and see if there are any changes in the personality, and if there is anything transcending the personality. The premise that observable and repeatable results can be obtained is to be understood as an intuitional realization or recognition of truth. So, while it is possible to show many illustrations and iconographical correlations in the scientific comparison of two forms of myth, the ultimate realization of the truth behind these is to be achieved in the understanding of the observer. The mystical scriptures have long held that if this procedure is followed, any person can discover the transcendental essence of Self. This is the scientific formula for Enlightened Sagehood or Sainthood, which mystical philosophy holds to be the only goal in and purpose of life. Thus, from ancient times, the Yogic and other authentic Mystical systems have defined themselves as sciences, since the

---

[28] *Memphite Theology*, Muata Ashby

[29] *The Tao of Physics*, Fritjof Capra

[30] *Dancing Wu Li Masters* by Gary Zukov

proper application of the correct philosophy, disciplines and principles of living leads to the same results of spiritual awakening in all human beings who apply them.

Due to the uniqueness of each person when dealing with human beings, there are variables in the degree of understanding and practice. Thus, in evaluating students of the Yogic and other Mystical sciences (spiritual aspirants or initiates), the results of spiritual practices cannot be assessed in terms of an all or nothing equation or within a given time frame or situation, since evolution is occurring even when outwardly there appears to be a backward movement. Also, spiritual evolution occurs over a long period of time encompassing many lifetimes. So these results cannot necessarily be seen in the form of data, but other criteria may be used to evaluate them: a calmer personality, a human being who is expanding in consciousness, discovering the inner depths of consciousness and the universality of life, increasing contentment and fearlessness, a stronger will, and magnanimousness, wisdom and inner fulfillment. Some of these evidences cannot be put on paper, and yet they can be experienced just as the message of a painting or the love of a relative can be intuited and felt, but not explained or proven to others. From time immemorial, the sages and saints of all world traditions have maintained the initiatic principles and technologies, the mystical philosophy and art of spiritual culture, that has been handed down through time. It has been found that when human beings are properly instructed and when they engage in certain disciplines of Yoga and mystical culture, they develop expanded consciousness and spiritual awareness, as well as intuitional realization of the divine presence in a predictable manner.

The correct practice of myth and mystical philosophy in yoga requires a scientific approach, using the personality as the subject, and the mind as the instrument for proving the existence of the transcendent. It is necessary to apply philosophy scientifically, incorporating intuition and spiritual culture when engaging in any study of religion, myth, mysticism, etc.

The following is a standard for our exploration into comparative mythology, which will be used to discover the validity of the hypothesis that Ancient Egyptian and Ancient Indian culture and civilization were related and share common cultural manifestations. This analysis will be accomplished by establishing what culture is and what factors within it can be identified and compared. Then the procedure to be followed in comparing them will be determined.

In a scientific investigation, opinions have no place beyond the stating of the hypothesis. Also, the constraints of social propriety do not apply. It is perfectly scientific to state a theory that the Ancient Egyptians were not black Africans, but rather Asiatics, or that Indian Vedic culture and not Kamitan culture gave rise to civilization. There is nothing wrong in making those statements. However, if the person stating these ideas wants to put them forth as "facts" or "reality" or consider these ideas as "proven," then a more rigorous process of supporting those ideas must be undertaken. The evidence must be accurate, available to all investigators, and it should be primary and not second-hand conjectures. Therefore, the opinions of other scholars, no matter how reputable they may be, must be based on primary evidence, and that evidence cannot be substituted by the scholars conclusions or opinions about it. Therefore, scholarly dictums[31] are worthless if the scholar cannot or does not support them with evidence. Other terms, often used synonymously in scientific discussions are "postulate" or "axiom."

---

[31] American Heritage Dictionary

An **axiom** is a self-evident or universally recognized truth; a maxim.

A **dictum** is an authoritative, often formal, pronouncement.

A **postulate** is a *statement or proposition that is to be assumed to be true without proof and that forms a framework for the derivation of theorems.*[32]

Many times scientists or others relying on them treat corollaries as proofs.

A **corollary** is *a proposition that follows with little or no proof required from one already proven, A deduction or an inference.*[33]

So corollaries, postulates, etc., are also useless in a presentation of scientific findings. They should not even be discussed because they have no merit. Sometimes merit is placed on dictums or corollaries due to the reputation of a scientist, or for political, social or economic reasons but these have no place in a scientific discussion. Thus, if a scientist is not dispassionate, an unconscious or conscious alternative agenda will be put forth. Further, if no evidence is produced to support a contention, then a scientist might be in danger of appearing biased, promoting a political or social point of view or expressing personal beliefs and sentiments about a particular issue. Over time, they themselves begin to believe in those opinions. This is the power and danger of the human mind.

The Factors That Make Cultures Distinct and the Methodology for Comparing Them

In the book *Comparative Mythology,* the author introduces two formats or models for the study of comparative mythology, based on the concepts of abstraction and generalization.

Comparative mythology of separately localized and attested traditions can be practiced on different levels of abstraction and generalization.

"Universal mythology" is essentially reduced to explaining accordances (and, if relevant, differences or contrasts) by appeal to human universals or at least common denominators based on similarities of psychological patterning, environment, or levels of culture. Needless to say, it has to pursue the typical and usual at the expense of the specific and unique.

"Diffusionary mythology" studies how traditions travel, charting the spread and transmission of myth. The trouble is precisely that myth does not "travel" very well and, when it does travel, frequently moves from its specific historical and geographical fulcrum into the international realm of legend, folktale, fairy tale, and other debased forms of originally mythical narrative.[34]

While the above author speaks primarily of mythological studies, the ideas are relevant to our study since mythology is an integral if not central aspect of culture. In our study, we will strive to

---

[32] American Heritage Dictionary
[33] American Heritage Dictionary
[34] *Comparative Mythology,* Jaan Puhvel

raise the methodology for the comparative cultural study to a high standard that goes beyond the universalistic aspects of culture, that is, those factors that are innate to all human beings.

The author quoted above also works with the premise that mythology becomes "debased" or degrades due to the changes and additions it experiences over time. While this model occurs and may even be considered as the norm, it is also possible to see a sustained practice of myth and other aspects of culture from one group to the next. We will also strive to determine if there is a degradation that can be discerned. The criteria here is the determination of the function and metaphorical significance of the cultural factors over time. That is, if the function and metaphorical significance of the cultural factors is lost over time, the model above is correct. However, if the function and metaphorical significance of the cultural factors are sustained over time, this indicates a closer connection between the two cultures, and the model is one of initiatic continuity (culture A has taught culture B directly) as opposed to blind diffusion of ideas without their full understanding. The closer bond can be expected in the contiguous relationship of a culture with its own legacy. That is, a modern culture can be expected to exhibit a lesser degree of deterioration of indigenous fundamental cultural factors as opposed to those that have been imported. The model presented in ordinary comparative mythology studies is that myth may retain its form but degrade in content. If a sustained (un-degraded) correlation can be shown between two cultures over time (one emerging after the other), then it is possible to maintain that the cultures are not separate and disparate but actually elements of a continuous manifestation of cultural expression. In other words, the two cultures are actually part of one evolving culture. Another factor to be considered is the concept of a study that works within the framework of different levels of abstraction and generalization. The principles under which this current study of Kamitan and Indian culture will be conducted is based on the contention that when several cultural factors can be correlated or matched, then the study becomes more concrete and specific as opposed to abstract and general. This of course raises the validity of the arguments and the conclusions drawn from them.

> "The twentieth-century search for universally applicable "patterns" that so clearly marks the ritualist and psychoanalytic approaches to myth is also characteristic of the trends that remain to be mentioned, the sociological and the structuralist. Whereas ritualism had its roots in England and psychoanalysis in the German cultural orbit, the French contribution is important here, starting with the sociological school of Emile Durkheim and Marcel Mauss. Durkheim's "collective representations," Mauss's seminal studies on gift giving and sacrifice, and Bronislaw Malinowski's views on myths as social "charters" all recognized the paramount role of myths as catalysts in cementing structured human coexistence. The structural study of myth, with Claude Levi-Strauss as its most flamboyant paladin, also stresses the role of myth as a mechanism of conflict resolution and mediation between opposites in the fabric of human culture and society, not least in the great dichotomy of nature versus culture itself. But Levi-Strauss's analytic method is one of binary oppositions influenced by structural linguistics (especially the work of Roman Jakobson) and folklore (starting with Vladimir Propp's *Morphology of the Folktale* [1928], which themselves are but manifestations of the vast structuralist movement in science and scholarship."[35]

The view that myth is a manifestation of ritual or of a psychological state is a barrier between scholarship and myth. This is because the very premise for the study is flawed. Created by sages, saints, seers, etc., mystical mythology is an "explanation" of something that is transcendental,

---

[35] Ibid

something that exists in a form that cannot be communicated by rational thinking or linear logical conceptualizations. When mystical mythology is reduced by scholars to a support for rituals, manifestations of the psyche or a tool to "glue" or bind members of a culture to a common concept, the original intent of myth is displaced and the resulting conclusions about myths, their import and pervasiveness, will be elusive. These models may be grouped together and referred to as logical models since they neglect to take into account the transcendental aspects of myth and indeed, also the human experience. The models that take into account the mystical nature and purpose of myth along with the disciplines of anthropology, archeology, philology and historical linguistics, phonetics and phonology, may be referred to as mystic or intuitional models. In another section, the author continues to outline the previous approaches taken by other mythologists in an attempt to determine the benefits or pitfalls of their concepts and methodologies.

> "While Levi-Strauss himself, after starting with the Oedipus myth, has for the most part resolutely ranged from Alaska to the Amazon, structuralist ideas have begun to seep into the study of classical myth and "historical" mythology in general. The obvious danger is that the approach is by nature generalist, universalizing, and ahistorical, thus the very opposite of text oriented, philological, and time conscious. Overlaying known data with binaristic gimmickry in the name of greater "understanding" is no substitute for a deeper probing of the records themselves as documents of a specific synchronic culture on the one hand and as outcomes of diachronic evolutionary processes on the other. In mythology, as in any other scholarly or scientific activity, it is important to recall that the datum itself is more important than any theory that may be applied to it. Hence historical and comparative mythology, as practiced in this book, is in the last resort not beholden to any one theory on the "nature" of myth or even its ultimate "function" or "purpose." But it is fully cognizant that myth operates in men's minds and societies alike, that it is involved in both self-image and worldview on an individual and a collective level (being thus tied to religion and its manifestations such as ritual and prayer, and to societal ideology as well), and that it creates potent tensions of language and history (speaking of timeless happening, narrating eternal events in the grammatical frame of tense forms for [usually]) past or [rarely] future occurrences [as in the case of prophecy], never in the generalizing present)."[36]

While there have been a wide range of scholars and writers who have taken note of and even asserted the similarities of the myths of widely varying cultures by citing simple similarities, there have been relatively few serious, rigorous, scholarly researches and documentations. Mostly, there have been many anecdotal and or unsubstantiated claims that do not reconcile history with the events that are being artificially connected. Further, there is little accounting for the discrepancies and inconsistencies that arise. While it is true that all humanity emerged from the same source, it is not necessarily correct to say that all cultures are related since people, having moved away from their original ancestral home (Africa) when humanity first appeared on earth, developed varying ways of life and cultural expression. So making the standard too tight or too loose leaves us with either biased conclusions or unsubstantiated conjecture respectively. The author ends his introduction to comparative mythology with a caveat for entering into those studies.

---

[36] Ibid

"Thus the twentieth-century lessons of ritualism, psychoanalysis, sociology, and structural anthropology alike deserve to be heeded by the historical and comparative student of myth and religion, but only to the extent that they offer viable insights into a study that is by definition historical, and more specifically philological, rooted in the minute and sensitive probing and comparison of primary written records."[37]

If the categories of cultural expression are found to match in several areas, the mythic principles will have survived the passage of time even as cultures interact with others and adopt new factors into their culture. The factors of cultural expression will remain embedded in the culture as layers upon which new traditions, names and idiosyncrasies[38] have been acquired. This layering of symbol, myth and metaphor is starkly evident in several examples that will be presented in this section. This pattern of diffusion was noticed early on in the study of the correlations between the myths of varied cultures. The writings of Count Goblet D' Alviella present a typical example, referring to the Sacred Tree symbolism.

"Each race, each religion has its independent type, which it preserves and develops in accordance with the spirit of its own traditions, approximating it, however, by the addition of extraneous details and accessories, to the equivalent image adopted in the plastic art of its neighbors. Thus the current which makes the Lotus of Egypt blossom on the Paradisaic Tree of India has its counter-current which causes the *Asclepias acida* of the Hindu Kush to climb upon the Sacred Tree of Assyria. Art and mythology comply, in this respect, with the usual processes of civilization, which is not the fruit of a single tree, but has always been developed by grafts and cuttings between the most favoured branches of the human race."[39]

The models (principles) presented in this book adopt the mystic understanding of myths and cultures in the determination of their compatibility. While this study will make use of such disciplines as anthropology, archeology, philology and historical linguistics, phonetics and phonology, it will lay heavy emphasis not so much on the historicity of the factors of cultural expression, although this forms an important aspect of the evidences related to prior contact, but rather on the substance or symbolic, philosophical and metaphoric significance of the items in question. Written records do constitute an essential aspect of the study but this definition needs to be broadened to include iconography, as symbol, metaphor, and iconography are also forms of language, as we will see. The following principles will be used in this comparative cultural study.

---

[37] Ibid

[38] A structural or behavioral characteristic peculiar to an individual or a group.

[39] *The Migration of Symbols,* Count Goblet D' Alviella, 1894

Principle 1: Single Event (one occurrence) Match Un-supported By Matches in Other Factors

Example: If one artifact looks the same (correlation of form) in two separate cultures, *this single event proposed correlation* may be explained as a coincidence. But if the primary factor upon which the conjecture is based, for example, *form,* is supported by correlations in other factors such as usage, philosophy, myth, etc., then the argument that it is only a coincidence becomes less tenable. That is, just because the *ontology*[40] of two cultures is expressed through mythology does not suggest a correlation between the two cultures. In order to be considered as a *proposed correlation* for the purpose of determining the congruence of the two cultures, the simple correlation must be supported by at least one or more matching elements of cultural expression. So if there is no other match beyond the initial apparent match this proposed correlation will be considered as being "unsupported."

A- Example of a *Unsupported single event proposed correlation:*

Primary Category proposed as a correlation between two cultures ➔ *Myth* ⬅
Supported by *Iconography*

In this example, one category, the myths of the two cultures match wholly or partially in iconography only.

Typically, the common forms of evidence used to support the theory of cultural connections is a Single Event (one occurrence) Unsupported Match in One Cultural Category which may or may not occur in the presence of other unrelated single event matches in the same or in related but separate cultural categories.

If the *single event proposed correlation* is devoid of additional supports (ex. correlation is of form only) but is found to be part of a group (occurring within the same culture) of several other *single event proposed unsupported correlations* in the same category or other cultural expression categories, then the conclusion that the correlating factors are simple coincidences is less supportable because the frequency of correlations rises beyond the threshold of chance as would be determined by statistical analysis of the normal probability of the existence of such correlations.[41] The correlations here are basic and superficial, usually of appearance, and yet they are suggestive of a deeper connection.

---

[40] Ontology, in philosophy, the branch of metaphysics that studies the basic nature of things, the essence of "being" itself.

[41] *Statistics-probability-* A number expressing the likelihood that a specific event will occur, expressed as the ratio of the number of actual occurrences to the number of possible occurrences. (American Heritage Dictionary)

Table 1: Example of Single Event (one occurrence) Unsupported Matches in One Cultural Category Occurring in the Presence of Other Unrelated Single Event Matches in the Same Cultural Categories

Single Event Unsupported Match	Culture A	Culture B	Culture A	Culture B	Culture A	Culture B	Supported Matches
The primary matching Categories	*Mythic Character 1*	*Mythic Character 1*	*Mythic ritual*	*Mythic ritual*	*Mythic ritual*	*Mythic ritual*	← Matches
The primary supporting factor →	*Iconography*	*Iconography*	*Iconography*	*Iconography*	*Iconography*	*Iconography*	← Matches

Table 2: Example of Single Event (occurrence) Unsupported Match in One Cultural Category Occurring in the Presence of Other Unrelated Single Event Matches in Related but Separate Cultural Categories

Single Event Unsupported Match	Culture A	Culture B	Culture A	Culture B	Culture A	Culture B	Supported Matches
The primary matching Categories	*Mythic Character 1*	*Mythic Character 1*	*Architecture*	*Architecture*	*Ritual*	*Ritual*	← Matches
The primary supporting factors →	*Iconography*	*Iconography*	*Style*	*Style*	*Tradition*	*Tradition*	← Matches

Additional criteria for Principle 1:

Single event proposed correlations that are unsupported by other factors and unrelated to other categories require a more rigorous standard of discernment in order to be included as evidence of congruence. A *single event proposed correlation* that is unsupported by other factors and unrelated to other categories will be accepted as evidence of congruence if it occurs in the presence of at least three or more other unrelated single event matches in the same or other cultural factor categories.

B- Example of a _Supported Single event proposed correlation:_

Primary factor proposed
as a correlation between two cultures➔ *Myth* ⬅ Supported by
⠀⠀⠀⠀⠀⠀⠀⠀⠀⠀⠀⠀⠀⠀⠀⠀⠀⠀⠀*Iconography*
⠀⠀⠀⠀⠀⠀⠀⠀⠀⠀⠀⠀⠀⠀⠀⠀⠀⠀⠀⬆⬆⬆
⠀⠀⠀⠀⠀⠀⠀⠀⠀⠀⠀⠀⠀⠀⠀⠀⠀⠀⠀⬆⬆⬆

Cultural elements that
may support the primary factor ➔➔➔➔ Plot,
⠀⠀⠀⠀⠀⠀⠀⠀⠀⠀⠀⠀⠀⠀⠀⠀⠀➔gender,
⠀⠀⠀⠀⠀⠀⠀⠀⠀⠀⠀⠀⠀⠀⠀⠀⠀➔theme,
⠀⠀⠀⠀⠀⠀⠀⠀⠀⠀⠀⠀⠀⠀⠀⠀⠀➔action,
⠀⠀⠀⠀⠀⠀⠀⠀⠀⠀⠀⠀⠀⠀⠀⠀⠀➔etc.

In this example, the myths of the two cultures match wholly or partially in iconography, plot, gender, theme, action, etc. Therefore, the initial correlation is supported by more than one factor (iconography).

Table 3: Supported Matching Cultural Factors

Supported Matching Cultural Factors	Culture A	Culture B	Supported Matches
The primary matching category ➔	*Myth* ⬆⬆⬆ **Supporting Factors**	*Myth* ⬆⬆⬆ **Supporting Factors**	⬅ **Matches**
The primary supporting factor ➔ Secondary supporting factor ➔ Tertiary supporting factor ➔ Quaternary supporting factor ➔ Quinternary supporting factor ➔	*Iconography* Plot, gender, theme, action, etc.	*Iconography* Plot, gender, theme, action, etc.	⬅ **Matches** ⬅ **Matches** ⬅ **Matches** ⬅ **Matches** ⬅ **Matches**

Additional criteria for Principle 1:

A *supported single event proposed correlation* between the categories being compared within the two cultures will be accepted as evidence of congruence if that *single event proposed correlation* is <u>supported</u> by at least one or more (secondary, tertiary, quaternary, etc.) cultural factors that match exactly in the two cultures (see table above).

Principle 2: Pattern-Multiple Correlations Occur Within the Same Cultural Category or Across the Landscape of Cultural Categories

Single event proposed <u>supported</u> correlations between two cultures that occur as a part of a pattern comprised of several *single event proposed supported correlations* will be accepted as evidence of congruence between the categories being compared among the two cultures. Pattern here implies consistency in the appearance of the number of correlating factors in the same or different categories.

Table 4: Example-Supported Matching Cultural Factors within the Cultural Factor/Category: Myth

Depth **(deepness-vertical)** *pattern of correlations*

If two or more independent factor matches within one category appear, they will be considered as a part of a pattern denoting congruence between the two cultures. These correlations will be considered as equivalencies within a particular category of expressions such as, art, architecture, myth, etc. This pattern is referred to as a *depth* (deepness-vertical) *pattern of correlations* and the category will be accepted as evidence in the determination of congruence between two cultures.

Depth pattern of correlations	Culture A	Culture B	Culture A	Culture B	Culture A	Culture B	Supported Matches
The primary matching categories	*Myth*	*Myth*	*Mythic Character 1*	*Mythic Character 1*	*Mythic Theme*	*Mythic Theme*	← Matches
The primary supporting factor →	⬆⬆⬆ **Supporting Factors** *Iconography* Plot, gender, theme, action, etc.	⬆⬆⬆ **Supporting Factors** *Iconography* Plot, gender, theme, action, etc.	⬆⬆⬆ **Supporting Factors** *Iconography* Plot, gender, theme, action, etc.	⬆⬆⬆ **Supporting Factors** *Iconography* Plot, gender, theme, action, etc.	⬆⬆⬆ **Supporting Factors** *Iconography* Plot, gender, theme, action, etc.	⬆⬆⬆ **Supporting Factors** *Iconography* Plot, gender, theme, action, etc.	← Matches ← Matches ← Matches ← Matches ← Matches

Table 5: Example-Supported Matching Cultural Factors within the wide range of Cultural Factor/Categories

Breadth **(wideness-horizontal)** *pattern of correlations*

The pattern may appear as a consistent number of single event correlations discovered in different cultural categories. For example, several correlations in a study of comparative culture may be found in any of the cultural categories discussed earlier. If two or more instances of matching factors arise then this pattern is referred to as a *breadth* (wideness-horizontal) *pattern of correlations* and the category will be accepted as evidence of congruence.

Breadth pattern of correlations Factors	Culture A	Culture B	Culture A	Culture B	Culture A	Culture B	Supported Matches
The primary matching Categories	*Mythic Character 1*	*Mythic Character 1*	*Architecture*	*Architecture*	*Ritual*	*Ritual*	← Matches
The primary supporting factor →	⬆⬆⬆ **Supporting Factors** *Iconography* Plot, gender, theme, action, etc.	⬆⬆⬆ **Supporting Factors** *Iconography* Plot, gender, theme, action, etc.	⬆⬆⬆ **Supporting Factors** *Iconography* Plot, gender, theme, action, etc.	⬆⬆⬆ **Supporting Factors** *Iconography* Plot, gender, theme, action, etc.	⬆⬆⬆ **Supporting Factors** *Iconography* Plot, gender, theme, action, etc.	⬆⬆⬆ **Supporting Factors** *Iconography* Plot, gender, theme, action, etc.	← Matches ← Matches ← Matches ← Matches ← Matches

Principle 3: Cross-Cultural Correlations

Principle #1 represents the most common form of evidence that can be presented as proof of congruence between two cultures. Therefore, this is the principle within which most simple correlations between cultures are to be found. However, the nature and exactness of the correlations of the factors between the two cultures may be deserving of greater weight. An example of this is the correlation between the relationship of the numbers used in Indian, Icelandic and Chaldean myth, presented in this text. Cross-cultural correlations (correlations between three or more cultures) may be observed in the unsupported or supported state. They may most likely be found in the breadth pattern of distribution. This pattern of correlation suggests a *diffusion* of the expressions of the cultural factors from one original source and / or a relationship between the cultures being studied.

Table 6: Single Event Unsupported Cross Cultural Correlations

Cross-Cultural Correlations	Culture A	Culture B	Culture C	Culture D	Culture E	Culture F	Supported Matches
The primary matching category	*Mythic Character 1*	*Mythic Character 1*	*Mythic Character 1*	*Mythic Character 1*	*Mythic Character 1*	*Mythic Character 1*	← Matches
The primary supporting factor →	Iconograph	Iconograph	Iconography	Iconography	Iconography	Iconograph	← Matches

In order for these principles to carry weight and to be considered a substantive arguments for theorizing that the given cultures are related and or that they adopted cultural factors from the other cultures, it is advisable to establish evidence of contact and a correlation of at least one additional factor of correlation. In this regard, once a factor has been preliminarily established to match, say as a mythic character appearing to possess the same iconography, if it can be determined that the mythic characters, for instance, perform the same function or if a mythic artifact or symbol carries the same usage in the mythic system, then it is possible to assert with greater confidence that there is a connection between the two cultures. The particular example used in this principle is one of the main patterns of cultural congruence discovered by mythologist Joseph Campbell, which he presented in his groundbreaking work *The Hero of A Thousand Faces*. The mythic, heroic character exhibits particular patterns in myths from various cultures which can be readily discerned. The myth of the Asarian Resurrection of Ancient Egypt, in which a prince is born, his father is killed by the uncle, the child flees into exile to be brought up by sages so that he/she may return and face the evil tyrant and reestablish order and justice, can be seen in the myth of Krishna of India, the story of Jesus, the story of Hamlet, and even in modern times with the story of the movie "Star Wars" and the even more recent "Lion King." The table gives an example of a single event supported cross-cultural correlation. Examples of multiple event supported cross-cultural correlations can be seen in the connections between Ancient Egyptian mythology, Indian mythology, Sumerian mythology, Greek mythology and Christian mythology.

Table 7: Single Event Supported Cross Cultural Correlations

Cross-Cultural Correlations	Culture A	Culture B	Culture C	Culture D	Culture E	Culture F	Supported Matches
The primary matching category	*Mythic Character 1*	*Mythic Character 1*	*Mythic Character 1*	*Mythic Character 1*	*Mythic Character 1*	*Mythic Character 1*	← Matches
The primary supporting factor →	*Iconograph*	*Iconograph*	*Iconography*	*Iconography*	*Iconography*	*Iconograph*	← Matches
Other possible additional supporting factors →→ ↘↘↘↘↘	Function Actions Gender Age Metaphoric significance	Function Actions Gender Age Metaphoric significance	Function Actions Gender Age Metaphoric significance	Function Actions Gender Age Metaphoric significance	Function Actions Gender Age Metaphoric significance	Function Actions Gender Age Metaphoric significance	← Matches ← Matches ← Matches ← Matches ← Matches

Final Standard

A. CULTURAL INFLUENCE- In order to establish the influence of one culture on another it must be possible to show concordances in any categories, including Evidence of Contact, but not necessarily including Ethnicity.

  a. Each category of cultural expression match must be supported by at least one Method of Correlation –

B. COMMON CULTURAL ORIGINS- In order to establish the common origins of two given cultures it must be possible to show a pattern of concordances in any of 6 or more categories including Evidence of Contact and Ethnicity.

  a. Each category of cultural expression match must be supported by at least two Methods of Correlation – Breadth Proof

and/or

  b. Each category of cultural expression match must be supported by at least two Methods of Correlation – Depth Proof

C. CULTURAL PRIMACY- In order to demonstrate that culture has come first in history and that the later (secondary) culture has drawn cultural factors from the primary culture, it is necessary to first establish Evidence of Contact, the exchange of cultural factors from the primary to the secondary culture, and next, it is necessary to show a chronology in which the primary culture is shown to have developed previous to the secondary culture.

The Fundamental Cultural Factors

What is it that distinguishes one culture from another? What factors determine whether or not a cultural factor is borrowed by one group from another, and what criteria determines that a culture is not simply influenced, but is actually part of another culture. As stated earlier, the principles under which this current study of Kamitan and Indian culture will be conducted is based on the contention that when several cultural factors can be correlated or matched, and when these matches can be supported by varied aspects within the two cultures, then the study becomes more concrete and specific as opposed to abstract and general. This of course raises the validity of the arguments and the conclusions drawn from them. But where is the threshold wherein it becomes obvious that a group of peoples is related to another? The following cultural principles are offered as criterion for such a determination. The latter four (Ethnicity, Myth, Philosophy and Rituals and Tradition) may be considered as the basic qualities which define a culture and which it carries forth over time. These cultural factors may be thought of as the core fundamental elements of culture which makes it unique from the standpoint of the determination of its kinship to another culture. Contact is considered here because interactions with other cultures can have a profound effect on the direction of a society and its cultural development.

Contact – evidence of prior contact (relationships)
Ethnicity – both groups matching in their ethnic background
Myth synchronism
Philosophical synchronism
Rituals and traditions synchronism

So under this model, even if people born in Kamit were to be found in India, if their lives and activities did not match in the other areas, they would not be considered as members of the same culture for the purposes of this study. Accordingly, it must be understood here that the term "ethnicity" does not relate to race. The word "ethnic" may have originated from the Biblical term "ethnos" meaning "of or pertaining to a group of people recognized as a class on the basis of certain distinctive characteristics, such as religion, language, ancestry, culture, or national origin."[124]

Ethnicity, Race as Culture Factors

Modern scientists and scholars say that race distinctions based on genetics is unscientific and wrong. The animosity and hatred of modern times, caused by distortion of religious scriptures when being rewritten or reinterpreted by various groups or ignorance of the true intent of the teachings of the religious holy books, has led to a situation where social problems have rendered practitioners of religion incapable of reaching a higher level of spiritual understanding. Many people in modern society are caught up in the degraded level of disputes and wars in an attempt to support ideas, which are in reality absurd and destructive in reference to the authentic doctrines of religion. Ironically, the inability of leaders in the church, synagogue or secular society to accept the truth about the origins of humanity comes from their desire to gain and maintain control and fear of losing control over their followers. Now that modern science is showing that all human beings originated from the same source, in Africa, and that racial distinctions are at least questionable and misleading and at worst, malicious lies and race baiting, it means that those who have perpetrated and sustained racism can no longer use science or religious teachings to support their iniquity and ignorant designs. They have no leg to stand on. The following excerpt was taken from Encarta Encyclopedia, and is typical of the modern scientific understanding of the question of human genetics and race issues.

"The concept of race has often been misapplied. One of the most telling arguments against classifying people into races is that persons in various cultures have often mistakenly acted as if one race were superior to another. Although, with social disadvantages eliminated, it is possible that one human group or another might have some genetic advantages in response to such factors as climate, altitude, and specific food availability, these differences are small. There are no differences in native intelligence or mental capacity that cannot be explained by environmental circumstances. Rather than using racial classifications to study human variability, anthropologists today define geographic or social groups by geographic or social criteria. They then study the nature of the genetic attributes of these groups and seek to understand the causes of changes in their genetic makeup. Contributed by: Gabriel W. Laser "Races, Classification of," Encarta." Copyright (c) 1994

It should be noted here that there is no evidence that racial classifications for the purpose of supporting racist views existed in Ancient Egypt. However, the concept of ethnicity, which is often erroneously confused with the modern concept of race, was acknowledged in ancient times. That is to say, the Ancient Egyptians recognized that some of the physical features and characteristics of the Asiatics, Europeans, and other groups were different from themselves and the Nubians. They recognized themselves as looking like the Nubians, but as possessing differences in culture. The Ancient Egyptian's depictions of themselves and their neighbors shows us beyond reasonable doubt, that they were dark skinned people like all other Africans, before the influx of Asiatics and Europeans to the country. Since genetics is increasingly being recognized as a false method of differentiating people the concept of phenotype has progressively more been used.

> **phe·no·type** (fē'nə-tīp') *n.* **1.a.** The observable physical or biochemical characteristics of an organism, as determined by both genetic makeup and environmental influences. **b.** The expression of a specific trait, such as stature or blood type, based on genetic and environmental influences. **2.** An individual or group of organisms exhibiting a particular phenotype.[42]

It has been shown that climactic conditions, geography, solar exposure, vegetation, etc., have the effect of changing the appearance of people. This means that while people (human beings) remain equally human internally, their physiognomy and shade of skin adapt to the conditions where they live. This means that the external differences in people have little to do with their internal humanity and therefore are illusory. The concept of social typing is therefore based on ignorance about the race issue and its misconceptions, and cannot be supported by the scientific evidences. Further, an advancing society cannot hold such erroneous notions without engendering strife, and confusion, within the society. An advancing society will not be able to attain the status of "civilization" while holding on to such spurious concepts.

One of the major problems for society and non-secular groups is that the teachings and scientific evidence presented here has not been taught to the world population at large as part of the public or private education system. Even if it were, it would take time for people to adjust to their new understanding. Most people grow up accepting the ignorance of their parents who

---

[42] American Heritage Dictionary

received the erroneous information from their own parents, and so on. Racism, sexism and other scourges of society are not genetically transmitted. They are transmitted by ignorant family members who pass on their ignorance, prejudices and bigotries to their children, and so on down through the generations.

The only fair and accurate standard to classify people is by means of education and ethics. Here education refers not just to trades or technical endeavors but to the origins of humanity and the contributions of all members (especially the Africans) of humanity to the evolution of world culture and the advancement towards civilization. This knowledge directly impacts a person's ethics, as once the common origins of humanity and the falseness of the race issue are understood and affirmed in a person's life, their ethics, and relations this will have an impact on how people view each other and consequently this will improve how people treat each other.

Below is a listing of the world's major cultures and a timeline of their rise and fall for the purpose of comparative study.

Timeline of World Cultures

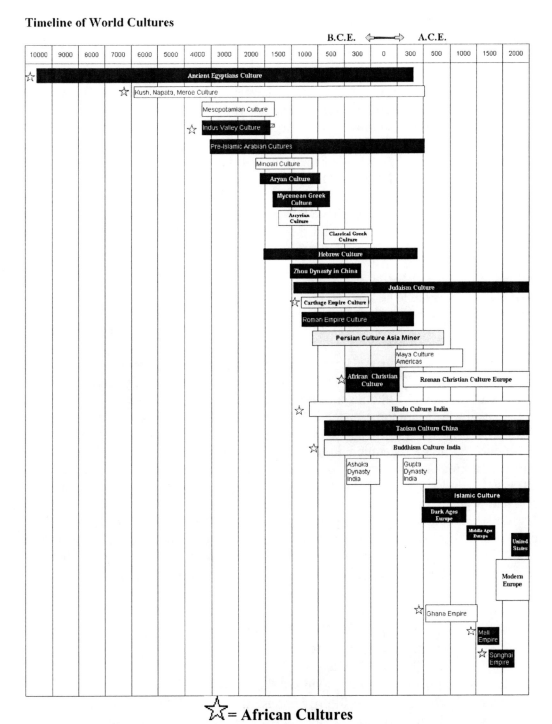

☆ = African Cultures

Example of Cultural Interaction (Application of the Cultural Comparison Criteria to Ancient Egptian/Nubian and Greek Cultures)

Early Cultural Interactions Between Greece, Rome, Egypt and Ethiopia.

The Greek and Roman epics are form the basis of Greco-Roman mythology and religion. These scriptures make specific and important references to Ancient Egypt and Ethiopia as foundations for Greco-Roman divinities and a special reverence for Ethiopia as the source of proper religious practice.

As Rome emerged as a powerful military force in the period just prior to the birth of Christ (200 B.C.E.-30 B.C.E.), they adopted Greek customs, religion and art, seeing these as their legacy. Just as the Greeks adopted *The Illiad* and *The Odyssey*, the Romans enthusiastically embraced *The Aeneid* as their national epic. Vergil or Virgil (70-19 B.C.E.) was a Roman poet who wrote *The Aeneid* in the Latin language.[43] *The Aeneid* is actually a story that was written in the same form as *The Odyssey* and *The Illiad* of the Greek writer Homer. It was widely distributed and read throughout the Roman Empire. Thus, *The Aeneid* is considered to be a classical Latin masterpiece of ancient world literature, which had enormous influence on later European writers.[44] Some portions of these texts have important implications to understand the relationship between the Egyptians, the Ethiopians and the Indians in ancient times. *(italicized portions are by Ashby)*

> Mixed in the bloody battle on the plain;
> *And swarthy Memnon in his arms he knew,*
> *His pompous ensigns, and his Indian crew.*
> — *The Aeneid*, Book I, Vergil or Virgil (70-19 BC)[45]

In Greek myth, Memnon was a king from Ethiopia, and was openly referred to as being "burnt of skin", i.e. "black."[46] He was the son of Tithonus, a Troyan (Trojan) prince, and Eos, a Greek goddess of the dawn. Tithonus and Eos represent the sky and romantic love, respectively. During the Troyan war, Memnon assisted Troy[47] with his army. Even though he fought valiantly, he was killed by Achilles. In order to comfort Memnon's mother, Zeus, the king of the Greek gods and goddesses, made Memnon immortal.[48] The Greeks revered a colossal statue of the Ancient Egyptian king Amenhotep III as an image of Memnon. During the times of Greek (332 B.C.E.-30 B.C.E.) and Roman (30 B.C.E.-450 A.C.E.) conquest of Egypt, it became fashionable for Greek and Roman royalty, nobles and those of means from all over the ancient world, especially Greece, to take sightseeing trips to Egypt. The "Colossi of Memnon" were big attractions. The Colossi of Memnon are two massive statues that were built under Amenhotep III, 1,417-1,379 B.C.E.[49] The statues fronted a large temple[50] which is now in ruin, mostly depleted of its stonework by nearby Arab inhabitants who used them to build houses.

---

[43] Random House Encyclopedia Copyright (C) 1983,1990

[44] "Vergil," Microsoft (R) Encarta. Copyright (c) 1994

[45] *The Aeneid By Virgil*, Translated by John Dryden

[46] Recall that the term Ethiopians means "land of the burnt (black) faces."

[47] Troy (Asia Minor), also Ilium (ancient Ilion), famous city of Greek legend, on the northwestern corner of Asia Minor, in present-day Turkey. "Troy (Asia Minor)," Microsoft (R) Encarta. Copyright (c) 1994

[48] "Memnon," Microsoft (R) Encarta. Copyright (c) 1994

[49] Random House Encyclopedia Copyright (C) 1983,1990

[50] *The Complete Temples of Ancient Egypt*, Richard Wilkinson, (C) 2000

Thus, the association of Amenhotep III with Memnon by the Greeks, supports their contention that the Ancient Egyptians and Nubians (Ethiopians) were not only related but looked alike (burnt or skin, i.e. what is today referred to as black).

This passage above is very important because it establishes a connection between Greece/Rome and Ethiopia, Egypt and India. Further, it establishes that the Indians made up the army of Memnon, that is to say, Ethiopia. Thus, in the time of Virgil, the cultural relationship between north-east Africa and India was so well known that it was mythically carried back in time to the reign of Pharaoh Amenhotep III, the father of the famous king Akhnaton. Pharaoh Amenhotep III was one of the most successful kings of Ancient Egypt. He ruled the area from northern Sudan (Nubia) to the Euphrates river. The Euphrates river is formed by the confluence of the Murat Nehri and the Kara Su Rivers. It flows from East Turkey across Syria into central modern day Iraq where it joins the Tigris River. The land referred to as Mesopotamia, along the lower Euphrates, was the birthplace of the ancient civilizations of Babylonia and Assyria, and the site of the ancient cities of Sippar, Babylon, Erech, Larsa, and Ur. The length of the river is 2,235mi (3.598km).[51] So again we have support for the writings of Herodotus and Diodorus who related the makeup of the ethnic groups in Mesopotamia as belonging to the Ancient Egyptian-Nubian culture.

At first inspection, this relationship appears to be perhaps an allusion to Virgil's times when it is well known and accepted that there was trade and cultural exchange, not only between India and Egypt, as we and other scholars have shown, but also between India and Greece.

Also, in contrast to present day society, there is no racist concept detected or being either implied or inferred, in the Greek writings. Also, there is no apparent aversion to having a personage of African descent (someone from a different ethnic group) in the Greek religion as a member of the family of Greek Gods and Goddesses. There is a remarkable feeling in reading the Greek texts that they had no compunction about admitting their association with Africa and Africans. The Greeks received much in terms of civilization and culture from Africa, in particular, Ethiopia and Ancient Egypt. This may be likened to modern college graduates who are proud to boast of their successful attendance at prestigious schools. There seems to be an eagerness to admit traveling to Egypt, as if it were a stamp of approval for their entry into society as professionals in their fields.

The Pharaoh Amenhotep III (referred to as the real life Memnon by the Greeks)

---

[51] Random House Encyclopedia Copyright (C) 1983,1990

The Colossi of Memnon- built under Amenhotep III, 1,417 B.C.E. -1,379 B.C.E. 59 feet tall

CHAPTER 1: BRIEF HISTORY OF ANCIENT EGYPT

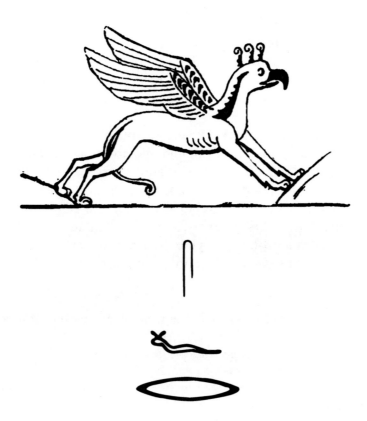

Who Were the Ancient Egyptians

The Ancient Egyptian religion (*Shetaut Neter*), language and symbols provide the first "historical" record of Mystical Philosophy and Religious literature. Egyptian Mysticism is what has been commonly referred to by Egyptologists as Egyptian "Religion" or "Mythology," but to think of it as just another set of stories or allegories about a long lost civilization is to completely miss the greatest secret of human existence. Mystical spirituality, in all of its forms and disciplines of spiritual development, was practiced in Ancient Egypt (Kemet) earlier than anywhere else in history. This unique perspective from the highest philosophical system which developed in Africa over seven thousand years ago provides a new way to look at life, religion, the discipline of psychology and the way to spiritual development leading to spiritual Enlightenment. Ancient Egyptian mythology, when understood as a system of *Smai Tawi*, that is, a system which promotes the union of the individual soul with the Universal Soul or Supreme Consciousness, gives every individual insight into their own divine nature, and also a deeper insight into all religions, mystical and Yoga systems.

In Chapter 4[52] and Chapter 17[53] of an Ancient Egyptian mystical text, the *Prt m Hru, The Ancient Egyptian Book of Enlightenment*, more commonly known as the *Book of the Dead*, the term "Smai Tawi" is used. It means "Union of the two lands of Egypt." The two lands refers to the two main districts of the country (North and South) and, in a mystical sense they refer to the gods Heru and Set, who are elsewhere referred to as the spiritual Higher Self and lower self of a human being, respectively. Thus, the term Smai Tawi is compatible with the Indian Sanskrit term "Yoga," which also means union of the Higher Self and lower self as well as other terms (Enlightenment, Kingdom of Heaven, Liberation, etc.) used by other systems of mystical spirituality.

Diodorus Siculus (Greek Historian) writes in the time of Augustus (first century B.C.):

"Now the Ethiopians, as historians relate, were the first of all men and the proofs of this statement, they say, are manifest. For that they did not come into their land as immigrants from abroad, but were the natives of it and so justly bear the name of autochthones (sprung from the soil itself), is, they maintain, conceded by practically all men..."

"They also say that the Egyptians are colonists sent out by the Ethiopians, Asar having been the leader of the colony. For, speaking generally, what is now Egypt, they maintain, was not land, but sea, when in the beginning the universe was being formed; afterwards, however, as the Nile during the times of its inundation carried down the mud from Ethiopia, land was gradually built up from the deposit...And the larger parts of the customs of the Egyptians are, they hold, Ethiopian, the colonists still preserving their ancient manners. For instance, the belief that their kings are Gods, the very special attention which they pay to their burials, and many other matters of a similar nature, are Ethiopian practices, while the shapes of their statues and the forms of their letters are Ethiopian; for of the two kinds of writing which the Egyptians have, that which is known as popular (demotic) is learned by everyone, while that which is called sacred (hieratic), is understood only by the priests of the Egyptians, who learnt it from their Fathers as one of the things which are not divulged, but among the Ethiopians, everyone uses these forms of letters. Furthermore, the orders of the priests, they maintain, have much the same position among both peoples; for all are clean who are engaged in the

---

[52] Commonly referred to as Chapter 17
[53] Commonly referred to as Chapter 176

service of the gods, keeping themselves shaven, like the Ethiopian priests, and having the same dress and form of staff, which is shaped like a plough and is carried by their kings who wear high felt hats which end in a knob in the top and are circled by the serpents which they call asps; and this symbol appears to carry the thought that it will be the lot who shall dare to attack the king to encounter death-carrying stings. Many other things are told by them concerning their own antiquity and the colony which they sent out that became the Egyptians, but about this there is no special need of our writing anything."

The Ancient Egyptian texts state:

> "Our people originated at the base of the mountain of the Moon,
> at the origin of the Nile river."

The ancient name for the land now called Egypt was:

"KMT" "Egypt," "Burnt," "Black people," "Black Land"

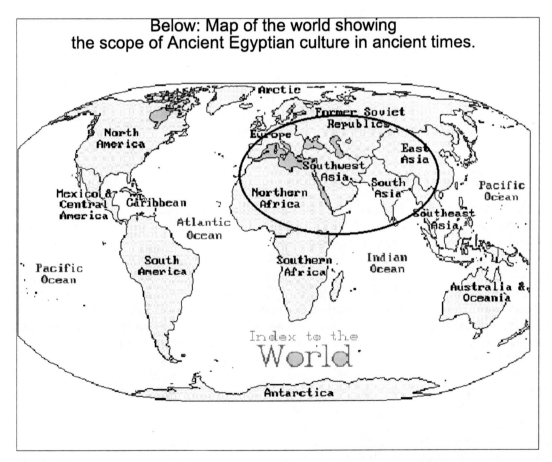

Below: Map of the world showing the scope of Ancient Egyptian culture in ancient times.

The World

In describing the Ancient Egyptians of his time Herodotus (Greek historian c. 484-425 BC), said: *"The Egyptians and Nubians have thick lips, broad noses, wooly hair and burnt skin... ...And the Indian tribes I have mentioned, their skins are all of the same color, much like the Ethiopians... their country is a long way from Persia towards the south..."* Diodorus, the Greek historian (c. 100 B.C.)

said the following, *"And upon his return to Greece, they gathered around and asked, "tell us about this great land of the Blacks called Ethiopia." And Herodotus said, "There are two great Ethiopian nations, one in Sind (India) and the other in Egypt."* Thus, the Ancient Egyptian peoples were of African origin and they had close ties in ancient times with the peoples of India.

Where is the land of Ancient Egypt?

A map of North East Africa showing the location of the land of *Ta-Meri* or *Kamit,* also known as Ancient Egypt.

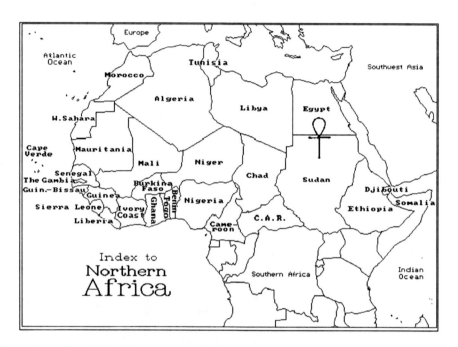

The Ancient Egyptians lived for thousands of years in the northeastern corner of the African continent in the area known as the Nile Valley. The Nile river was a source of dependable enrichment for the land and allowed them to prosper for a very long time. Their prosperity was so great that they created art, culture, religion, philosophy and a civilization which has not been duplicated since. The Ancient Kamitans (Egyptians) based their government and business concerns on spiritual values and therefore, enjoyed an orderly society which included equality between the sexes, and a legal system based on universal spiritual laws. The *Prt m Hru* is a tribute to their history, culture and legacy. As historical insights unfold, it becomes clearer that modern culture has derived its basis from Ancient Egypt, though the credit is not often given, nor the integrity of the practices maintained. This is another important reason to study Ancient Egyptian Philosophy, to discover the principles which allowed their civilization to prosper over a period of thousands of years in order to bring our systems of government, religion and social structures to a harmony with ourselves, humanity and with nature.

Christianity was partly an outgrowth of Judaism, which was itself an outgrowth of Ancient Egyptian culture and religion. So who were the Ancient Egyptians? From the time that the early Greek philosophers set foot on African soil to study the teachings of mystical spirituality in Egypt (900-300 B.C.E.), Western society and culture was forever changed. Ancient Egypt had such a profound effect on Western civilization as well as on the native population of Ancient India (Dravidians) that it is important to understand the history and culture of Ancient Egypt, and the nature of its spiritual tradition in more detail.

The history of Egypt begins in the far reaches of history. It includes The Dynastic Period, The Hellenistic Period, Roman and Byzantine Rule (30 B.C.E.-638 A.C.E.), the Caliphate and the Mamalukes (642-1517 A.C.E.), Ottoman Domination (1082-1882 A.C.E.), British colonialism (1882-1952 A.C.E.), as well as modern, Arab-Islamic Egypt (1952- present).

Ancient Egypt or Kamit had a civilization that flourished in Northeast Africa along the Nile River from before 5,500 B.C.E. until 30 B.C.E. In 30 B.C.E., Octavian, who was later known as the Roman Emperor, Augustus, put the last Egyptian King, Ptolemy XIV, a Greek ruler, to death. After this Egypt was formally annexed to Rome. Egyptologists normally divide Ancient Egyptian history into the following approximate periods: The Early Dynastic Period (3,200-2,575 B.C.E.); The Old Kingdom or Old Empire (2,575-2,134 B.C.E.); The First Intermediate Period (2,134-2,040 B.C.E.); The Middle Kingdom or Middle Empire (2,040-1,640 B.C.E.); The Second Intermediate Period (1,640-1,532 B.C.E.); The New Kingdom or New Empire (1,532-1,070 B.C.E.); The third Intermediate Period (1,070-712 B.C.E.); The Late Period (712-332 B.C.E.).

In the Late Period the following groups controlled Egypt. The Nubian Dynasty (712-657 B.C.E.); The Persian Dynasty (525-404 B.C.E.); The Native Revolt and re-establishment of Egyptian rule by Egyptians (404-343 B.C.E.); The Second Persian Period (343-332 B.C.E.); The Ptolemaic or Greek Period (332 B.C.E.- c. 30 B.C.E.); Roman Period (c.30 B.C.E.-395 A.C.E.); The Byzantine Period (395-640 A.C.E) and The Arab Conquest Period (640 A.C.E.-present). The individual dynasties are numbered, generally in Roman numerals, from I through XXX.

The period after the New Kingdom saw greatness in culture and architecture under the rulership of Ramses II. However, after his rule, Egypt saw a decline from which it would never recover. This is the period of the downfall of Ancient Egyptian culture in which the Libyans ruled after The Tanite (XXI) Dynasty. This was followed by the Nubian conquerors who founded the XXII dynasty and tried to restore Egypt to her past glory. However, having been weakened by the social and political turmoil of wars, Ancient Egypt fell to the Persians once more. The Persians conquered the country until the Greeks, under Alexander, conquered them. The Romans followed the Greeks, and finally the Arabs conquered the land of Egypt in 640 A.C.E to the present.

However, the history which has been classified above is only the history of the "Dynastic Period." It reflects the view of traditional Egyptologists who have refused to accept the evidence of a Predynastic period in Ancient Egyptian history contained in Ancient Egyptian documents such as the *Palermo Stone, Royal Tablets at Abydos, Royal Papyrus of Turin,* the *Dynastic List* of *Manetho.* The eye-witness accounts of Greek historians Herodotus (c. 484-425 B.C.E.) and Diodorus (Greek historian died about 20 B.C.E.) corroborate the status and makeup of Kamitan culture in the late dynastic period which support the earlier accounts. These sources speak clearly of a Pre-dynastic society which stretches far into antiquity. The Dynastic Period is what most people think of whenever Ancient Egypt is mentioned. This period is when the pharaohs (kings) ruled. The latter part of the Dynastic Period is when the Biblical story of Moses, Joseph, Abraham, etc., occurs (c. 2100? -1,000? B.C.E). Therefore, those with a Christian background generally only have an idea about Ancient Egypt as it is related in the Bible. Although this biblical notion is very limited in scope, the significant impact of Ancient Egypt on Hebrew and Christian culture is evident even from the biblical scriptures. Actually, Egypt existed much earlier than most traditional Egyptologists are prepared to admit. The new archeological evidence related to the great Sphinx monument on the Giza Plateau and the ancient writings by Manetho, one of the last High Priests of Ancient Egypt, show that Ancient Egyptian history begins earlier than 10,000 B.C.E. and may date back to as early as 30,000-50,000 B.C.E.

It is known that the Pharaonic (royal) calendar based on the Sothic system (star Sirius) was in use by 4,240 B.C.E. This certainly required extensive astronomical skills and time for observation. Therefore, the history of Kamit (Egypt) must be reckoned to be extremely ancient. Thus, in order to grasp the antiquity of Ancient Egyptian culture, religion and philosophy, we will briefly review the history presented by the Ancient Egyptian Priest Manetho and some Greek Historians.

The calendar based on the Great Year was also used by the Ancient Egyptians. The Great year is based on the movement of the earth through the constellations known as the precession of the Equinoxes and confirmed by the History given by the Ancient Egyptian Priest Manetho in the year 241 B.C.E. Each Great Year has 25,860 to 25,920 years and 12 arcs or constellations, and each passage through a constellation takes 2,155 – 2,160 years. These are the "Great Months." The current cycle or year began around the year 10,858 B.C.E. At around the year 36,766 B.C.E., according to Manetho, the Creator, Ra, ruled the earth in person from his throne in the Ancient Egyptian city of Anu. By this reckoning our current year (2,000 A.C.E.) is actually the year 38,766 based on the Great Year System of Ancient Egyptian history.

Below left: A map of North East Africa showing the location of the land of *Ta-Meri* or *Kamit*, also known as Ancient Egypt and South of it is located the land which in modern times is called Sudan.

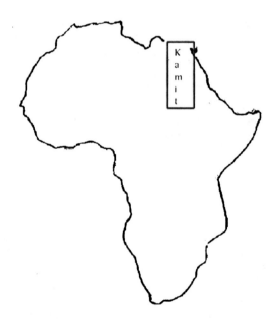

Below- The Land of Ancient Egypt-Nile Valley and major cities in ancient times.

The cities wherein the theology of the Trinity of Amun-Ra-Ptah was developed were: A- Sais (temple of Net), B- Anu (Heliopolis- temple of Ra), C-Men-nefer or Hetkaptah (Memphis, temple of Ptah), and D- Sakkara (Pyramid Texts), E- Akhet-Aton (City of Akhnaton, temple of Aton), F- Abdu (temple of Asar), G- Denderah (temple of Hetheru), H- Waset (Thebes, temple of Amun), I- Edfu (temple of Heru), J- Philae (temple of Aset). The cities wherein the theology of the Trinity of Asar-Aset-Heru was developed were Anu, Abydos, Philae, Denderah and Edfu.

The Two Lands of Egypt

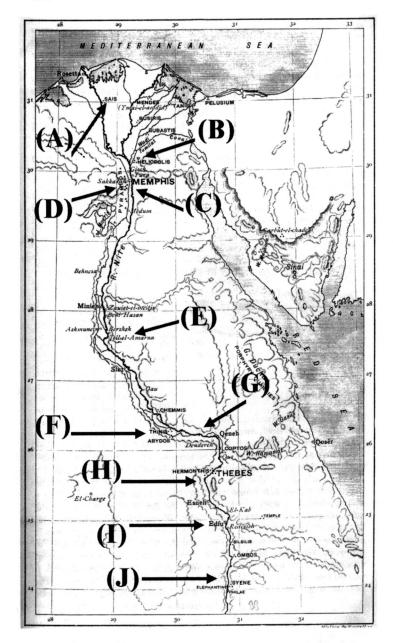

In Chapter 4[54] and Chapter 17[55] of the Ancient Egyptian mystical text, the *Prt m Hru, The Ancient Egyptian Book of Enlightenment*, more commonly known as the *Book of the Dead*, the term "Smai Tawi" is used. It means "Union of the two lands of Egypt." The two lands refers to the two main districts of the country (North and South) and, in a mystical sense they refer to the gods Heru (the north) and Set (the south land), who are elsewhere referred to as the spiritual Higher Self and lower self of a human being, respectively. Thus, the term Smai Tawi is compatible with the Indian Sanskrit term "Yoga," which also means union of the Higher Self and

---

[54] Commonly referred to as Chapter 17
[55] Commonly referred to as Chapter 176

lower self as well as other terms (enlightenment, Kingdom of Heaven, Liberation, etc.) used by other systems of mystical spirituality.

Diodorus Siculus (Greek Historian) writes in the time of Augustus (first century B.C.):

"Now the Ethiopians, as historians relate, were the first of all men and the proofs of this statement, they say, are manifest. For that they did not come into their land as immigrants from abroad, but were the natives of it and so justly bear the name of autochthones (sprung from the soil itself), is, they maintain, conceded by practically all men..."

"They also say that the Egyptians are colonists sent out by the Ethiopians, Asar having been the leader of the colony. For, speaking generally, what is now Egypt, they maintain, was not land, but sea, when in the beginning the universe was being formed; afterwards, however, as the Nile during the times of its inundation carried down the mud from Ethiopia, land was gradually built up from the deposit...And the larger parts of the customs of the Egyptians are, they hold, Ethiopian, the colonists still preserving their ancient manners. For instance, the belief that their kings are Gods, the very special attention which they pay to their burials, and many other matters of a similar nature, are Ethiopian practices, while the shapes of their statues and the forms of their letters are Ethiopian; for of the two kinds of writing which the Egyptians have, that which is known as popular (demotic) is learned by everyone, while that which is called sacred (hieratic), is understood only by the priests of the Egyptians, who learnt it from their Fathers as one of the things which are not divulged, but among the Ethiopians, everyone uses these forms of letters. Furthermore, the orders of the priests, they maintain, have much the same position among both peoples; for all are clean who are engaged in the service of the gods, keeping themselves shaven, like the Ethiopian priests, and having the same dress and form of staff, which is shaped like a plough and is carried by their kings who wear high felt hats which end in a knob in the top and are circled by the serpents which they call asps; and this symbol appears to carry the thought that it will be the lot who shall dare to attack the king to encounter death-carrying stings. Many other things are told by them concerning their own antiquity and the colony which they sent out that became the Egyptians, but about this there is no special need of our writing anything."

How Some Western and Arab Scholars Distort Evidence Pointing to the Older Age of Ancient Egyptian Culture

After examining the writings of many Western scholars the feeling by many Afrocentrists and Africologists (researchers into African culture) of African descent and some western scholars, is that traditional Egyptologists, a group composed almost entirely of people of European descent or trained by western scholars, have over the years sought to bring down the estimated date for the commencement of the dynastic period in Egypt in order to show that Ancient Egyptian culture emerged after Mesopotamian culture. Presumably, this was done because Mesopotamia is held by many Western scholars to be their (Western Culture's) own, if not genetic, cultural ancestral homeland. The reader should understand the context of this issue which goes to the heart of cultural relations between Western culture and Eastern and African cultures. From the perspective of many people of non-European descent they see a culture which has sought to establish its socio-economic supremacy by suppressing and undermining the capacity of indigenous peoples to govern themselves and control their own resources. This is verified by the documented evidence of the African slave trade,[56] military and covert intervention to destabilize governments, distortion of history,[57][58] colonial and neocolonial systems,[59] etc., either set up or supported by Western countries in the past 500 years. In order to perpetuate this control the image of superiority demands that Western culture should be able to project an ancestral right as it were to control other countries. Therefore, twisting evidence in order to make Western culture appear ancient, wise, beneficial, etc., necessitates a denial that there is any civilization that is older or at least better than Western civilization or that there could be any genetic or cultural relation with non-western cultures which are being subjugated and thereby a common ancestry with the rest of humanity. An example of this twisting of history by Western scholars is the well known and documented deliberate misinterpretation of the Bible story of Noah so as to make it appear that the Bible advocated and condones the enslavement of the children (descendants) of Ham (all Hamitic peoples- people of African descent) by the children (descendants) of Japheth (all peoples of Germanic (European) descent).

Genesis 9:26-27:

> 26 And he said, Blessed [be] the LORD God of Shem; and Canaan shall be his servant. {his servant: or, servant to them}
> 27 God shall enlarge Japheth, and he shall dwell in the tents of Shem; and Canaan shall be his servant. {enlarge: or, persuade}

The perceived continued denial of the past and the continued process of benefiting from past wrongdoing is a strong concern for many people around the world who feel they have been misled, abused by Western culture. A case often cited is distortion of the biblical story of Ham. In the Bible itself there is an attempt to show that the main Jewish ancestors comes from the blood-line of Shem (Genesis 11:10-26). This is done in an effort to follow up on the idea given in Genesis 9:26-27, that the Canaanites should be serving the Jews. These Biblical statements, like "be fruitful and multiply" (Genesis 1:28) and other "commands" of God are in reality mandates or directives written into the Bible for guiding the goals and objectives of the Jews. They are similar to political edicts, and acted to reinforce a particular agenda for the masses of people to believe in and pursue. They give a purpose and meaning to the lives of the Jews but they are not to be understood as spiritual edicts to be followed literally. They were written for a certain time and purpose which is several thousands of years removed from the present.

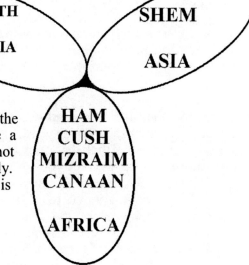

Figure 1: The Descendants of Noah-From the Judeo-Christian Biblical System.

[56] *The Middle Passage : White Ships Black Cargo* by Tom Feelings, John Henrik, Dr Clarke
[57] Stolen Legacy, George James
[58] *Black Athena, The Afroasiatic Origins of Classical Civilization* by Martin Bernal
[59] *Destruction of Black Civilization: Great Issues of a Race from 4500bc to 2000ad* by Chancellor Williams

It is notable that if Noah was angry with Ham, why did he not curse Ham? Instead he cursed Canaan. This is perhaps because the land of Canaan was the place where the Hebrews had always lived as wanderers and some of them were the writers of the Bible scriptures. They always longed to have a homeland in Canaan and the scriptures of the Old Testament are therefore directed at rallying people together in a movement towards conquering the land of Canaan and its people. The early Jews wanted to live in Canaan (Palestine) and not in Ethiopia (Ham). Judging from the times they were recorded, the clear implication is that the inhabitants of the land of Canaan, who were not followers of Judaism, were to be conquered by the Jews and used by them for their survival. This theme of the inferiority of the "Hamitic" peoples (Africans and Palestinians) and the superiority of the descendants of the Japhethian peoples-Eurasians was repeated and promoted by secular and non-secular western scholars and became a reality in the minds of many people. Continuing deceptions by government agencies, businesses and others, for profit, power, fame or fortune, continue to manifest in society. These problems are not the exclusive province of Western culture but they are exacerbated in Western culture by the superiority complex-mentality and the power bestowed by technological advancement and economic domination. Speaking from a yogic point of view, the past negative actions and continued abuses by Western culture in the distribution of material resources but also in distorted scholarship due to intellectual arrogance and hoarding of technological advancement for profit have created negative will towards the West. This has led to mistrust and animosity that will continue until their is a realization of the mistake and a subsequent move to redress the injustices and the ways of thinking that they engender which only serve to perpetuate the ignorance and misery of life when there is human conflict and strife.

Desiring to envision their own history as a civilized culture stretching back into antiquity and having realized that Greek culture is too late in history and not wanting to acknowledge that Ancient Greece essentially owes[60] its civilization to Ancient Egypt,[61] a process of downplaying the importance of Ancient Egypt in history by means of reducing the chronology of its history took place. How could this obfuscation of the record occur?

Along with the natural stubbornness of ordinary human beings to accept change due to the their identification with prestige of their culture and heritage as a source of self-worth instead of truth and virtue, two methods of discrediting the early achievements of Ancient Egypt have been used.

One method that was used was to examine the surviving mummies and apply undetermined forensic techniques in order to assign "causes of death" to the entire Ancient Egyptian culture and then conclude that the Ancient Egyptians had a short life span due to "primitive living conditions" so the average life expectancy of a Pharaoh would appear to be no more than 20 years or so. The cause of death can often not be determined even in modern times, so how can any technique be applied to a mummified body of 3,000 or more years ago and achieve consistent conclusive results? This and other rationales are not considered and as the erroneous pronouncements are repeated more and more it becomes accepted as truth by scholars and lay persons for a variety of reasons. Many scholars also do not look at the evidence themselves since they are comfortable in their positions. The laity may be unwilling, due to blind faith, or mental weakness to examine the evidences, or they may be unable to do so due to socio-economic obstacles, physical barriers preventing access to information, training, etc. Since we have lists of the Pharaohs of the Dynastic period we can easily use that figure, do the math by multiplying

[60] *Stolen Legacy,* George G.M. James
[61] *From Egypt to Greece,* M. Ashby C. M. Books 1997

that number by the reduced number of the life expectancy and come up with a figure that is less than 3,000 B.C.E. as a date for the beginning of the dynastic period. However, this methodology does not make sense if we consider the ample documentation showing that Ancient Egypt was reputed to have the "best doctors" in the ancient world. Further, even if it were true that ordinary people received "primitive living conditions" does it make sense that the Kings and Queens would get the worst health care out of the entire population? Or as a scholar, is it prudent to apply this number to the royalty? Also, we have documented evidence to show that kings and queens as well as other members of the society lived normal healthy lives by modern standards as there are surviving records and statues as well as illustrations of kings, mummies and other royalty who lived well into their 80's and 90's. One might also envision the wretchedness of such a life if one dies so young. No sooner does one realize the potential of life one dies as a mere child. Life would not be worth living and since spiritual evolution requires maturity in ordinary human terms, that is, sufficient time to grow up and discover the meaning of life, a short life-span would make the vast number of texts that are extant from Ancient Egypt, treating the subject of spiritual enlightenment impossible to create and useless because there would not be sufficient time to take advantage of them if they were available.

Two ways of invalidating Ancient Egyptian history are misunderstanding or supporting erroneous theories. A method that was used to discredit the Kamitan history is to arbitrarily claim that when the Ancient Egyptians spoke of years they were actually talking about months.[62] This practice is patently false and demeaning. Thus the corrupt nature of the historian and those who perpetuate such iniquitous misrepresentations is evident.

Still another motivation has been to try to synchronize the events such as those described in Ancient Egyptian texts or the Greek histories with those of the Bible. An example of this kind of writing can be found in a book by W.G. Waddell, called _Manetho_. Some people feel this kind of distortion was done to establish the prestige of the Judeo-Christian tradition since having other traditions which are recognized as older and having more honor, heritage and prominence would undermine the perception that the Bible is ancient and infallible. Others feel the reason was out of an effort to prove that Ancient Egyptian culture existed within the timeframe that the Bible has given for the Creation. The Creation was dated by the 17th-century Irish archbishop James Ussher as 4004 BC.[63] If the world was more than 6,000 years old, as postulated by the archbishop, this would refute the teaching presented in the church and would legitimize the existence of culture, philosophy and most of all, religion, prior to the emergence of Christianity. The work of Darwin (theory of evolution) and other scientists caused major controversies in society. A case in point is the attempt to correlate the events of Exodus with those of Ramses II of Ancient Egypt. First, there is no record of any conflict between the Jews and the Egyptians in any Ancient Egyptian record yet discovered beyond an inscription at the Karnak temple in Egypt stating that the Jews were one of the tribes under Egyptian rule in Palestine. Secondly, there is no corroborating record of the Bible in any of the contemporary writings from countries who had contact with the Jews and the Ancient Egyptians. Thirdly, there were at least 11 Kings who went by the title Rameses (Rameses I, II, III, III, etc.), spanning a period dated by traditional Egyptology from 1307 B.C.E. to 1070 B.C.E. Further, some localities were also referred to as Rameses. The oldest scholarly dating for the existence of Moses, if he did exist, is c. 1200 B.C.E. However, most Bible scholars agree that the earliest texts of the Bible were composed around 1000 B.C.E or later, and were developed over the next millennia. Also, most scholars are now

---

[62] _Manetho_, W. G. Waddell
[63] Encarta Encyclopedia, Copyright (c) 1994

beginning to accept the Ancient Egyptian and therefore, African ethnicity of the original Jewish People. An example of modern scholarship on the question of the origins of the Jewish People occurs in the book *Bible Myth: The African Origins of the Jewish People,* in a section entitled "Contradictory Biblical Evidence," the author, Gary Greenberg states:

> Dating the Exodus is problematic because evidence of its occurrence appears exclusively in the Bible, and what little it tells is contradictory. Exodus 12:40-41, for example, places the Exodus 430 years after the start of Israel's sojourn in Egypt (i.e., beginning with Jacob's arrival), whereas Genesis 15:13-14 indicates that four hundred years transpired from the birth of Isaac to the end of the bondage. Both claims cannot be true. Jacob was born in Isaac's 60th year,[64] and he didn't arrive in Egypt until his 130th year.[65] If the sojourn lasted 430 years, then the Exodus would have to have occurred 620 years after Isaac's birth.[66] On the other hand, if the Exodus occurred 400 years after Isaac was born, then the sojourn could only have been 210 years long.[67] Other biblical passages raise additional problems.[68]

The story of Sargon I points to another source and purpose for the Moses story. According to the biblical tradition, at about 1200? B.C.E., the Hebrews were in Egypt, serving as slaves. A Jewish woman placed her son in a basket and allowed it to float downstream where the Egyptian queen found it and then adopted the child. The child was Moses, the chosen one of God, who would lead the Jews out of bondage in Egypt. Moses was taken in by the royal family and taught all of the wisdom related to rulership of the nation as well as religious wisdom in reference to running the Egyptian Temples and the Egyptian religion. He was being groomed to be king and high priest of Egypt. This is why the Bible says he was knowledgeable in the wisdom of the Egyptians (Bible: Acts 7:22 and Koran C.144-(Verses 37 to 76)).

A story similar to the birth of Moses, about a child being placed in a basket and put in a stream which was later found by a queen, can be found in Zoroastrian mythology as well.[58] Also, the Semitic ruler, Sargon I, was rescued in the same manner after he was placed in a basket and sent floating down a river. Sargon I reigned about 2335-2279 B.C.E. He was called "Sargon The Great." He was one of the first known major Semitic conquerors known in history. He was successful in conquering the entire country of Sumer. Sumer is an ancient country of southwestern Asia, which corresponds approximately to the land known as Babylonia of biblical times. Babylon was an ancient city of Mesopotamia, which was located on the Euphrates River about 55mi (89km) South of present-day Baghdad. Sargon I created an empire stretching from the Mediterranean to the Persian Gulf in c.2350 B.C.E. The adoption of the child into royalty and rulership motif was apparently a popular theme in ancient times for those who wanted to legitimize their ascendancy to power by creating the perception that it was divinely ordained.[69]

Despite the myriad of ongoing excavations that have been conducted, many sponsored by Christian or Jewish groups, no substantial evidence has been unearthed that supports the

---

[64] Gen. 25:26

[65] Gen. 47:9

[66] 60+130+430=620.

[67] 400-130-60=210.

[68] *Bible Myth: The African Origins of the Jewish People* Gary Greenberg

[69] *The Power of Myth*, Joseph Campbell

historicity of the Bible. However, new discoveries have been brought forth that corroborate Herodotus' statements and the histories relating to the fact that the land that is now called Palestine, was once part of Ancient Egypt.

> An approximately 5,000-year-old settlement discovered in southern Israel was built and ruled by Egyptians during the formative period of Egyptian civilization, a team of archaeologists announced last week.
> The new find, which includes the first Egyptian-style tomb known to have existed in Israel at that time, suggests that ancient Egypt exerted more control over neighboring regions than investigators have often assumed, contends project director Thomas E. Levy of the University of California, San Diego.

> Source: Science News, Oct 5, 1996 v150 n14 p215(1).
> Title: Ancient Egyptian outpost found in Israel.
> (Halif Terrace site in southern Israel upsets previous estimates of Egyptian imperialism) Author: Bruce Bower

Speaking out on the stronghold which modern European and American Egyptologists have created, the Egyptologist, scholar and author, John Anthony West, detailed his experiences and those of others attempting to study the Ancient Egyptian monuments and artifacts who are not part of the "accepted" Egyptological clique. He describes the situation as a kind of "Fortress Egypt." He describes the manner in which not only the Ancient Egyptian artifacts are closely protected from the examination of anyone outside but also the interpretation of the meaning of them as well. It is as if there is a propaganda machine which like the medical establishment has set itself up as sole purveyors of the "correct" knowledge in the field and thereby invalidate the findings of other scholars or scientists. In discussing the way in which mistakes made by scholars are treated, mister West says the following.

> In academia, the rules vis-à-vis mistakes change according to location. Only those within the establishment are allowed to 'make mistakes.' Everyone else is a "crank" "crackpot" or "charlatan," and entire lifetimes of work are discredited or dismissed on the basis of minor errors.

Also, the treatment of any scholar who reads metaphysical import in the teachings, literature or iconography of Ancient Egypt is ridiculed by orthodox Egyptologists generally. For instance, anyone suggesting that the Great pyramids (no mummies or remnants of mummies have ever been discovered in them) were not used as burial chambers but rather as temples is openly called a "Pyramidiot."[70] West describes the ominous power that orthodox Egyptologists have taken to themselves and the danger this power poses to humanity.

> A tacit territorial agreement prevails throughout all Academia. Biochemists steer clear of sociology; Shakespearean scholars do not disparage radio astronomy. It's taken for granted that each discipline, scientific, scholarly or humanistic, has its own valid self-policing system, and that academic credentials ensure expertise in a given field.
> With its jealous monopoly on the impenetrable hieroglyphs,± its closed ranks, restricted membership, landlocked philosophical vistas, empty coffers, and its lack of impact upon virtually every other academic, scientific or humanistic field, Egyptology has prepared a near-impregnable strategic position for itself - an

---

[70] *Traveler's Key to Ancient Egypt*, John Anthony West

academic Switzerland but without chocolate, cuckoo clocks, scenery or ski slopes, and cannily concealing its banks. Not only is it indescribably boring and difficult to attack, who'd want to?

But if Swiss financiers suddenly decided to jam the world's banking system, Swiss neutrality and impregnability might suddenly be at risk. That is partially analogous to the situation of Egyptology. The gold is there, but its existence is denied, and no one is allowed to inspect the vaults except those whose credentials make them privy to the conspiracy and guarantee their silence. To date, only a handful of astute but powerless outsiders have recognized that the situation poses real danger. But it's not easy to generate a widespread awareness or appreciation of that danger.

If you think of Egyptologists at all, the chances are you conjure up a bunch of harmless pedants, supervising remote desert digs or sequestered away in libraries, up to their elbows in old papyrus. You don't think of them as sinister, or dangerous. The illuminati responsible for the hydrogen bomb, nerve gas and Agent Orange are dangerous; if you reflect upon it you see that the advanced beings who have given us striped toothpaste and disposable diapers are also dangerous ... but Egyptologists?

Possibly they are the most dangerous of all; dangerous because false ideas are dangerous. At any rate *some* false ideas are dangerous. Belief in the flat earth never hurt anyone though it made navigation problematic. Belief in a geocentric universe held back advances in astronomy but otherwise had certain metaphysical advantages. Academic Egyptology is dangerous because it maintains, in spite of Schwaller de Lubicz's documented scholarly evidence, and the obvious evidence of our own eyes and hearts when we go there, that the race responsible for the pyramids and the temples of Karnak and Luxor was less, advanced' than ourselves. As long as academic Egyptology prevails, children will be brought up with a totally distorted view of our human past, and by extension, of our human present. And millions of tourists will continue to visit Egypt every year, and have the experience of a lifetime vitiated and subverted by a banal explanation that the greatest art and architecture in the world to superstitious primitives.

So the fabulous metaphysical gold of Egypt remains hidden; it's existence stridently denied. For orthodox Egyptology is really little more than a covert operation within the Church of Progress. Its unspoken agenda is to maintain the faith; not to study or debate the truth about Egypt.[71]

±NOTE: Who will claim authority to challenge the accepted translations of the texts, even when these read as nonsense? Actually, a number of independent scholars have learned the hieroglyphs for themselves and produced alternative less insulting translations of some of the texts. But since these are either ignored or dismissed out of hand by orthodox Egyptologists, there is no way to know if these translations come closer to the real thinking of the ancients or if they are themselves no more than figments of the translators' imaginations, and in consequence no more representative and satisfactory than the standard translations.

Noting further difficulties of sustaining independent or "alternative" Egyptology studies, West remains hopeful that the pressure not just from alternative Egyptologists but also from

---

[71] *Serpent in the Sky,* John Anthony West, p. 239

geologists who bring to bear an irrefutable and exacting science to the dating of Ancient Egyptian monuments as opposed to the methods which other reputable sociologists and historians have found to be unreliable. Out of all the major accepted methods to establish a chronology to understand the origins of civilization and the history of the world, Astronomical Time, Geological Time, Archaeological Time and Political or Historical Time, the use of Scriptural chronology is recognized as "extremely uncertain because various local chronologies were used at different times by scriptural writers, and different systems were used by contemporaneous writers."[72]

An alternative Egyptology is less easily managed. Almost no one can earn a living from it. Serious research is difficult to accomplish on a spare-time basis, and research requires access to the few major Egyptological libraries scattered around the world. In Egypt itself, excavation and all work on or in the pyramids, temples and tombs is controlled by the Egyptian Antiquities Organizations. No one without academic credentials can expect to obtain permission to carry out original work[73] Infiltration from within is also peculiarly difficult. At least a few people I know personally have set out to acquire degrees in Egyptology, hoping to devote themselves full time to Egypt and ultimately to legitimize the symbolist interpretation. So far, none have been able to stick out the boredom or dutifully parrot the party line for the years necessary to get the diploma, knowing better from the onset.

It seems unlikely that symbolist Egypt will ever establish itself from within its own ranks. But pressure from outside Egyptology but within academia could force a change. Academics with an interest but no personal stake in the matter must sooner or later realize that the support of highly qualified geologists (of a fundamentally geological theory) must overrule either the clamor or the silence of the Egyptological/archeological establishment. At some point they must express those views.[74]

Having read the preceding excerpts published in 1993 by West one might think that orthodox Egyptology has never been successfully challenged. The same problems are faced by African

[72] "Chronology," Microsoft (R) Encarta Encyclopedia. Copyright (c) 1994

[73] West ads the following footnote: Prior to the development of modern day Egyptology by the western nations, native Egyptians showed little regard or respect for their distant dynastic ancestors; the temples were quarried for stone, anything movable was cheerfully sold to antiquities dealers. Islam, along with Christianity and Judaism, tended to regard ancient Egypt as pagan and idolatrous. But today, at least in private, Egyptian Egyptologists often display a much higher degree of understanding and sensitivity toward the Pharaonic achievement than their European and American colleagues. It would not surprise me to find some closet symbolists among them. Egyptian licensed tour guides (a much coveted job) must have degrees in academic Egyptology and pass an exacting test to qualify. Over the course of years of research and leading tours myself, at least a few dozen have approached me, eager to learn more about symbolist Egypt. But within the closed ranks of practicing, professional Egyptology, academic prestige (such as it is), is still wielded by the major European and American Universities. So even though all ancient Egyptian sites are now entirely under Egyptian control, an Egyptian Egyptologist would be as unlikely to try to break the "common front of silence" as anyone else, whatever his or her private convictions.

[74] _Serpent in the Sky,_ John Anthony West, p. 241

American and African Egyptologists. By simply trying to show that Ancient Egyptian civilization was originally created by African people and that people of African descent played a crucial role in the development of Ancient Egyptian culture and its interactions with other world cultures, a major storm of repudiation and ridicule began in the 1970's. African and African American scholars such as Chancellor Williams, George G.M. James, John H. Clarke, Yosef A. A. ben-jochannan[75] and Cheikh Anta Diop[76] were ridiculed and their struggle to be heard even in their own communities was hampered by the constant rhetoric and derision from orthodox Egyptologists. Catching orthodox Egyptology by surprise, however, Cheikh Anta Diop not only challenged their opinion about the African origins of Ancient Egyptian culture, religion and philosophy but offered overwhelming proof to support his contentions at the 1974 Unesco conference in which he faced 18 of the (at that time) leaders in orthodox Egyptology. Describing the evidence presented at the Unesco conference, scholar Asa G. Hilliard, described the proceedings as recorded by a news media reporter.[77]

> In a scientific forum such opinions are unlikely to be expressed, they will be unable to compete with data-based arguments for, example, Dr. Diop presented eleven categories of evidence to support his argument for a native black African KMT, including eye witness testimony of classical writers, melanin levels in the skin of mummies, Bible history, linguistic and cultural comparisons with the rest of Africa, Kamitan self descriptions, Kamitan historical references, physical anthropology data, blood type studies, carvings and paintings, etc.[78] That is why the reporter at the Cairo Symposium wrote the following in the minutes of the meeting:

>> "Although the preparatory working paper ... sent out by UNESCO gave particulars of what was desired, not all participants had prepared communications comparable with the painstakingly researched contributions of Professors Cheikh Anta Diop and Obenga. There was consequently a real lack of balance in the discussions."[79]

> At this conference, there was either expressed or implied consensus on the following points. (No objections were raised to them.)

1. In ancient KMT the south and the north were always ethnically homogeneous.
2. Professor Vercoutter's suggestion that the population of KMT had been made up of "black skinned whites" was treated as trivia.

---

[75] *Black Man of The Nile and His Family* by

[76] *The African Origin of Civilization, Civilization or Barbarism,* Cheikh Anta Diop

[77] *Egypt Child of Africa* Edited by Ivan Van Sertima, *Bringing Maat, Destroying Isfet: The African and African Diasporan Presence in the Study of Ancient KMT* by Asa G. Hilliard III

[78] Diop, Cheikh Anta (1981) "Origin of the ancient Egyptians" In Moktar, G. *(Ed.) General history of Africa: volume II, Ancient Civilizations of Africa.* Berkeley, California: University of California Press, pp. 27-57

[79] UNESCO, (1978) *The peopling of ancient Egypt and the deciphering of Meroitic script: The general history of Africa, studies and documents I, Proceedings of the symposium held in Cairo from 28 January to 3 February, 1974.* Paris: United Nations Educational, Scientific and Cultural Organization, p. 102.

3. There were no data presented to show that Kamitan temperament and thought were related to Mesopotamia.

4. The old Kamitan tradition speaks of the Great Lakes region in innerequatorial Africa as being the home of the ancient Kemites.

5. There was no evidence of large scale migration between Kemet and Mesopotamia. There were no Mesopotamian loan words in Kamitan: (therefore the two cultures could have no genetic linguistic relationship or be populated by the same people.) For comparison purposes, mention was made of the fact that when documented contact with Kemet was made by Asian Hyksos around 1700 B.C.E., loan words were left in ancient Kemet.

6. No empirical data were presented at the conference to show that the ancient Kemites were white. (Generally, there is a tendency for some historians to *assume* that developed populations are white, but to require proof of blackness.)

7. Muslim Arabs conquered Kemet during the 7th century of the Common Era. Therefore, Arabic culture is not a part of Kemet during any
part of the 3,000 years of dynastic Kemet.

8. Genetic linguistic relationships exist between the African languages of Kamitan, Cushitic (Ethiopian), Puanite (Punt or Somaliland), Berber, Chadic and Arabic. Arabic only covered territory off the continent of Africa, mainly in adjacent Saudi Arabia, an area in ancient times that was as much African as Asian.

9. Dr. Diop invented a melanin dosage test and applied it to royal mummies in the Museum of Man in Paris, mummies from the Marietta Excavations. All had melanin levels consistent with a "black" population. The symposium participants made a strong recommendation that all royal mummies be tested. To date there is no word that this has been done. Dr. Diop struggled for the remaining years of his life to have access to the Cairo museum for that purpose, but to no avail.

Hilliard Concludes:

> *Significantly, it was at the urging of African scholars, led by Dr. Cheikh Anta Diop, that this UNESCO sponsored scientific gathering was convened. Interestingly, the reporter's comments quoted above actually used one of the aspects of MAAT, "balance," to describe Diop and Obenga's work. Truly open dialogue brings MAAT and destroys ISFET. We know this but have not required the open dialogue.*

Careful to avoid any future such exchanges which might prove to be further injurious to the orthodox Egyptological dogma, Diop was refused further access to materials or monuments for detailed research. However, by that time the injury to the orthodox Egyptological position had been done. Since that time other evidences such as those presented in this book and by other scholars, have steadily chipped away at the orthodox Egyptological dogmas. In this sense the struggle over the "guardianship" or as some might consider "ownership," over the prestige that comes with being able to consider oneself as an Ancient Egyptian Scholar will continue because this is apparently a war of information in which western countries have taken the lead. All kinds of information are valued but the information on the origins of humanity and the metaphysics of spiritual evolution are both feared and awed by most ordinary human beings and perhaps particularly the orthodox Egyptologists because this information truly changes everything, from the concept of human origins to what is life all about. Reflect on what would happen if those people in positions of authority in religions, governments and schools were suddenly faced with the realization that their knowledge is deficient and that ordinary people are beginning to understand that they are higher beings that should not be taken advantage of? This is the power of understanding the glory and truth about Ancient Egypt. All humanity, not just Africans or Europeans, can be transformed through it. The illusion which orthodox Egyptologists have promoted and have self-hypnotized themselves with will gradually awaken them as well or else they will be left behind just as the Model "T" left the horse drawn buggy behind and electricity left oil lamps behind.

The Far Reaching Implications of the New Evidence Concerning the Sphinx and Other New Archeological Evidence in Egypt and the Rest of Africa

In the last 20 years traditional Egyptologists, archeologists and others have been taking note of recent studies performed on the Ancient Egyptian Sphinx which sits at Giza in Egypt. Beginning with such students of Ancient Egyptian culture and architecture as R. A. Schwaller de Lubicz in the 1950's, and most recently, John Anthony West, with his book *Serpent In the Sky*, many researchers have used modern technology to study the ancient monument and their discoveries have startled the world. They now understand that the erosion damage on the Sphinx could not have occurred after the period 10,000-7,000 B.C.E. because this was the last period in which there would have been enough rainfall in the area to cause such damage. This means that most of the damage which the Sphinx displays itself, which would have taken thousands of years to occur, would have happened prior to that time (10,000 B.C.E.).

Many scholars have downplayed or misunderstood the new geological evidences related to the Great Sphinx. One example are the authors of the book *In Search of the Cradle of Civilization*, Georg Feuerstein, David Frawley (prominent western Indologists), and Subhash Kak, in which the authors state the following: (highlighted text is by Ashby)

> In seeking to refute current archeological thinking about the Sphinx, West relies on a *single geological feature*. Understandably, most Egyptologists have been less than accepting of his redating of this monument, *hoping* that some other explanation can be found for the *strange* marks of erosion. P. 6

The characterization of the evidence as a "single geological feature" implies it stands alone as an anomaly that does not fit into the greater picture of Ancient Egyptian history and is completely without basis. In support of orthodox Egyptologists, the authors agree with them, stating that their attitude is understandable. Now, even if there were only a single form of evidence, does this mean that it is or should be considered suspect especially when considering the fact that Egyptology and archeology are not exact sciences and geology is an exact science? Further, the authors mention the wishful thinking of the orthodox Egyptologists as they search in vein (hoping) for some other way to explain the evidence. Yet, the authors seem to agree with the Egyptological view and thereby pass over this evidence as an inconsistency that need not be dealt with further.

> The following evidences must also be taken into account when examining the geology of the Sphinx and the Giza plateau.
>
> ➢ The surrounding Sphinx Temple architecture is similarly affected.
>
> ➢ Astronomical evidence agrees with the geological findings.

➢ Ancient Egyptian historical documents concur with the evidence.

It is important to understand that what we have in the Sphinx is not just a monument now dated as the earliest monument in history (based on irrefutable geological evidence). Its existence signifies the earliest practice not only of high-art and architecture, but it is also the first monumental statue in history dedicated to religion. This massive project including the Sphinx and its attendant Temple required intensive planning and engineering skill. Despite its deteriorated state, the Sphinx stands not only as the most ancient mystical symbol in this historical period, but also as the most ancient architectural monument, and a testament to the presence of Ancient African (Egyptian) culture in the earliest period of antiquity. Further, this means that while the two other emerging civilizations of antiquity (Sumer and Indus) were in their Neolithic period (characterized by the development of agriculture, pottery and the making of polished stone implements), Ancient Egypt had already achieved mastery over monumental art, architecture and religion as an adjunct to social order, as the Sphinx is a symbol of the Pharaoh (leader and upholder of Maat-order, justice and truth) as the god Heru. The iconography of the Sphinx is typical of that which is seen throughout Ancient Egyptian history and signals the achievement of the a culture of high morals which governs the entire civilization to the Persian and Greek conquest.

Plate 1: The Great Sphinx of Ancient Egypt-showing the classical Pharaonic headdress popularized in Dynastic times. Also, the water damage can be seen in the form of vertical indentations in the sides of the monument.

> The water erosion of the Sphinx is to history what the convertibility of matter into energy is to physics.
>
> -John Anthony West *Serpent In the Sky*

Many people have heard of the new evidence concerning the water damage on the Sphinx and how it has been shown to be much older than previously thought. However, as we saw earlier, detractors usually claim that this is only one piece of evidence that is inconclusive. This is the usual opinion of the uninformed. The findings have been confirmed by seismographic tests[80] as well as examination of the water damage on the structures related to the Sphinx and the Sphinx Temple, as compared to the rest of the structures surrounding it which display the typical decay due to wind and sand. It has been conclusively found that the Sphinx and its adjacent structures (Sphinx Temple) were built in a different era and that the surrounding structures do not display the water damage. Therefore, the wind and sand damaged structures belong to the Dynastic Era and the Sphinx belongs to the Pre-Dynastic Era. Therefore, the evidence supporting the older dating of the Sphinx is well founded and confirmed.

Plate 2: Sphinx rump and Sphinx enclosure show detail of the water damage (vertical damage).

The new evidence related to the Sphinx affects many other forms of evidence which traditional Egyptologists have also sought to dismiss. Therefore, it is a momentous discovery on

---

[80] *Traveler's Key to Ancient Egypt*, John Anthony West

the order the discernment of the Ancient Egyptian Hieroglyphic text. It requires an opening up of the closely held chronologies and timelines of ancient cultures for revision, thereby allowing the deeper study of the human experience on this earth and making the discovery of our collective past glory possible. Thus, it is clear to see that the problem in assigning dates to events in Ancient Egypt arises when there is an unwillingness to let go of closely held notions based on biased information that is accepted as truth and passed on from one generation of orthodox Egyptologists to the next generation, rather than on authentic scholarship (constant search for truth). This deficiency led to the exclusion of the ancient historical writings of Ancient Egypt (*Palermo Stone, Royal Tablets at Abydos, Royal Papyrus of Turin,* the *Dynastic List* of Manetho). However, now, with the irrefutable evidence of the antiquity of the Sphinx, and the excavations at Abydos and Hierakonpolis, the mounting archeological evidence and the loosening grip of Western scholars on the field of Egyptology, it is no longer possible to ignore the far reaching implications of the Ancient Egyptian historical documents.

The History of Manetho

The evidence concerning the new dating of the Sphinx affects the treatment of the History of Manetho. Manetho was one of the last Ancient Egyptian High Priests who retained the knowledge of the ancient history of Egypt. In 241 B.C.E. he was commissioned to compile a series of wisdom texts by King Ptolemy II, one of the Macedonian (Greek) rulers of Egypt after it was captured and controlled by the Greeks. One of Manetho's compositions included a history of Egypt. However, Manetho's original writings did not survive into the present. Therefore, the accounts of his writings by the Greeks who studied his work constitute the current remaining record of his work, and some of the accounts differ from each other in certain respects. His history has come down to us in the form of translation, part of which are missing certain portions. However, it has been ascertained that he grouped the Dynastic Rulers of Ancient Egypt into 30 Dynasties containing around 330 Pharaohs in a period of around 4,500 years (going back from his time-241 B.C.E.). According to Manetho Ancient Egyptian chronology included the following periods:

1- The Gods - This period was the genesis. It began with the emergence of the great Ennead or Company of gods and goddesses headed by Ra, the Supreme Being. According to the creation myth, the God, Ra himself, ruled over the earth.

2- The Demigods - After the Gods, the Demigods ruled the earth. Then came a descendent line of royal rulers followed by 30 rulers in the city of Memphis. These were followed by another set of royal rulers. The Heru Shemsu often mentioned in various texts referring to the ancient worship of Heru as the Supreme Spirit belong to this age. (Ra is an aspect of Heru).

3- The Spirits of the Dead - After the period of the Demigods came the Spirits of the Dead.

According to the Turin Papyrus (original Ancient Egyptian document dating to c.1440 B.C.E.), the dates of the periods are:

1- The Gods – 23,200

2- The Demigods – 13,420

3- The Spirits of the Dead – cannot be deciphered due to damage
on the document.

Total: A minimum of 36,620 years before the unification (fist Dynasty).

According to Eusebius, the dates of the periods of Ancient Egypt *before* Menes, the uniter
of the two lands into one empire, total: 28,927 years before the unification.

According to Diodorus of Sicily, the dates of the periods total 33,000 before the
unification.

These periods were then followed by the Dynastic Period which is the only period of Ancient
Egypt of which most people have knowledge (c. 5,000 B.C.E.-30 B.C.E.). Due to the
deficiencies in the historical record, an exact dating for each period preceding the Dynastic is not
available. However, it is reasonably certain that the total number of years outlined above goes
back in history to at least 28,927 years from the time when Manetho was writing in 241 B.C.E.
This gives a total of number of years around the beginning of the preceding Kamitan "Great
Year" former to the commencement of our current one.

Support for this remote date comes from the writings of Herodotus. According to Herodotus,
he was told by one of his Egyptian guides in 450 B.C.E. that "the sun had risen twice where it
now set, and twice set where it now rises." This statement has been recognized by scholars as a
reference to the processional cycles. This means that the Ancient Egyptians witnessed the
beginning of the previous Great Year to our current one. Since the beginning of the current Great
Year is reckoned at 10,858 B.C.E., this would mean that the beginning of Ancient Egyptian
records goes back to 36,748 (10,858 + 25,890 the period of the previous great year =36,748).

4- Mortal Men – i.e. The Pre-Dynastic and Dynastic Periods- Rulership by
Pharaohs (Kings and Queens).

This period must be divided into the Pre-Dynastic age and the Dynastic age, for the Dynastic
age that is often used to represent the beginning of Ancient Egyptian civilization only refers to
the time of the major unification of all the kingdoms (nomes) of the Southern ands Northern
portions of the country into one single nation.

The Pharaonic (royal) calendar based on the Sothic system (star Sirius) containing cycles of
1,460 years, was in use by 4,241 B.C.E. This certainly required extensive astronomical skills and
time for observation. The Sothic system is based on the *Heliacal* (i.e. appears in the sky just as the
sun breaks through the eastern horizon) rising of the star Sirius in the eastern sky, signaling the
New Year as well as the inundation season. Therefore, the history of Kamit (Egypt) must be
reckoned to be extremely ancient. Thus, in order to grasp the antiquity of Ancient Egyptian
culture, religion and philosophy, we will review the calendar systems used by the Ancient
Egyptians.

The Stellar Symbolism related to the Pole Star and the Opening of the mouth and Eyes Ceremony in Ancient Egypt

As introduced earlier, Herodotus, in his book of history, quoted one of his guides as having told him that in Egyptian history had lasted for a period of time in which, "the sun had twice risen where it now set, and twice set where it now rises."[81]

> "This remark Schwaller de Lubicz interpreted as a description of the passage of one and a half precessional cycles. This would place the date of foundation around 36,000 BC, a date in broad agreement with the other sources."[82]

There are three constellations that circulate around the North Pole of the planet earth. These are Draco, Ursa Major and Ursa Minor. The Great Pyramid was discovered to have a shaft that points to the North Pole. Precession is the slow revolution of the Earth's axis of rotation (wobbling) about the poles of the ecliptic. The eclipticis a great circle inscribed on a terrestrial globe inclined at an approximate angle of 23°27' to the equator and representing the apparent motion of the sun in relation to the earth during a year. It is caused by lunar and solar perturbations acting on the Earth's equatorial bulge and causes a westward motion of the stars that takes around 25,868 years to complete.[83] During the past 5000 years the line of direction of the North Pole has moved from the star Thuban, or Alpha (a) Draconis, in the constellation Draco, to within one degree of the bright star Polaris, also known as Alpha (a) Ursae Minoris, in the constellation Ursa Minor (Little Dipper), which is now the North Star. Polaris is a binary star of second magnitude, and is located at a distance of about 300 light-years from the earth. It is easy to locate in the sky because the two stars opposite the handle in the bowl of the dipper in the constellation Ursa Major (Big Dipper), which are called the Pointers, point to the star Polaris. [84]

---

[81] *Histories,* Herodotus
[82] *Serpent in the Sky,* John Anthony West, p. 97
[83] Random House Encyclopedia Copyright (C) 1983,1990
[84] "North Star," Microsoft (R) Encarta. Copyright (c) 1994 Microsoft Corporation. Copyright (c) 1994 Funk & Wagnall's Corporation.

The Kamitan Zodiac and the Precession of the Equinoxes and the History of Ancient Egypt

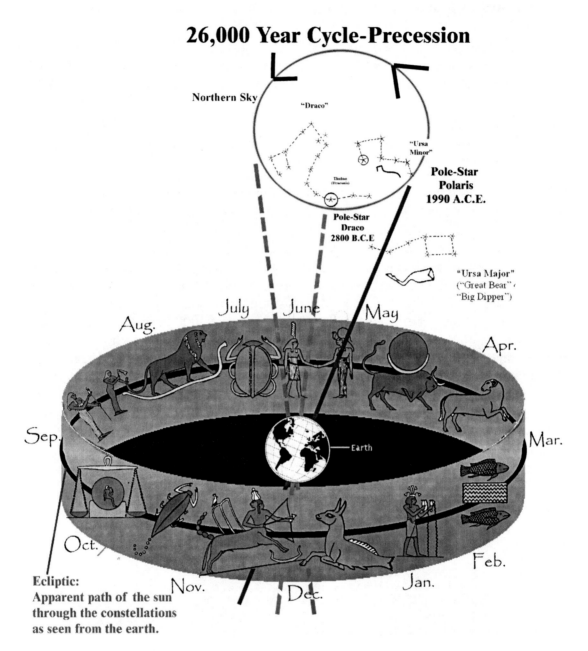

26,000 Year Cycle-Precession

Northern Sky

"Draco"

"Ursa Minor"

Thuban (Draconis)

Pole-Star Polaris 1990 A.C.E.

Pole-Star Draco 2800 B.C.E

"Ursa Major" ("Great Bear" "Big Dipper")

July   June   May

Aug.   Apr.

Sep.   Earth   Mar.

Oct.   Feb.

Nov.   Dec.   Jan.

Ecliptic:
Apparent path of the sun
through the constellations
as seen from the earth.

The Zodiac is an imaginary belt in the celestial sphere, extending about 8° on either side of the ecliptic. The ecliptic is a line that traces the apparent path of the Sun among the stars. It is believed that the width of the zodiac was originally determined so as to include the orbits of the Sun and Moon and of the five planets that were believed to have been known by people in ancient times (Mercury, Venus, Mars, Jupiter, and Saturn). The zodiac is divided into 12 sections of 30° each, which are called the signs of the zodiac. Because of the precession of the equinoxes about the ecliptic, a 25,920-year cycle or "Great Year" period, the first point of Aries retrogrades about 1° in 72 years, so that the sign Aries today lies in the constellation Pisces. In about 13,061 years, when the retrogression will have completed the entire circuit of 360°, the zodiacal signs and constellations will again coincide. It is believed that the zodiacal signs originated in

74

Mesopotamia as early as 2000 B.C.E. and the Greeks adopted the symbols from the Babylonians and passed them on to the other ancient civilizations. The Chinese also adopted the 12-fold division, but called the signs rat, ox, tiger, hare, dragon, serpent, horse, sheep, monkey, hen, dog, and pig. Independently, the Aztec people devised a similar system.[85]

The calendar based on the Great Year was also used by the Ancient Egyptians. The Great Year is founded on the movement of the earth through the constellations known as the *Precession of the Equinoxes.* It is confirmed from the history given by the Ancient Egyptian Priest Manetho in the year 241 B.C.E. Each Great Year has 25,860 to 25,920 years and 12 arcs or constellations. Each passage through a constellation takes 2,155 – 2,160 years. These are known as the "Great Months" of the "Great Year." As explained earlier, the current cycle or year began at around 10,858 B.C.E. At about the year 36,766 B.C.E., according to Manetho, the Creator, Ra, ruled the earth in person from his throne in the Ancient Egyptian city of Anu (Greek-Heliopolis-city of the sun). By this reckoning our current year (2,002 A.C.E.) is actually the year 12,860 G.Y. based on the Great Year System of Ancient Egyptian reckoning.

The period of 36,525 years is also 25 times 1,460 which is the cycle of the helical rising of Sirius (when Sirius rises not only in the east but on the ecliptic, i.e. with the sun). The Sirian calendar was another time reckoning system based on the star Sirius and its relation with the sun of our solar system which contains a cycle of 1,460 years. An inscription by Censorinus informs us that the rising of Sirius occurred in 139 A.C.E. This means that the Sirian cycle also occurred in the years 1321 B.C.E, 2781 B.C.E, and 4241 B.C.E. By means of two inscriptions from the 18th Dynasty, it has been reliably established that the date for the 18th Dynasty is 1580 B.C.E.

According to the reckoning based on Manetho's history, if we take the average number of years in the Great Year and add it to the known year of the beginning of the current Great Year we get a total of 36,748 (25,890 + 10,858=36,748). If we compare this number with the history of Manetho we find a difference of 18 years, accountable by the deterioration in the translated records and the variance in the number of years in the Great Year cycle. Thus, we have match that supports the History and the practice of reckoning time by the Great Year. So we have reliable confirmations that the Sirian calendar was in use in Ancient Egypt at least as early as 4241 B.C.E.[86] and that a greater form of reckoning, the Great Year, corroborates the History of Manetho which takes Ancient Egyptian chronology and civilized use of mathematics, astronomy and time reckoning back to 36,748 B.C.E. This longer duration cycle system of time reckoning was supported by recent discoveries.

"That the Egyptians handled astronomical cycles of even greater duration is indicated by inscriptions recently found by Soviet archeologists in newly opened graves during the period of their work on the Aswan Dam.[87] Here the cycles appear to cover periods of 35,525 years, which would be the equivalent of 25 cycles of 1461 years. The apparent discrepancy of one year in this recording of cycles is due to the sothic cycle of 1460 years being the equivalent of a civil cycle of 1461 years. According to Muck (researcher), there were three main cycles: one

---

[85] "Zodiac," Microsoft (R) Encarta. Copyright (c) 1994 Microsoft Corporation. Copyright (c) 1994 Funk & Wagnall's Corporation.

[86] *Echoes of the Old Darkland,* Charles Finch

[87] Between the years 1960-1970

75

of 365 X 4 = 1460; another of 1460 X 25 = 36,500; and a third of 36,500 X 5 = 182,500 years."[88]

Let us recall the brilliant discovery by Joseph Campbell introduced earlier in relation to the same great age period being used in India, Iceland and Babylon and the unlikelihood of this arising by chance.

"There are, however, instances that cannot be accounted for in this way, and then suggest the need for another interpretation: for example, in India the number of years assigned to an eon[89] is 4,320,000; whereas in the Icelandic *Poetic Edda* it is declared that in Othin's warrior hall, Valhall, there are 540 doors, through each of which, on the "day of the war of the wolf,"[90] 800 battle-ready warriors will pass to engage the antigods in combat.' But 540 times 800 equals 432,000!
Moreover, a Chaldean priest, Berossos, writing in Greek ca. 289 B.C., reported that according to Mesopotamian belief 432,000 years elapsed between the crowning of the first earthly king and the coming of the deluge.
No one, I should think, would wish to argue that these figures could have arisen independently in India, Iceland, and Babylon."[91]

When we compare the Indian, Icelandic and Babylonian system of Ages of time with that of Ancient Egypt some startling correlations can be observed; the same numbers appear.

Ancient Egyptian Age	Ancient Indian Age
25,920 Great Year	----------------------------------
25,920 ÷ 6 = 4320	432,000 Kali Yuga – Iron Age 4,320,000 Maha Yuga – Great Age or Cycle
25,920 ÷ 4 = 8640	
25,920 ÷ 2 = 1296	864,000 Dwapar Yuga – Copper Age
25,920 ÷ 15 = 1728	1,296,000 Treta Yuga – Silver Age
	1,728,000 Satya Yuga – Golden or Truth Age

[88] *Secrets of the Great Pyramid,* Peter Tompkins
[89] A "Great Cycle" *(Mahayuga)* of cosmic time.
[90] I.e., at the ending of the cosmic eon, Wagner's *Götterdämmerung.*
[91] *The Mythic Image*, Joseph Campbell

The *Royal Papyrus of Turin* gives a complete list of the kings who reigned over Upper and Lower Egypt from Menes to the New Empire, including mention of the duration of each reign. Before the list comes a section devoted to the Pre-Dynastic era. This section lists the kings who reigned before Menes, and the duration of each reign, establishing that there were nine Dynasties. According to Schwaller de Lubicz, some of these were called:

> ... the (venerables) of Memphis, the venerables of the North, and finally the *Shemsu-Hor,* usually translated as the 'Companions of Heru'.

> Fortunately, the last two lines have survived almost intact, as have indications regarding the number of years:

> venerables Shemsu-Hor, 13,429 years
> 'Reigns up to Shemsu-Hor, 23,200years (total 36,620)
> King Menes.[92]

The Turin Papyrus names the following neteru (gods and goddesses) as rulers in the Pre-Dynastic ages:

Ptah, Ra, Shu, Geb, Asar, Set, Heru, Djehuti, Maat

In support of the above, Diodorus of Sicily reports that several historians of his time reported Egypt was ruled by gods and heroes for a period of 18,000 years. After this Egypt was ruled by mortal kings for 15,000 years.[93] While it is true that this account differs with that of Manetho and the Turin Papyrus, the inescapable fact remains that every account refers to ages of rulers that go back beyond 30,000 B.C.E. as the earliest period of record keeping. The implications are far reaching. Consider that if we were to add the figure above for the period prior to the first king (King Menes) of our era and use the first confirmed date for the use of the calendar (4240 B.C.E.) we indeed would have a date over 40,000 B.C.E. for the beginnings of Ancient Egyptian history (36,620+4240).

---

[92] Sacred Science by Schwaller de Lubicz
[93] Diodorus Book 23

Below left-The Great Heru m Akhet (Sphinx) of Ancient Egypt.

Below -The Great Heru m akhet (Sphinx) of Egypt-with the Panel of Djehutimes between its Paws. (19th century rendition of the Sphinx) [94]

_____

[94] This illustration appeared in the book *History of Egypt*-Samuel Sharp 1876 A.C.E.

The Great Sphinx, covered in sand - Drawing by early Arab explorers[95]

The Sphinx is the oldest known monument and it relates to the solar mysticism of Anu as well as to the oldest form of spiritual practice known. From it we also derive certain important knowledge in reference to the antiquity of civilization in Ancient Egypt. The picture of the Great Sphinx above-right appeared in 1876. Notice the broad nose and thick lips with which it is endowed. Any visitor to Egypt who examines the Sphinx close up will see that even with the defacement of the nose, it is clearly an African face and not an Asiatic or European personality being depicted. Many other early Egyptologists concluded the same way upon gazing at the monument and this picture is but one example of their conviction on the subject.

The Per-Aah (Pharaoh) Djehutimes IIII (Thutmosis) makes offerings to the Great Heru m Akhet (Sphinx)

The Heru-em-akhet (Horemacket Ra-Herakhti (Herukhuti, Heruakhuti - Great Sphinx) Stele is a panel placed directly in front of the chest of the monument in between the two front paws. It recounts the story of how the prince Djehutimes IIII (Thutmosis IV- 18th Dynasty 1401-1391

---
95 *Descriptions of Egypt*

B.C.E.) fell asleep at the base of the Sphinx on a hot day and the spirit of the Sphinx came to him. The inscription that survived with the Ancient Egyptian Sphinx also has serious implications for the revision of the dating of Ancient Egyptian history. The Sphinx came to him and offered him kingship and sovereignty over the world if Djehutimes would repair him and make devout offerings and worship. Having complied with the wishes of the Divine, to maintain the great monument and sustain the worship of Ra-Herakhti, Djehutimes became king and Egypt prospered under his reign with the favor of the Divine. According to Egyptologist Maspero, this was not the first time that the Sphinx was cleared:

> The stele of the Sphinx bears, on line 13, the cartouche of Khephren in the middle of a gap .... There, I believe, is the indication of an excavation of the Sphinx carried out under this prince, and consequently the more or less certain proof that the Sphinx was already covered with sand during the time of Cheops and his predecessors.[96]

R. A. Schwaller de Lubicz reports that legends support the contention that at a very early date in Ancient Egyptian history, the Old Kingdom fourth Dynasty (Cheops {Khufu} reigned 2551-2528 B.C.E., Khephren {Ra-ka-ef} reigned 2520-2494), the Sphinx was already considered ancient and as belonging to a remote past of Ancient Egyptian Culture.

> A legend affirms that even in Cheops' day, the age of the Sphinx was already so remote that it was impossible to situate it in time. This Sphinx is a human and colossal work. There is an enigma about it that is linked with the very enigma posed by the Sphinx itself.

It has been proposed, as a support of the use of the Great Year calendar, that the Ancient Egyptians instituted the use of different symbolisms in religion and government in accordance with the current symbolism of the particular age in question.[97] Thus, during the age (great month) of Leo, the lion symbolism would be used. What is compelling about this rationale is that the new evidence in reference to the age of the Sphinx coincides with the commencement of the New Great Year and the month of Leo, which began in 10,858 B.C.E. However, when it is understood that the damage on the Sphinx would have required thousands of years to produce, and when the history of Manetho as well as the conjunction of the Sphinx with the constellation Leo when it makes its heliacal rising at the beginning of each Great Year is taken into account, it becomes possible to understand that the Sphinx was already in existence at the commencement of our current Great Year, and to envision the possibility that the Sphinx was created at the beginning of the previous Great Year anniversary (36,748 B.C.E.).

The Great Sphinx and its attendant monuments as well as other structures throughout Egypt which appear to be compatible architecturally should therefore be considered as part of a pinnacle of high culture that was reached well before the Dynastic age, i.e. previous to 5,000 B.C.E. The form of the Sphinx itself, displaying the lion body with the human head, but also with the particularly "leonine" headdress including the lion's mane, was a legacy accepted by the Pharaohs of the Dynastic Period. In the Ancient Egyptian mythological system of government, the Pharaoh is considered as a living manifestation of Heru and he or she wields the leonine

---

[96] G. Maspero, *The Passing of the Empires* (New York, 1900).
[97] *Echoes of the Old Darkland*, Charles Finch

power which comes from the sun, Ra, in order to rule. Thus, the Pharaohs also wore and were depicted wearing the leonine headdress. The sundisk is the conduit through which the Spirit transmits Life Force energy to the world, i.e. the Lion Power, and this force is accessed by turning towards the Divine in the form of the sun. Hence, the orientation of the Sphinx towards the east, facing the rising sun. All of this mystical philosophy and more is contained in the symbolic-metaphorical form and teaching of the Sphinx. Thus, we have a link of Ancient Egyptian culture back to the Age of Leo and the commencement of the current cycle of the Great Year in remote antiquity.

Heru-m-akhet or "Heru in the Horizon" or "manifesting" in the horizon, the "Sphinx," actually represents an ancient conjunction formed by the great Sphinx in Giza, Egypt and the heavens. This conjunction signals the beginning of the "New Great Year." It has been noted by orthodox as well as nonconformist Egyptologists alike, that the main symbolisms used in Ancient Egypt vary over time Nonconformist Egyptilogists see this as a commemoration of the zodiacal symbol pertaining to the particular Great Month in question. What is controversial to the orthodox Egyptologists is the implication that the Ancient Egyptians marked time by the Great Year, and this would mean that Ancient Egyptian civilization goes back 12 millenniums, well beyond any other civilization in history. This further signifies that all of the history books and concepts related to history and the contributions of Africa to humanity would have to be rewritten. Also, since it has been shown that the Ancient Egyptians commemorated the Zodiacal sign of Leo at the commencement of the Great Year it means that the knowledge of the precession of the equinoxes, the Great Year and the signs of the Zodiac proceeded from Ancient Egypt to Babylon and Greece and not the other way around. The twelve zodiacal signs for these constellations were named by the 2nd-century astronomer Ptolemy, as follows: Aries (ram), Taurus (bull), Gemini (twins), Cancer (crab), Leo (lion), Virgo (virgin), Libra (balance), Scorpio (scorpion), Sagittarius (archer), Capricorn (goat), Aquarius (water-bearer), and Pisces (fishes).

> That is precisely what the records reveal. Mentu the bull disappears and is superceded by the ram of Amon. The character of the architecture loses its monolithic simplicity. While still within its recognizable tradition, there is no mistaking a change of 'character'. The Pharaohs incorporate Amon in the names they assume: Amenhotep, Amenophis, Tutankhamun.
>
> Egyptologists attribute the fall of Mentu and the rise of Amon to a hypothetical priestly feud, with the priests of Amon emerging victorious. There is nothing illogical or impossible about this hypothesis, but at the same time there is no evidence whatever to support it.
>
> The evidence shows a shift of symbolism, from duality under Gemini, to the bull, to the ram. These shifts coincide with the dates of the astronomical precession.
>
> Further corroboration of Egyptian knowledge and use of the precession of the equinoxes, and of the incredible coherence and deliberation of the Egyptian tradition, was deduced by Schwaller de Lubicz from a detailed study of the famous zodiac from the Temple of Denderah. This temple was constructed by the Ptolemies in the first century BC, upon the site of an earlier temple. The hieroglyphs declare that it was constructed according to the plan laid down in the time of the 'Companions of Heru' - that is to say, prior to the beginnings of

Dynastic Egypt. Egyptologists regard this statement as a ritual figure of speech, intended to express regard for the tradition of the past.[98]

One striking form of symbolism that is seen from the beginning to the end of the Ancient Egyptian history is the Sphinx/Pharaonic Leonine headdress.

Above- The Heru-m-akhet (Sphinx) Pharaonic headdress.[99]

Below- Drawing of the Sphinx from a sculpture in Egypt

Constellation Leo-The Lion

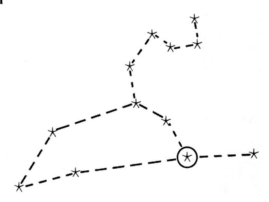

The Great Sphinx faces due east and in the year c. 10,800 B.C.E. a perfect conjunction is created as the Sphinx faces the rising sun and the constellation Leo, the lion.

---

[98] Se*rpent in the Sky,* John Anthony West, p. 100

[99] These illustrations appeared in the book *The Ancient Egyptians: Their Life and Customs*-Sir J. Garner Wilkinson 1854 A.C.E.

The Sphinx faces due east at the beginning of the Great year and faces the Constellation Leo as it makes its Heliacal Rising.

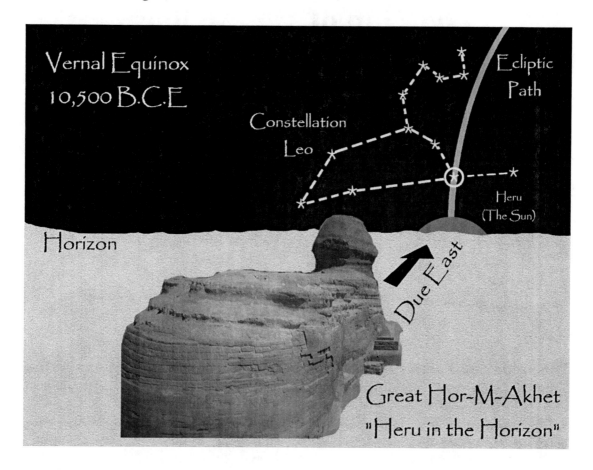

Ra-Herakhti

Human Head-Lion Body
Spirit (Mind) -Matter
Subtle-Gross
Heaven-Earth
Human-Animal

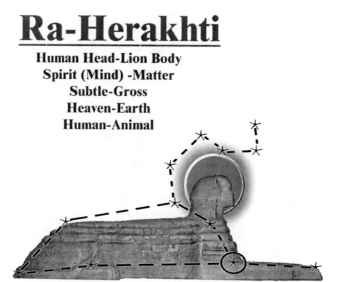

Constellation Rw Ua-ti:
The Lion of the Zodiac
in conjunction with Ra, the Sun at the beginning
of the Great Year produces Her-m-akht
"Heru manifesting in the horizon."

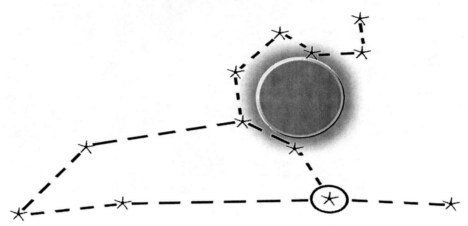

The Sphinx on Earth (Rw or Ru) as a Counterpart to the Sphinx in the Heavens.

The Sphinx on earth as a counterpart to the Sphinx in the heavens (Astral Plane), i.e. the horizon of the earth plane and the horizon of the astral plane. In this view, the Sphinx on earth and the Sphinx in heaven complement each other and form two halves of the akher-akhet symbol, but turned facing each other, looking at the sun which is between them, i.e. turning away from the earth plane and towards the Transcendental Spirit.

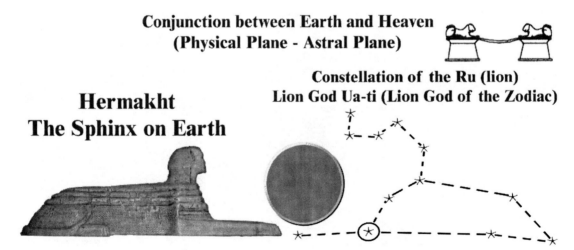

Conjunction between Earth and Heaven
(Physical Plane - Astral Plane)

Constellation of the Ru (lion)
Lion God Ua-ti (Lion God of the Zodiac)

Hermakht
The Sphinx on Earth

84

Below- The Ancient Egyptian zodiacal signs for the ages of the Ram, Bull and Lion

Opening of the Mouth with the Imperishable Stars

In the Hermetic Texts, which are the later development in Ancient Egyptian scripture, Hermes, the Greek name ascribed to the Ancient Egyptian god Djehuti, states to his pupil Asclepius (Egyptian Imhotep) that *"Did you know, O Asclepius, that Egypt is made in the image of heaven?"*[100] The Ancient Egyptian Pyramid Texts and the Pert M Heru (Book of Enlightenment) texts contain more references to stellar mysticism. The stellar symbolism of Ancient Egypt relates to the passage of time but also to mystical awakening and spiritual realization.

> As to these all, Maat and Djehuti, they are with Isdesba[101] Lord of Amentet. As to the divine beings behind Asar, they are again Mseti, Hapy, Duamutf, and Kebsenuf. They are behind the Chepesh[102] in the northern heavens.
>
> From Prt M Hru Chap. 4, V. 22

The Chepesh has important mystical symbolism. Mythically it represents the foreleg of the god Set which was torn out and thrown into the heavens by the god Heru during their epic battle. A similar teaching occurs in the Babylonian epic of Gilgemesh[103\104] when the "foreleg of the Bull of Heaven" is ripped out and thrown at the goddess Ishtar, who was the goddess or Queen of Heaven in Mesopotamia. It symbolizes the male generative capacity and is one of the offerings of Hetep given in Chapter 36 (usually referred to as #30B) of the Pert M Heru (Egyptian Book of the Dead). Its cosmic and mystical implications provides us with insight into Kamitan philosophy as well as ancient history.

---

[100] *Hermetica,* Asclepius III, Solos Press ed., p. 136

[101] A protector god in the Company of Gods and Goddesses of Djehuti.

[102] Big Dipper, common name applied to a conspicuous constellation in the northern celestial hemisphere, near the North Pole. It was known to the ancient Greeks as the Bear and the Wagon and to the Romans as Ursa Major (the Great Bear) and Septentriones (Seven Plowing Oxen). The seven brightest stars of the constellation form the easily identified outline of a giant dipper. To the Hindus, it represents the seven Rishis, or holy ancient Sages. "Big Dipper," Microsoft (R) Encarta. Copyright (c) 1994 Microsoft Corporation. Copyright (c) 1994 Funk & Wagnall's Corporation.

[103] Col. V. l, 161

[104] **Gilgamesh,** legendary king of Babylonia, hero of an epic poem written on clay tablets, found in the ruins of Nineveh; epic has affinities with Old Testament, contains story of the flood. Excerpted from *Compton's Interactive Encyclopedia.* Copyright (c) 1994, 1995

Also, in ancient times the Chepesh symbol represented the "Northern path" of spiritual evolution. Since the constellation of the Ursa Major ("Great Bear" or "Big Dipper"), known to the Ancient Egyptians as "Meskhetiu," contains *seven* stars and occupied the location referred to as the "Pole Star." As it occupies the pole position it does not move, while all the other stars in the sky circle around it. This constellation, whose symbol is the foreleg, ⌒, was thus referred to as "the imperishables" in the earlier Pyramid Texts: "He (the king-enlightened initiate) climbs to the sky among the imperishable stars."[105]

Akhemu Seku - never setting stars – imperishable

Akhemu Urdu - never resting stars – setting

The Great Pyramid in Egypt, located in the area referred to as "The Giza Plateau" in modern times, incorporated this teaching. The main chamber in the Great Pyramid incorporates two shafts that pointed in ancient times to the Chepesh (Ursa {Bear} Major {Great} - the foreleg) in the north sky and to Orion (Sahu or Sah), the star system of Asar (Osiris) in the southern sky. The imperishable constellation refers to that which is unchanging, absolute, transcendental and perfect.

---

[105] Pyramid Texts 1120-23. *Egyptian Mysteries,* Lucie Lamy

CHAPTER 2: THE ANCIENT KAMITANS, AND THEIR CULTURE

The Ancient Egyptian (Kamitan) religion (*Shetaut Neter*), language and symbols provide the first "historical" record of Mystical Philosophy and Religious literature. Egyptian Mysticism is what has been commonly referred to by Egyptologists as Egyptian "Religion" or "Myth," but to think of it as just another set of stories or allegories about a long lost civilization is to completely miss the greater teaching it has to offer. Mystical spirituality, in all of its forms and disciplines of spiritual development, was practiced in Ancient Egypt (Kemet) earlier than anywhere else in history. This unique perspective from the highest philosophical system which developed in Africa over seven thousand years ago provides a new way to look at life, religion, the discipline of psychology and the way to spiritual development leading to spiritual Enlightenment. Ancient Egyptian myth, when understood as a system of *Smai Tawi* (Egyptian Yoga), that is, a system which promotes the union of the individual soul with the Universal Soul or Supreme Consciousness, gives every individual insight into their own divine nature, and also a deeper insight into all religions, mystical and Yoga systems.

Ancient Egyptian culture and philosophy is crucial to the understanding of world history and spirituality. It is especially important for people of African descent to know and understand their roots and thereby become powerful and dynamic members of the world community. The study of Kamitan Spirituality is also important for people of Indian descent as they too share in the Kamitan legacy. This knowledge will allow them to understand the depth of their own culture and spiritual tradition as well as aid in the restoration of positive interactions with people of African descent and Africa itself.

The Term Kamit and Its Relation to Nubia

As we have seen, the terms "Ethiopia," "Nubia," "Kush" and "Sudan" which all refer to "black land" and/or the "land of the blacks." In the same manner we find that the name of Egypt which was used by the Egyptians also means "black land" and/or the "land of the blacks." The hieroglyphs below reveal the Ancient Egyptian meaning of the words related to the name of their land.

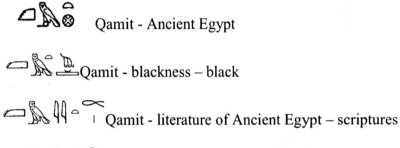

Qamit - Ancient Egypt

Qamit - blackness – black

Qamit - literature of Ancient Egypt – scriptures

Qamiu - Ancient Egyptians-people of the black land

"QMT" (KMT, Kemet, Kamit), "Egypt," "Burnt," "Black people," "Black Land"

The African Ancestry of the Ancient Egyptians

Many of the same writers who lived in the times of the Ancient Egyptians described them and confirmed that they were of African descent. Some of the descriptions state that they had wooly hair and were burnt (black) of skin. Some say that they also had thick lips as the Ethiopians and other Africans. This shows that the Ancient Egyptian Philosophy, though universal in its scope, is a creation of ancient African peoples. Who did not hoard their wisdom but shared it freely with the world. This is a matter of truth which must be affirmed whenever the origins of the teachings is discussed. It underscores the African contributions to the emergence of western culture and modern civilization.

"...several Egyptians told me that in their opinion the Colchidians were descended from soldiers of Sesotris. I had conjectured as much myself from two pointers, firstly because **they have black skins and kinky hair...**and more reliably for the reason that alone among mankind the Egyptians and the Ethiopian have practiced circumcision since time immemorial." (Herodotus, Book II, 104)

"The **Egyptians and Nubians (Ethiopians) have thick lips, broad noses, wooly hair and burnt skin...**
...And the Indian tribes I have mentioned, their skins are all of the same color, much like the Ethiopians... their country is a long way from Persia towards the south..."

Herodotus

"And upon his return to Greece, they gathered around and asked, "tell us about this great **land of the Blacks called Ethiopia**." And Herodotus said, **"There are two great Ethiopian nations, one in Sind (India) and the other in Egypt."**
Recorded by Diodorus (Greek historian 100 B.C.)

Dialogue:

Lycinus (describing an Egyptian): **'this boy is not merely black; he has thick lips** and his legs are too thin...his hair worn in a plait shows that he is not a freeman.'
Timolaus: **'but that is a sign of really distinguished birth in Egypt,** Lycinus. All freeborn children plait their hair until they reach manhood...' (Lucian, _Navigations_, paras 2-3)

Dialogue:

Danaos (describing the Aegyptians (Egyptians)): 'I can see the crew with their **black limbs** and white tunics.' (Aeschylus, _The Suppliants_, vv. 719-20, 745)

The Egyptians were **"very black"** and the Ethiopians **'wooly haired."**
(See Aristotle, Physiognomy, Chap. VI).

Ancient Egyptian Depictions of Egyptians and Nubians

The Ancient Egyptians and Their Neighbors

From the Tomb of Ramses III: The four branches of mankind, according to the Egyptians: A- Egyptian as seen by himself, B- Indo-European, C- Other Africans, D- Semites (Middle Easterners). (Discovered by Cheikh Anta Diop)

Ancient Nubian/Egyptian man.

Ancient Asiatic man.

The images above clearly show that the Ancient Egyptian and the Nubians looked alike. One reason for the confusion about the ethnicity of the Ancient Egyptians is the misunderstanding about their depictions of themselves. There are three distinct forms, the red or reddish-brown, the brown and the black. Both of these are used interchangeably and this is what the early Egyptologists such as Champollion witnessed before the colors on many depictions had been damaged or lost. However, there are several images that have survived and from these it is possible to clearly see that the Ancient Egyptians depicted themselves with colors that were the same as those used to illustrate the Nubians. The pictures below are only one example. In any case, the depictions that have survived are supported by the statements of the ancient Greek writers themselves as well as the testimony and drawings of the European explorers of the early nineteenth century, who first uncovered the monuments and tomb inscriptions that were covered in sand, which had preserved the images up to that time but many of which have suffered due to vandalism by Arab/Muslim zealots, tourism, pollution ever since.

The images above from the tomb of Rameses III shows an Ancient Egyptian rendition of another man from the Sudan (Kush – Ethiopia). It is clear to see that the Egyptian peoples were originally of African descent and later mixed with the peoples from the neighboring lands and became a multicultural country.

The renowned Africologist Basil Davidson presented Dr. Diop briefly in Davidson's documentary program "Africa" and commented on this ancient ethnography and remarked that it was "rare," thus dismissing it as an anomaly. However, the following picture was discovered by Dr. Muata Ashby in the book *Arts and Crafts of Ancient Egypt* by Flinders Petrie but not ascribed as an ethnography including Ancient Egyptians, but rather unknown "Abyssinians."

Ancient Egyptian Depiction of Ethnic Groups (New Kingdom Dynastic Period)[106]

The picture above is an Ancient Egyptian depiction of the four ethnic groups of the ancient world. Described by Petrie as "the Four Races" the picture is one of the rare ethnographies that have come down to us from Ancient Egypt. To the far left is the face of a "Negro" (native African man). The next, from left to right, is a "Syrian" man, the third is described as an "Abyssinian" and the last is a "Libyan." Notice that there is supposed to be an Ancient Egyptian person in these class of art and having assigned the other "races" the Egyptian person has been omitted in the description of the group. This picture is a variation of the previous picture, discovered by Dr. Diop. If the picture is rendered as the original it would mean that the first man on the left that Petrie is refereeing to as a "Negro" is actually an Ancient Egyptian man. Since the practice of scarification is rare or unknown in Ancient Egypt the "Abyssinian" man would be the Nubian (Ethiopian) and the other person of African descent would have to be the Egyptian.

---

[106] *Arts and Crafts of Ancient Egypt,* Flinders Petrie

The term "Abyssinian" refers to languages often distinguished as belonging to the subgroup of Hamitic languages. The words Semitic (Asia Minor) and Hamitic (African) are derived from the names of Noah's sons, Shem and Ham (Christian Bible-Gen. 10). Ethiopia, formerly Abyssinia, is a republic in eastern Africa, currently bounded on the northeast by Eritrea and Djibouti, on the east and southeast by Somalia, on the southwest by Kenya, and on the west and northwest by Sudan. In ancient times the country was bounded in the north by Ancient Egypt. In ancient times Ethiopia and Egypt were strongly related. In fact, Ethiopia was the birthplace of the early Egyptians and also, according to Herodotus, the Indians as well. They appeared the same to him at the time of his travels through those countries. Thus, the picture shows that the Ancient Egyptians looked no different from other Africans.

> *"And upon his return to Greece, they gathered around and asked, "tell us about this great land of the Blacks called Ethiopia." And Herodotus said, "There are two great Ethiopian nations, one in Sind (India) and the other in Egypt."*

—Herodotus (c. 484-425 BC)

Jean Franςois Champollion (1790-1832), the main decipherer of the hieroglyphic text in the early 19th century remarked at the art he saw, which at the time was fully colored since the tombs and many other structures had been closed since the middle ages. He described images of the Ancient Egyptians created by them in which they made themselves look like the Ethiopians and concluded that they were of the same "race" as the modern day Nubians. It is unfortunate that due to the mishandling of the monuments due to the push for tourism, destruction and neglect by the Arab peoples and the harsh elements, many of the images that he saw cannot be seen today in their original form except for a limited amount of originals, like the one discovered by Dr. Diop or drawings made by people in his and other expeditions to Egypt. However, we have sufficient images and corroborating texts to say with certainty that the ethnicity of the original peoples who created the culture and civilization of the Nile Valley (Ancient Egypt) were the same in appearance as those people living in modern day Nubia, i.e. they were indeed "black" Africans.

One reason for the confusion about the ethnicity of the Ancient Egyptians is the misunderstanding about their depictions of themselves. There are two distinct forms, the red or reddish-brown and the black. Both of these are used interchangeably and this is what the early Egyptologists such as Champollion witnessed before the colors on many depictions had been damaged or lost.

References to the Nubian Genealogy of Kamitans in Kamitan Texts and Monuments

In the didactic treatise known as *The Prophesies of Neferti,* it is stated that Amunmhat I was the "son of a woman of Ta-Seti, a child of Upper Egypt. The term "Ta-Seti" means "Land of the Bow." This is one of the names used by the Ancient Egyptians to describe Nubia. Thus we are to understand that contrary to the assertions of orthodox Egyptologists, there are several Ancient Egyptian kings that can be recognized as "Nubian" besides those of the 25th dynasty. The late period Greeks and Romans accepted Pharaoh Amunhotep III (Memnon -18th Dyn.) as a Nubian in appearance and as Pharaoh. Yet there is a consistent effort to deny the obvious. When their histories and genealogies are examined, along with their statuary, it becomes clear that the

Ancient Egyptians and their rulers were not just Africans but "black" skinned and also possessed the same physical features as other Africans.

One issue that western and Arab scholars who want to characterize the appearance of "Nubian features" in Ancient Egyptian art is that these are either rare or that they appear almost exclusively in the period of the 25th Dynasty when it is universally accepted that the Nubians from the south took over the all of Egypt. However, a cursory study of the Ancient Egyptian statues and relief provides insights into the insufficiency of any arguments pretending to suggest that there are no records besides the Greek classical writers which show that the Ancient Egyptians saw and depicted themselves as "black Africans," not just during the 25th Dynasty, but throughout the history of Ancient Egypt to the Greek and Roman periods.

The evidences above are corroborated by the Greek writer Herodotus. Herodotus, a Greek historian who traveled the area around 484-425 B.C.E.,[107] journeyed through the ancient world, including Asia Minor, Mesopotamia, Babylon, and Egypt. He described the Ethiopians as: "The tallest, most beautiful and long-lived of the human races." Recall also some of the other statements he made in reference to the Ethiopians and the Egyptians: ***"There are two great Ethiopian (Black) nations, one in Sind (India) and the other in Egypt"*** and ***"The Colchians, Ethiopians and Egyptians have thick lips, broad noses, wooly hair, and they are burnt (dark) of skin color."***

Below Left- Peraah (Pharaoh) Muntuhotep II (Muntuhotep)[108] – 11th Dynasty

Below Center- Peraah Senusert I statue – 12th Dynasty

Below Right- Peraah Senusert I relief – 12th Dynasty

(A)   (B)

(C)

---

[107] Random House Encyclopedia.
[108] Metropolitan Museum New York

The images above are representative of the reliefs and statuaries that the Greek classical writers and the seventeenth- and eighteenth-century European travelers in Egypt saw in full color. Notice the features of the first two (A-B) faces. They clearly exhibit the characteristic traits that have been described as "Black African", including the "puffed up face." Plate (C) is actually a relief representing the same personality as plate (B). Notice that the features in the statues are more pronounced than in the reliefs. This same pattern of iconography can be observed in the statuary and reliefs of King Akhnaton. What we are witnessing is an Ancient Egyptian artistic standard practice of representing the personality in a more naturalistic form in the statuary, and a more standardized manner in the reliefs.[109] In all cases however, the features denote the "bloated face, puffed up eyes, flat nose, and thick lips, and woolly hair as well as the brown-red or black skin tone painting.

Below left, Per-aah Akhnaton Statue (18 Dynasty) – Cairo Museum

Below right, Per-aah Akhnaton Relief (18 Dynasty)

---

[109] *The projection of figures or forms from a flat background, as in sculpture, or such a projection that is apparent only, as in painting.* – American Heritage Dictionary

The Controversy Over the "Race" of the Ancient Egyptians (Kamitans) in European Scholarship and the Move to Refute the Testimony of the Seventeenth- and Eighteenth-century European Travelers to Egypt

The move to deny the appearance of the Ancient Egyptians and promote the idea that they were not African at all has been put forth by many western writers, even in the face of the writings of the Ancient Egyptians themselves who attest that

1. They are ancestors of the Nubians, to the south, in Africa.
2. Their own depictions of themselves as dark or "black" skinned people.
3. The descriptions of them as "black" people, by the Greek classical writers.
4. The genealogies provided by the Ancient Egyptians themselves stating that their parents are Nubian (such as Amunmhat I).

Jean Fransçois Champollion (1790 A.C.E.-1832 A.C.E.), the main decipherer of the hieroglyphic text in the early 19th century, who is often referred to as the "Father of Egyptology", remarked at the art he saw, which at the time was fully colored since the tombs and many other structures had been closed since the Middle Ages (Dark Ages). He described images of the Ancient Egyptians, created by them, in which they made themselves look like the Ethiopians, and concluded that they were of the same "race" as the modern day Nubians, who are "black" skinned African peoples, saying in a letter to his brother that he wrote while in Egypt examining the reliefs and studying the hieroglyphs: *"We find there Egyptians and Africans represented in the same way"*.[110] Jean Fransçois Champollion later states that based on the images he saw it was clear that the Ancient Egyptians looked like the people presently living in Nubia, i.e. they were "black Africans."

In this same manner, Count Volney wrote after a trip to Egypt between 1783 and 1785:

> "Just think that this race of black men, today our slave and the object of our scorn, is the very race to which we owe our arts, sciences and even the use of speech! Just imagine, finally, that it is in the midst of people who call themselves the greatest friends of liberty and humanity that one has approved the most barbarous slavery and questioned whether black men have the same kind of intelligence as whites!"[111]

Some of the these travelers were being referred to were *Livingstone, Speke, Baker and Junker*. Documenting the observations of travelers such as Livingstone, and others J. A Rogers recorded the following statements by them in his book *Sex and Race Vol. I*:

> "Livingstone said that the Negro face as he saw it reminded him more of that on the monuments of ancient Assyria than that of the popular white fancy.[112] Sir Harry Johnston, foremost authority on the African Negro, said that "the Hamite,"

---

[110] Published in 1833 by the son of Champollion-Figeac, brother of Jean Fransçois Champollion.
[111] Ruins of Empires by Count Volney, (Diop, 1974, p. 28).
[112] The Zambesi and Its Tributaries, p. 526. N. Y., 1866.

that Negroid stock which was the main stock of the ancient Egyptians, is best represented at the present day by the Somali, Galla, and the blood of Abyssinia and Nubia."[113] Sergi compares pictorially the features of Ramases II with that of Mtesa, noted Negro king of Uganda, and show the marked resemblance.[114] Sir M. W. Flinders Petrie, famed Egyptologist says that the Pharaohs of the Xth dynasty were of the Galla type, and the Gallas are clearly what are known in our day as Negroes. He tells further of seeing one day on a train a man whose features were "the exact living, type" of a statue of ancient Libya, and discovered that the man was a American mulatto.[115]"

The stir that the early descriptions of the Egyptians based on their own depictions, as described and reproduced by early explorers and artists, created in Europe in the early years of Egyptology after the translation of the hieroglyphic language by Champollion (1822 A.C.E.) was an unforeseen controversy that later Egyptologists tried desperately to refute. The following memoir recorded by Champollion-Figeac, the brother of Jean Fransçois Champollion in 1829 denotes the "problem," which the western researchers who recognized the importance of Ancient Egyptian civilization, were facing. It was obvious that the writings were beginning to reveal religion, philosophy and evolved culture, all of which contradict the basic tenets used to justify the denigration of the "Negro" race and their enslavement in Africa, Europe and the "New World" (the Americas). Therefore, it became necessary to refute and even attempt to explain away the reason for the findings. (underlined portions by Ashby)

The opinion that the ancient population of Egypt belonged to the Negro African race, is an error long accepted as the truth. Since the Renaissance, travelers in the East, barely capable of fully appreciating the ideas provided by Egyptian monuments on this important question, have helped to spread that false notion and geographers have not failed to reproduce it, even in our day. A serious authority declared himself in favor of this view and popularized the error. Such was the effect of what the celebrated Volney published on the various races of men that he had observed in Egypt. In his *Voyage,* which is in all libraries, he reports that the Copts are descended from the ancient Egyptians; that <u>the Copts have a bloated face, puffed up eyes, flat nose, and thick lips, like a mulatto; that they resemble the Sphinx of the Pyramids, a distinctly Negro head</u>. He concludes that the ancient Egyptians were true Negroes of the same species as all indigenous Africans. To support his opinion, Volney invokes that of Herodotus who, apropos the Colchians, recalls that the <u>Egyptians had black skin and woolly hair. Yet these two physical qualities do not suffice to characterize the Negro race</u> and Volney's conclusion as to the Negro origin of the ancient Egyptian civilization is evidently forced and inadmissible.

It is recognized today that the inhabitants of Africa belong to three races, quite distinct from each other for all time: 1. Negroes proper, in Central and West Africa; 2. Kaffirs on the east coast, who have a less obtuse facial angle than

---

[113] The Uganda Protectorate, Vol. II, p. 472. London, 1902.
[114] The Mediterranean Races, p. 243. N. Y., 1901.
[115] Royal Soc. of Arts Jour., Vol. XLIX, p. 594. 1901.

Blacks and a high nose, <u>but thick lips and woolly hair</u>; 3. Moors, <u>similar in stature, physiognomy and hair to the *best-formed* nations of Europe and western Asia</u>, and differing only in skin color which is tanned by the climate. <u>The ancient population of Egypt belonged to this latter race, that is, to the white race.</u> To be convinced of this, we need only examine the human figures representing Egyptians on the monuments and above all the great number of mummies that have been opened. <u>Except for the color of the skin, blackened by the hot climate, they are the same men as those of Europe</u> and western Asia: <u>frizzy, woolly hair is the true characteristic of the Negro race</u>; the Egyptians, however, had long hair, identical with that of the white race of the West.[116]

Firstly, Champollion-Figeac affirms that the ancient "Egyptians had black skin and woolly hair." However, he and then goes on to say that these are not sufficient to characterize the Negro race. He thus contradicts himself later by saying <u>"frizzy, woolly hair is the true characteristic of the Negro race."</u> Obviously this is a contradiction in terms that is inescapable. In an attempt to formulate a thesis that the Ancient Egyptians were essentially "white people," like "the best-formed" Europeans, <u>"except for the color of the skin, blackened by the hot climate,"</u> he stumbles on his own argument which is unreasonable at the outset. At no time previous or since has there been recognized anywhere on earth, a "race" of white-black people. This argument is based on observing the so-called "three races" of Africa of his time, as if these were representative of the ancient ethnicity of Africa and could have any baring on the question of the "race" of the Ancient Egyptians. This argument is of course contradictory and unworkable such as it is, but even more so when it is kept in mind that the Ancient Egyptians mixed with Asiatics and Europeans (Greeks) and even still the descriptions of the classical Greek writers unanimously considered them as what in the present day would be called "Negros." Also, the present day Copts, descendants of the Ancient Egyptians, of Champollion-Figeac's time were even then recognized as having "Negroid" features. By Champollion-Figeac's reasoning it would be necessary to conclude that Africans are white Europeans. The Kaffirs (Muslim word for pagans) being referred to are those people whom the Muslim Arabs found in Africa as they entered Africa from the Sinai Peninsula, which is the bridge between Asia Minor and Africa. From there they captured the countries in North Africa from Egypt, to Libya, Tunisia, Algiers and Morocco as well as Spain. Through limited genealogies left by the Moors it has been determined that they were a mixture of Arab and African blood.

Thus, the comparisons used by Champollion-Figeac are wholly useless for determining the "race" of the Ancient Egyptians, but they can however be used for comparisons to the Copts, who like the Moors, appeared to "<u>have a bloated face, puffed up eyes, flat nose, and thick lips, like a mulatto</u>" like the Moors, and also like the present day peoples of African descent living in the Diaspora (African Americans, African Brazilians, Africans in Jamaica, etc.). When this kind of comparison is made it is clear that the "mulatto" arises from a combination of African and Semite (Arab) or European. This of course means that the African features, (<u>color of the skin, thick lips and woolly hair</u>) must have been present in the past if they are present in the current population of mixed peoples, that is to say, the population goes from "black" skin to "lighter" skin color and not the other way around. Except for the effects of climactic changes on

---

[116] *Egyptiene ancienne.* Paris: Collection l'Univers, 1839, pp 26-27

populations over a long period of time (thousands of years), which have been shown to cause changes in physical appearance, there is no record of "Black" populations arising from "white" populations. Lastly, in the time of the Ancient Egyptians, before the coming of the Greeks, there were no Europeans in Africa at all. The only populations recognized by the Egyptians were themselves, the other Africans, the Libyans and the Asiatics, all of whom vary in skin tone from dark "black" to light "brown" coloration. So if there are any "white" people in present day Africa they are descendants of the documented influx of Greeks who came in as invading forces with Alexander the Great (330 B.C.E.) and or the documented influx of Arabs which came with the advent of the expansion of Islam (650 B.C.E.) and after. In any case, when discussing the Ancient Egyptians of the Old and Middle Kingdoms and the Pre-Dynastic Period, we are not discussing "mulattos" since the admixture with other ethnic groups had not occurred until the New Kingdom period, and even more so in the Late period, through contact with the conquering Asiatic and European forces. Therefore, to look at the images of the Egyptians during the mixture period and to say that these are representative of the Ancient Egyptian ethnic origins is the worst kind of scholarship. This is a tactic used by some Western and Arab scholars to escape the conclusion that the Ancient Egyptians were "black." How is this possible? In places such as the United States of America, the "rule" established by the "white" ruling class has always been that "one drop of black blood make one black." This means that everyone from dark black skin color to the light brown or swarthy complexion, are recognized as being descendants of the African slaves, and are subject to being segregated and discriminated against. But in this argument it is also possible to say that those mulattos are not 100% African since they are mixed with European, Arab, etc. So they are trying to say that the Ancient Egyptians were either a mixed race or better yet, an indigenous Asiatic group that developed independently of the "black Africans." In any case, even in the late period the Greek classical writers witnessed the population of Kamit as being overwhelmingly "black" (Nubian). So we are not talking about "light skinned black people" or "dark skinned white people" but <u>dark skinned black people</u>," like those who can be met even today (2002 A.C.E.) in the city of Aswan (Upper (southern) Egypt – see picture above).

There were several prominent and respected Linguists and Egyptologists who affirmed that the Ancient Egyptians were "African" or "Negros." Sir Henry Rawlinson, prominent linguist and decipherer of the mideastern scripts and widely regarded as the "father of Middle-Eastern Studies," said *"Seti's face is thoroughly African, strong, fierce, prognathous, with depressed nose, thick lips and a heavy chin..."*[117] Showing that certain foremost Egyptologists accept the "Negro" composition of the Ancient Egyptian people, J. A Rogers recorded the following statements by the famous British Egyptologist Flinders Petrie, in his book *Sex and Race Vol.I*:

> "Egyptian civilization, from its beginning to the Christian era, lasted for more than seven thousand years, that is, about four times as long as from "the birth of Christ" to the present, therefore, most of the records have been lost, and the little that remains must be pieced together. There are often great gaps. Between the Bushman period of 9000 B.C. and the First Dynasty (4477-4514 B.C.) very little is known. Some of the faces of the rulers of this dynasty are clearly Negroid. The founder of the Third Dynasty, Sa-nekht, was a full-blooded Negro, a type

---

[117] Rawlinson, G. *The Story of Egypt*, p. 252. London. 1887.

commonly seen in the Egyptian army today. Petrie says of him, "It will be seen how strongly Ethiopian the characters of it (the portrait) is even more so than Shabaka, most marked of the Ethiopian dynasty. The type is one with which we are very familiar among the Sudanese of the Egyptian police and army; it goes with a dark-brown skin and a very truculent character."

In the late 19th century (A.C.E.) the French director general of the Egyptian Service of Antiquities and regarded as a foremost Egyptologist, Gaston Maspero (1846-1916 A.C.E.), wrote about the controversy about the origins and descriptions of the Ancient Egyptians as it stood in his times. (underlined portions by Ashby)

> "In our day the origin and ethnographic affinities of the population _have inspired lengthy debate_. First, the seventeenth- and eighteenth-century travelers, _misled by the appearance of certain mongrelized Copts_, certified that their predecessors in the Pharaonic age had a _puffed up face, bug eyes, flat nose, fleshy lips_. And that they presented certain _characteristic features of the Negro race_. This error, common at the start of the century, vanished once and for all as soon as the French Commission had published its great work."[118]

One of the questions that arise here is why was the unanimous reaction of the seventeenth- and eighteenth-century European travelers in Egypt so upsetting to the late eighteenth and twentieth century western scholars? They were the first Europeans in modern times to see the Ancient Egyptian reliefs and paintings and their reaction was the same as the Greek classical writers when it came to describing the peoples of Kamit and the rest of the Nile Valley. In fact, they did not base their assessment of the Ancient Egyptian ethnicity just by examining their descendants, the Copts, but on images left behind by the Kamitans, some that had been buried under the encroaching dessert sands, which for this reasons were preserved in very good condition. It is interesting to note that the appearance of the Copts was acknowledged as presenting the "mongrelized" features (puffed up face, bug eyes, flat nose, fleshy lips) and that these are understood as being generally representative of the "Negro race." This observation has been widely accepted by all who agree with the concept of ethnic differentiations among human populations. Yet, when it comes to acknowledging these features in the images of Ancient Egypt they become somehow unrepresentative or unreliable or insufficient in assisting in the determination about where those people came from and to which population they are related.

This move to obfuscate the issue gained momentum in the 20th century and became widely accepted by society in general, despite all the evidence to the contrary. Even in the late 20th century there are anthropologists and Egyptologists staunchly supporting the baseless construct of an other than "Negro" origin of the Ancient Egyptians. What has changed is the willingness to say that they were Africans. What has not changed is the reluctance to accept their "blackness." Being unable to refute the pictorial evidences or the writings by the Egyptians themselves, many present day researches who seek to prove that the Ancient Egyptians were not "black" Africans attempt to use other means to discredit the findings which do not support their contentions.

The work of a western scholar by the name of Martin Bernal, author of _Black Athena : The Afroasiatic Roots of Classical Civilization (The Fabrication of Ancient Greece 1785-1985_, (published in 1989), a scathing report on the western falsification of the evidences pointing to an African

---

[118] _Historie ancienne des peubles de l'Orient._

origin of Greek (i.e. Western civilization) received a storm of criticism from some researchers who propose that his treatment of the statements by the classical Greek writers as "eager credulity." Jacques Berlinerblan, the author of *Heresy in the University: The Black Athena Controversy and the Responsibilities of American Intellectuals* (1999) examines the charge against Bernal.

> "With this generous reading now rendered I would like to note that Bernal has offered no viable alternative or corrective to the approaches which he believes are responsible for the fall of the Ancient Model. Nor does he distinguish among better or worse types of exegetical and hermeneutic approaches, leaving us with the impression that he believes all are equally corrupt. His methodological credo seems to be *The Ancients could very well be telling us the truth.* While this is plausible, it is incumbent upon the author to advance a method which might help us to determine how scholars might go about distinguishing truthful accounts from untruthful ones. As Egyptologist John D. Ray asked, "Where are the final criteria to lie?" To this point, Bernal has neglected to articulate such criteria, and this leaves him vulnerable to Mary Lefkowitz's charge of "eager credulity" toward the ancient sources."[119]

There is an interesting process of selective acceptance of certain evidences from the ancient writers and overlooking or minimizing certain other evidences when it is convenient to explain a particular point. This is noticeable in the work of some western scholars of Ancient Egypt, Greece as well as India. Bernal's book drew such criticism, not because the information was new, since other writers such as Cheikh Anta Diop had presented it in his book *African Origins of Civilization, Myth or Reality.* The problem was that Bernal is a "white" European scholar, part of the establishment, and the information he presented was perceived by some of his peers as precipitating the fall of the walls of western academia's characterization of African civilization, and consequently the history of western civilization, and their prestige as western scholars with it. The objective here also seems to call into question the veracity of the ancient writers, or to say that they were gullible, or to make it appear that their Egyptian "guides" or "informants" were trying to impress the Greeks by telling them wild stories that they wanted to hear. In the third chapter of *Not Out of Africa: How Afrocentrism Became an Excuse to Teach Myth As History* (August 1997), Mary Lefkowitz reviews the texts which Bernal used in order to build his Ancient and Revised Ancient Models. "The idea that Greek religion and philosophy has Egyptian origins," she asserts, "may appear at first sight to be more plausible, because it derives, at least in part, from the writings of ancient Greek historians." The scholar Jacques Berlinerblan explains Lefkowitz's position, which he himself admittedly shares. (Underlined portions by Ashby)

> "Lefkowitz advances an unyieldingly critical appraisal of the writings of Herodotus, Diodorus, Plato, Strabo, and the Church Fathers on the subject of Egypt. These figures cannot be counted on to offer us objective accounts due to their "respect for the antiquity of Egyptian religion and civilization, and a desire somehow to be connected with it." This admiration inclined them to overemphasize their dependency on, and contacts with, the land of the Pyramids.

---

[119] *Heresy in the University: The Black Athena Controversy and the Responsibilities of American Intellectuals* by Jacques Berlinerblan

But the presence of a pro-Egyptian bias in Greek thought is not the only drawback which Lefkowitz discovers. In true Hard Modern fashion she enumerates the failings of the ancients qua historical researchers. The Greeks were not <u>sufficiently skeptical or critical of their informants and sources</u>. They did not speak Egyptian, nor did they draw upon Egyptian archives. They misunderstood the very Egyptian phenomena they studied. Their linguistic surmises were predicated on <u>simplistic and erroneous assumptions</u>. <u>They looked at Egypt "through cultural blinkers,"</u> producing an image that was "astigmatic and deeply Hellenized."[120] Again and again Lefkowitz pounds the point home-how poorly the Greeks performed when compared to us:

Unlike modern anthropologists, who approach new cultures so far as possible with an open mind, and with the aid of a developed set of methodologies, Herodotus tended to construe whatever he saw by analogy with Greek practice, as if it were impossible for him to comprehend it any other way.

Lest there exist any remaining question as to the reliability of the ancients, Lefkowitz proceeds to pulverize the final link in the chain of historical transmission. Not only were <u>the Greeks unreliable, but so were their Egyptian informants. Jewish and Christian Egyptians supplied the gullible Greeks with self-aggrandizing information</u> as "a way of asserting the importance of their culture, especially in a time when they had little or no political powers."[121]

We must keep in mind that scholars such as Lefkowitz are trying to discredit the ancient authors but the arguments of such scholars are not based on rationality or on evidences to prove their contentions.

1. People from different periods in time, removed in some cased by several hundreds of years, which means that they did not have an opportunity to conspire with each other to fabricate the same "fantasies".
2. They did not speak to the same people upon visiting Egypt or in such cases as Pythagoras and Plato, becoming students of the Egyptian masters for several years.
3. They had no reason to lie about their experiences as do present day western scholars, who need to uphold a view of the past that support western superiority and independence from the very people whose oppression is rationalized by saying that they had no culture, religion, philosophy or civilization.
4. The Greek classical writers (Herodotus, Plutarch, Pythagoras, Plato, Aristotle, Diodorus, Strabo, and others) did not rely simply on what they were told by their "informants." They presented evidences and described what they saw with their own eyes and when these descriptions are compared they are in agreement with their statements and with the evidences that can be examined by any person who takes the time to visit a serious museum of Egyptian antiquities or the monuments and tombs of Ancient Egypt themselves.

---

[120] George, *Crimes of Perception,* xi (emphasis added); Peters, *Heresy and Authority,* 15, 17.

[121] P. L. Berger, Heretical Imperative, 28. Foucault, History *of* Sexuality, vol. 1, 93. On Foucault's use of this term, see James Miller, Passion *of* Michel Foucault, 108. Char, "Partage formel XXII," 0euvres completes, 160.

5. The use of the term "informants" in itself reveals the demeaning attitude and prejudicial manner of dealing with the Greek Classical writers, presumably because there is no other area that these scholars can attack in order to prove their theory.

6. There are ample forms of evidence besides the writings of the Greek classical authors upon which to investigate the ethnicity of the Ancient Egyptians and their contributions to early Greek culture. These other evidences, such as the adoption of Ancient Egyptian customs, tradition and religion by the Greeks are irrefutable and inescapable and therefore, not to be mentioned. By creating a stir in one area, the western researchers hope to cloud the issue and taint an objective observer's view of other evidences.

In any case, such attacks can be easily dismissed since they are entirely without basis. The problem arises in the fact that they speak from a self-serving pulpit, the "western scholarly establishment" that is supported by the western media, which accepts documentaries that are made for television by these scholars or approved by the "legitimate" schools that they represent, rather than from conclusive evidence. Anyone who has worked in the western university setting knows that there is a lot of politics involved with attaining the coveted status as tenured professor. Of course, anyone who does not agree with the established opinions will have a difficult time breaking through the invisible walls of the western "ivory towers." The Western academia, which controls the scholars through the process of selectively accepting those who support the pre-established doctrines and rejecting those who do not. Scholarly criticism is one thing, but dismissing something just because it does not agree with one's views is simply unscientific and evidence of an ulterior motive or hidden agenda. Having the most powerful voice to speak with and being supported by the government, the western scholarly establishment has the capacity to put out skewed images of reality, that when repeated again and again over a period of time, attains a status of being "truth" and "real," but when examined closely, are found to be nothing more that the cries of unhappy children who cannot accept the evidences before them. A fault that was noted in Lefkowitz's work not by the Africentrists or by Bernal but by her own colleague Jacques Berlinerblan, which reveals her duplicitous manner of handling the statements of the Greek classical writers.

> In my own work on the Hebrew Bible I have argued, with no less passion, that we simply cannot believe what this text reports. Accordingly, I concur with her objections, and I find Lefkowitz's overarching skepticism justified. Yet in her haste to skewer Bernal, Lefkowitz avoids considering the drawbacks or implications of her - I should say "our"-position. At one point in Not Out of Africa she speaks of the "important," "generally accurate," and "useful information" which Herodotus makes apropos of the Nile, Egyptian monuments, and individual pharaohs. The problem is that Lefkowitz never pauses to tell us why she considers these particular observations to be "generally accurate." Further, she and other critics of Bernal often evince their own "eager credulity" toward ancient texts, especially when it permits them to criticize Bernal. Lefkowitz, for instance, is not averse to citing and accepting Herodotus's testimony if it helps her to refute Black Athena's historical claims.[122]

---

[122] Bernal, Black Athena 1: 2 (emphasis in original).

Lefkowitz's double standard sabotages her own integrity and thus invalidates her statements and motives as a scholar. When the empty attempts to impugn the statements of the Greek classical writers fails there is no recourse but to engage in attempts to discredit the scholars who advance their positions using the "unacceptable" evidences by referring to them as <u>"wild,"</u> <u>"flaky,"</u> etc., and refer to their positions as based on <u>"fantasies."</u> A western writer by the name of Steven Howe characterized the work of noted Africentric scholars in this way in his book. Without providing any evidence to refute their positions, a practice that is widely regarded as the hallmark of the western scientific process, he presented the opinions of other scholars who agree with him, they also being devoid of evidences to back up their positions. This of course is no scholarship at all, but merely the addition of one more voice to the cacophony of western scholarly discontent over the undeniable and overwhelming evidences contradicting their positions. The absence of real evidence to support their opinions is substituted with forceful opinions and emotional appeals and these cannot be accepted as science, but as disgruntled and frustrated outbursts. Mr. Howe makes the following assertions without supporting these with any evidence either in Egyptology, anthropology, genetics, geology or any other recognized science.

1. The ancient Egyptians belonged to no race, they were neither black nor white but Egyptian.
2. The white race did not evolve from the black.
3. The race concept did not exist in Ancient Egypt.
4. Arabs did not overrun or destroy north Africa.

The obvious misconceptions or misinformation or errors in Mr. Howe's arguments can be easily and concisely proven to be false, since there is no real evidence being presented:

A. The first point is bogus on its face. Even in the present day, the spurious concept of "racism" recognizes no such race as "Egyptian." All human beings have been regarded by the western race concept as either "white," meaning European, or of some "Negroid" stock, meaning descendant or affiliated with African ancestry, or fitting into some range of color between "black" and "white."

B. All the evidences from anthropology and genetic sciences point to a common origin for all modern human beings as having originated in Africa. Therefore, Mr. Howe is either misinformed or deliberately misdirecting the public. Inherent in the treatment of Egyptology is the practice of ignoring the findings of scientific disciplines which are widely regarded as being empirical as opposed to theoretical. These are ignored because they contradict the orthodox dogmatic position. These other sciences support the "black" African origins of Ancient Egyptian culture.

C. Mr. Howe proposes the idea that the Ancient Egyptians did not indeed have a concept of race in order to support the idea that there was no difference between how they saw themselves and the other peoples of the world. The Ancient Egyptians were not racists and consequently no record of race classifications, or racial practices such as those of modern Western Culture have been discovered even after 200 years of Egyptological research. However, the concept of ethnic differentiation did exist. The Ancient Egyptians did recognize and acknowledge the concept of ethnicity which includes an awareness of the differences in physical features like skin color, etc. Several examples of these "ethnographies" survive to this day. So the Ancient Egyptians saw themselves as being the same in appearance to the Nubians and other Africans and different from the Asiatics and the later Greeks (Europeans). Thus, the Greeks (Europeans) could not be Egyptians since the Egyptians depicted themselves as "black" Africans. It is interesting that some scholars try to hold on to the idea that race is not important based on the genetic evidence which shows the race concept to be bogus, when it suits the ideal of asserting that the Egyptians had no race so as not to be forced to admit that they were "black Africans," but when it comes to accepting people of non-European descent into European countries, equality in economics, social settings and government, the practice of segregation and discrimination based on racial bias, remains enforced.

D. Ample records and evidences from African peoples as well as the Assyrian, Persian, Greek and Arab conquerors attest to the fact of the movement from Europe, imposing Roman Christianity, and from Asia Minor into North Africa, imposing Islam and the destruction of "Kaffir" (pagan) monuments, temples and cultures which were seen as contradictory with the formation of a world dominated by Christianity, and later Islam.

Thus, even at the end of the 20th century the world is still contending with the agenda of some duplicitous or ignorant western scholars and writers of characterizing African culture as primitive and insignificant, and to elevate Western Culture and western scholarship without any footing in science. This is why the work of those who study Ancient Egyptian culture, religion and philosophy needs to confront the issue of history and the means to present evidences with rigorous standards that will lead to reasonable and useful conclusions, as opposed to disparaging remarks and insults calling the work of their opponents "wild", "flaky", "fantasies", opinion and innuendo.

Finally, this author (Ashby), knows of no African American Africentric scholar or African Africentric scholar who would say that Western civilization, as we know it today, is based on African civilization, it does however owe its existence to Ancient Africa since what the European countries built cannot be said to be in keeping with either the principles or philosophy of civilization enjoined by the Ancient Egyptian sages, nor the tenets that were learned by the Greek philosophers who were students of the Kamitan sages, who attempted to enlighten the early Greeks with the knowledge of the Land of the Pyramids. When asked by a western reporter what he thought about western civilization, the Indian leader Mahatma Ghandi is said to have replied: *That is a good idea!* He responded in this way because western civilization remains an idea yet to be realized. Technological advancement and material wealth or military power do not in themselves constitute "civilization." Western Culture cannot be considered to be a civilization since civilization means to be "civilized" in one's actions, constructions, and views towards the world. Being civilized means being civil (Civility = **1.** *Courteous behavior; politeness.* **2.** *A courteous act or utterance.* –American Heritage Dictionary) to other people. Civility is one of the most important concepts of Ancient Egyptian Maat philosophy. Being civilized does not mean just being courteous in social situations, but then taking advantage of the same people in another or promoting the welfare of one's own group, but promoting the welfare of all people in general, otherwise one's civilization is biased and therefore duplicitous and hypocritical, which disqualifies it from being regarded as a "civilization" in any stretch of the concept. Civilization benefits the world community as it sees all human beings as citizens of humanity. Being civilized cannot be equated with the denigration of women in the culture, the concept of a male god and the exclusion of women in religion, the global domination of people through economic manipulation and hoarding of resources, the enslavement of entire populations, the murder of entire populations and stealing their land, etc. These are not values of the ancient African culture, which was based on the principle of Humanism (Ubuntu/Maat) and required the provision of resources to meet the needs of all members of the population as well as the balance between male and female, etc. So Africa cannot be claimed to be the source of such acts of inhumanity, selfishness and greed. So wherever these were learned, they developed independently, perhaps due to the inability of people in Europe to heed the teachings of the Ancient Egyptian sages and their early Greek students. Thus, even though the early Greek philosophers created a spark in their home country that provided an impetus for the later development of European culture, that culture cannot yet be considered to be a civilization in the contexts of what was accomplished in Ancient Egypt (Africa).

Ancient Egyptian Origin of the Hieroglyphic Writing & Greek Alphabet

There is a misconception about the Ancient Egyptian hieroglyphic language that it arrived with no development at all as if by magic to the African continent. This notion plays into the speculation that it was not produced and developed in Africa, by Africans. If the text itself is examined and if the writings from linguists who have studied it are examined, it becomes quickly obvious that there was a period of development of the language. Precisely, in relation to the developing a solution to the problem of confusion in the reading, the Ancient Egyptian scribes developed what are called determinatives, to be added to the word so as to make the meaning more accurate. However, there still remained some ambiguities, so then came the development of "alphabetic" signs. This development is recognized by linguists as being *"not derived from Mesopotamian writing, and demonstrates the <u>total</u> autonomy of the development of the hieroglyphic system."*

While all of the scriptures of the Ancient Egyptians are written in Hieroglyphic or Hieratic script, certain differences ascribe the literature to different periods. This is not a determination for dating, but rather for determining relative periods to which they belong. In the case of Ancient Egyptian, the varied schools were not opposed to each other. Therefore, a sage from the school of Amun would be harmonious in treating the texts of the Asar school, and a sage from the Aset (Isis) school would have no problem treating the texts of the Memphite school, etc., because they are all understood as being related, presenting varied views but of the same underlying teaching.

The most ancient writings in our historical period are from the Ancient Egyptians. These writings are referred to as hieroglyphics. The original name given to these writings by the Ancient Egyptians is *Medu Neter,* meaning "the writing of God" or *Neter Medu* or "Divine Speech." These writings were inscribed in temples, coffins and papyruses and contained the teachings in reference to the spiritual nature of the human being and the ways to promote spiritual emancipation, awakening or resurrection.

Up to the late 20th century it had been thought that the alphabet that is used in western countries was derived from the Phoenicians through a man called Cadmus. However, scholarship has determined that the Phoenician alphabet, that was later used in Asia Minor and even later, taken over and altered by the Greeks, was derived from a "**Proto-Canaanite**" – also known as "**Proto-Siniatic**" which was itself developed mostly by taking characters from the Ancient Egyptian Hieroglyphic script (signs).[123]

This scholarship supports the claims of the Ancient Egyptians. According to ancient Greek legends Cadmus was a Phoenician prince who founded Thebes in Boeotia,[124] and among several other things *invented the alphabet*. In spite of the popularity of this tradition (supported by Herodotus, 450 B.C.), this was doubted even in ancient times. For instance, Tacitus[125] says:

> **The Egyptians also claim to have invented the alphabet, which the Phoenicians appropriated the glory, giving out that they had discovered what they had really been taught. (*Annals* 11.14)**

Diodorus (1st Cent. B.C.) states that Cadmus was an Egyptian citizen and also expresses caution in the acceptance of this Phoenician "invention":

> Cadmus, who was a citizen of Egyptian Thebes… (*Lib. Hist.*, Book 1. 23. 1-5)

> Men tell us . . . that the Phoenicians were not the first to make the discovery of letters; but that they did no more than change the form of the letters; whereupon the majority of mankind made use of the way of writing them as the Phoenicians devised. (*Lib. Hist.*, Book V).

So the use of the alphabet appears to have been derived from the Ancient Egyptian signs, which were taken by Asiatics and developed in to a Proto-Syniatic system which in turn developed into Canaanite, Cuneiform, Aramaic, Phoenician, Hebrew, Arabic, Greek, Roman and from Roman into the Romance languages, English, Spanish, French, etc.

EVOLUTION OF THE ALPHABET

3400 BCE.   2000 BCE   1100 BCE 800-600 BCE
⇓   ⇓   ⇓   ⇓

Ancient Egyptian → proto-Sinaitic→ Phoenician→ Greek→ Etruscan→ Roman→ modern

---

[123] Reading the Past, Egyptian Hieroglyphs, by W.V. Davies

[124] An ancient region of Greece north of Attica and the Gulf of Corinth. The cities of the region formed the **Boeotian League** in the seventh century B.C. but were usually under the dominance of Thebes.

[125] Roman public official and historian whose two greatest works, *Histories* and *Annals,* concern the period from the death of Augustus (A.D. 14) to the death of Domitian (96).

CHAPTER 3: SUMMARY OF SHETAUT NETER – ANCIENT EGYPTIAN RELIGION

The Spiritual Culture and the Purpose of Life in Ancient Egypt: Shetaut Neter

"Men and women are to become God-like through a life of virtue and the cultivation of the spirit through scientific knowledge, practice and bodily discipline."

-Ancient Egyptian Proverb

THE RELIGION OF ANCIENT EGYPT

A full treatment of Ancient Egyptian religion is impossible in this small booklet. However, there are some important factors to understand about Ancient Egyptian religion and Yoga Philosophy. The first sophisticated system of religion and yoga mystical philosophy in historical times (5,000 B.C.E.) occurred in Ancient Egypt. This system included all of the gods and goddesses which in later times became individually popular in various cities throughout Ancient Egypt. At the heart of this system of gods and goddesses was *Shetai*, the hidden and unmanifest essence of the universe, also known as *Neberdjer* and *Amun*. The system of religion of Ancient Egypt was called *Shetaut Neter* or the *Hidden Way of The Unmanifest Supreme Being*.

The entire system of mystical philosophy of the hidden Supreme Being, as well as the method through which that Being manifests in the form of the phenomenal physical universe and individual human consciousness, was explained in progressive stages in the theology of the Trinity known as Amun-Ra-Ptah, which was said to have arisen out of the Supreme Being: Neberdjer. As Ancient Egyptian history moved on through thousands of years, each segment of this Trinity was adopted by a particular priesthood and locality which then set about to explain and expound the philosophy of that particular segment of the Trinity. The priests of the Ancient Egyptian city of Anu adopted Ra, the priesthood of the Ancient Egyptian city of Hetkaptah adopted Ptah, and the Ancient Egyptian city of Waset or Newt (Thebes) adopted Amun.[126]

Fundamental Concepts of Kamitan Spirituality

Ancient Egyptian Religion is predicated upon a simple but profound concept which is based in the mystical experience. Elevated initiates discovered that all Creation is actually an expression of one indivisible being. That being manifests as the apparent objects and multiplicity in Creation. This being was referred to as "Neter" and its expressions were termed "Neteru." Neter means "Divinity" and Neteru means "Aspects of the original divinity." Another term that is used to describe the neteru is "Gods and Goddesses." The gods and goddesses are like the children and the Supreme Being, Neter, is the ultimate parent of all. This Ancient Egyptian system of divinities was adopted by the Ancient Greeks by their own admission. Therefore, it is no surprise to see that the fundamental concepts, iconographies and many aspects of Greek mythology appear to be copies of the earlier Ancient Egyptian creations. This religion centers around the concept of the single, undivided being. Therefore, the religion of Ancient Egypt may be referred to as "Neterianism." The following is an overview of Ancient Egyptian religious philosophy.

What is Shetaut Neter? The Ancient Egyptians were African peoples who lived in the north-eastern quadrant of the continent of Africa. They were descendants of the Nubians, who had themselves originated from farther south into the heart of Africa at the great lakes region, the sources of the Nile River. They created a vast civilization and culture earlier than any other society in known history and organized a nation which was based on the concepts of balance and order as well as spiritual enlightenment. These ancient African people called their land Kamit

[126] See *Egyptian Yoga Vol. I: The Philosophy of Enlightenment* and *Egyptian Yoga Vol. II: The Supreme Wisdom of Enlightenment* by Dr. Muata Ashby

and soon after developing a well ordered society they began to realize that the world is full of wonders but life is fleeting and that there must be something more to human existence. They developed spiritual systems that were designed to allow human beings to understand the nature of this secret being who is the essence of all Creation. They called this spiritual system "Shtaut Ntr."

Shetaut means secret or mystery.

Who is Neter?

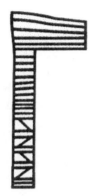

"Ntr"

Who is Ntr?

The symbol of Neter was described by an Ancient Kamitan sage as:

"That which is placed in the coffin"

The term Ntr , or Ntjr , come from the Ancient Egyptian hieroglyphic language which did not record its vowels. However, the term survives in the Coptic language as *"Nutar."* The same Coptic meaning (divine force or sustaining power) applies in the present as it did in ancient times, It is a symbol composed of a wooden staff that was wrapped with strips of fabric, like a mummy. The strips alternate in color with yellow, green and blue. The mummy in Kamitan spirituality is understood to be the dead but resurrected Divinity. So the Nutar is actually every human being who does not really die, but goes to live on in a different form. Further, the resurrected spirit of every human being is that same Divinity. Phonetically, the term Nutar is related to other terms having the same meaning, the latin "Natura," Spanish Naturalesa, English "Nature" and "Nutriment", etc. In a real sense, as we will see, Natur means power manifesting as Neteru and the Neteru are the objects of creation, i.e. "nature."

Neter means Divinity.

Neter and the Neteru

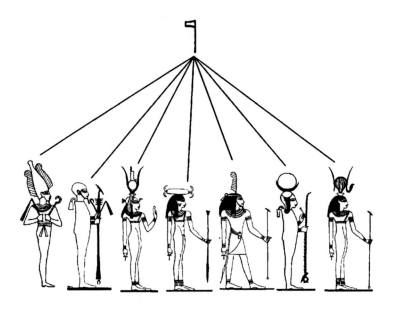

The concept of Neter and Neteru binds and ties all of the varied forms of Kamitan spirituality into one vision of the gods and goddesses all emerging from the same Supreme Being. Therefore, ultimately. Kamitan spirituality is not polytheistic, nor is it monotheistic, for it holds that the Supreme Being is more than a God but an all-encompassing Absolute Divinity.

The Neteru

"Neteru"

The term "Neteru" means "gods and goddesses." This means that from the ultimate and transcendental Supreme Being, "Neter," come the Neteru. There are countless Neteru. So from the one come the many. These Neteru are cosmic forces that pervade the universe. They are the means by which Neter sustains Creation and manifests through it. So Neterianism is a monotheistic polytheism. The one Supreme Being expresses as many gods and goddesses and at the end of time, after their work of sustaining Creation is finished, these gods and goddesses are again absorbed back into the Supreme Being.

All of the spiritual systems of Ancient Egypt (Kamit) have one essential aspect that is common to all; They all hold that there is a Supreme Being (Neter) who manifests in a multiplicity of ways through nature, the Neteru.

Like sunrays, the Neteru emanate from the Divine and they are its manifestations. So by studying the Neteru we learn about and are led to discover their source, the Neter. And with this discovery we are enlightened.

The Neteru may be depicted anthropomorphically or zoomorphically in accordance with the teaching about Neter that is being conveyed through them.

The Neteru and Their Temples

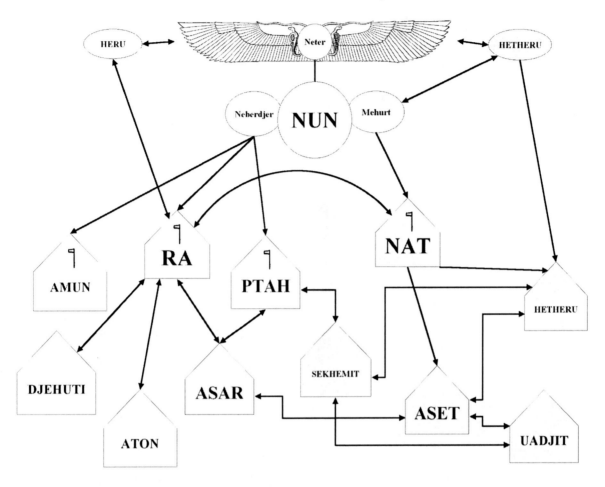

The sages of Kamit instituted a system by which the teachings of spirituality were espoused through a temple organization. The major divinities were assigned to a particular city and that divinity became the "patron" of that city. Also, the priests and priestesses of that temple were in charge of seeing to the welfare of the people in that district as well as to maintain the traditions and disciplines of the traditions based on the particular divinity being worshipped. So the original concept of "Neter" became elaborated through the "theologies" of the various traditions and variations on the teachings emerged that expressed nuances of variation in perspective on the teachings to suit the needs of varying kinds of personalities in the people of different locales.

The primary or main divinities are denoted by the Neter symbol (⌐). The house structure represents the temple for that particular divinity. The interconnections with the other temples are based on original scriptural statements which were espoused by the temples that linked them with the other divinities. So this means that the divinities should be viewed not as separate entities operating independently but rather as family members who are in the same "business" together, i.e. the enlightenment of society, albeit through variations in form of worship, name and form, etc. Ultimately, all the divinities are referred to as Neteru and they are all said to be emanations from the ultimate and Supreme Being. Thus, the teaching from any of the temples leads to understanding of the others and these lead back to the source, the highest Divinity and with this attainment comes spiritual enlightenment, the Great Awakening.

The same Supreme Being, Neter, is the winged all-encompassing transcendental Divinity, the Spirit, which is in the early history called "Heru." The physical universe in which the Heru lives is called "Hetheru" or the house of Heru. This Divinity is also the Nun or primeval substratum from which all matter is composed and from this mass are composed the various Divinities and the material universe. Neter is actually androgynous and Heru, the Spirit, is also related as a male aspect of that androgyny. Heru gives rise to the solar principle and this is seen in both the male and female divinities.

The Neteru and Their Interrelationships

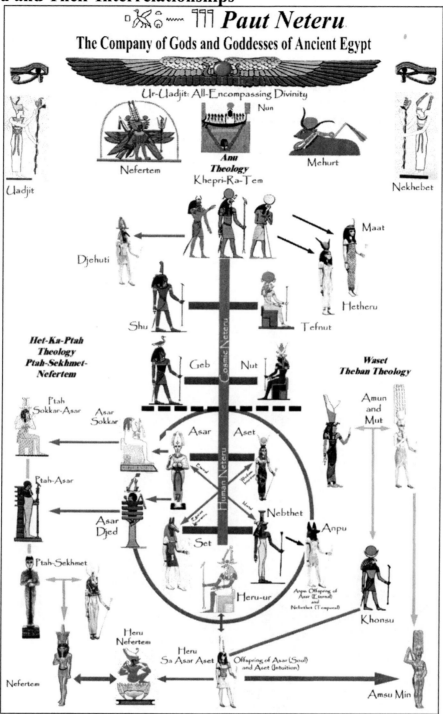

The image above provides an idea of the relationships between the divinities of the three main Neterian spiritual systems (traditions). The traditions are composed of companies or groups of gods and goddesses. Their actions, teachings, interactions, with each other and with human beings, provide insight into their nature as well as that of human existence and Creation itself. The lines indicate direct scriptural relationships and the labels also indicate that some divinities from one system are the same in others with only a name change. Again, this is attested to by the scriptures themselves in direct statements, like those found in the *Prt m Hru* text Chapter 4 (17).[127]

The Cities in Ancient Egypt Where the Greek Philosophers Studied

The land of Ancient Egypt

Solon, Thales, Plato, Eudoxus and Pythagoras went to Egypt and consorted with the priests. Eudoxus they say, received instruction from Chonuphis of Memphis,* Solon from Sonchis of Sais,* and Pythagoras from Oeniphis of Heliopolis.*

–Plutarch (Greek historian c. 46-120 A.C.E.)

*(cities in Ancient Egypt-see below)

---

[127] See the book *The Egyptian Book of the Dead* by Muata Ashby

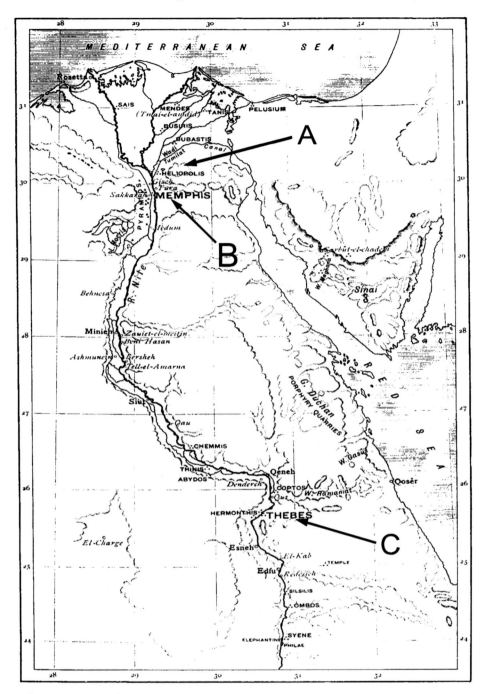

Key to the Map above: Egypt is located in the north-eastern corner of the African Continent. The cities wherein the theology of the Trinity of Amun-Ra-Ptah was developed were: A- Anu (Heliopolis), B-Hetkaptah (Memphis), and C-Waset (Thebes).

Sacred Scriptures of Shetaut Neter

The following scriptures represent the foundational scriptures of Kamitan culture. They may be divided into three categories: *Mythic Scriptures*, *Mystical Philosophy* and *Ritual Scriptures*, and *Wisdom Scriptures* (Didactic Literature).

MYTHIC SCRIPTURES Literature	Mystical (Ritual) Philosophy Literature	Wisdom Texts Literature
Shetaut Asar-Aset-Heru The Myth of Asar, Aset and Heru (Asarian Resurrection Theology) - Predynastic **Shetaut Atum-Ra** Anunian Theology Predynastic **Shetaut Net/Aset/Hetheru** Saitian Theology – Goddess Spirituality Predynastic **Shetaut Ptah** Memphite Theology Predynastic **Shetaut Amun** Theban Theology Predynastic	**Pyramid Texts** (c. 5500 B.C.E.-3800 B.C.E.) **Coffin Texts** (c. 2040 B.C.E.-1786 B.C.E.) **Papyrus Texts** (c. 1580 B.C.E.-Roman Period)[128] Books of Coming Forth By Day Example of famous papyri: Papyrus of Any Papyrus of Hunefer Papyrus of Kenna Greenfield Papyrus, Etc.	**Wisdom Texts** (c. 3,000 B.C.E. – Ptolemaic Period) Precepts of Ptahotep Instructions of Any Instructions of Amenemope Etc. Maat Declarations Literature (All Periods) Songs of the Blind Harper

---

[128] After 1570 B.C.E they would evolve into a more unified text, the Egyptian Book of the Dead.

Medu Neter

"Medu Neter"

The teachings of the Neterian Traditions are conveyed in the scriptures of the Neterian Traditions. These are recorded in the Medu Neter script.

Old Period Hieroglyphic Script

Above: A section from the pyramid of Teti in Sakkara Egypt, known as the "Pyramid Texts" (Early Dynastic Period) showing the cross

The Medu Neter was used through all periods by Priests and priestesses – mostly used in monumental inscriptions such as the Pyramid texts, Obelisks, temple inscriptions, etc. – since Pre-Dynastic times. It is the earliest form of writing in known history.

Hekau, Medu Neter and Shetitu

"hekau"

The concept of the divine word or *Hekau,* is an extremely important part of Ancient Egyptian religion and is instructive in the study of all African religion. The only difference between Ancient Egyptian religion and other African religions in this area was the extensive development of the "written word." As explained earlier, the word religion is translated as Shetaut Neter in the Ancient African language of Kamit.

Shetitu

This Shetaut (mysteries- rituals, wisdom, philosophy) about the Neter (Supreme Being) are related in the ⌂ꞏ|||*Shetitu* or writings related to the hidden teaching. And those writings are referred to as *Medu Neter* or "Divine Speech," the writings of the god Djehuti (Ancient Egyptian god of the divine word) – also refers to any hieroglyphic texts or inscriptions generally. The term Medu Neter makes use of a special hieroglyph, ⎮ , which means "*medu*" or "staff - walking stick-speech." This means that speech is the support for the Divine, ⌐. Thus, just as the staff supports an elderly person, the hieroglyphic writing (the word) is a prop (staff) which sustains the Divine in the realm of time and space. That is, the Divine writings contain the wisdom which enlightens us about to the Divine, *Shetaut Neter.*

If Medu Neter is mastered then the spiritual aspirant becomes Maakheru or true of thought, word and deed, that is, purified in body, mind and soul. The symbol medu is static while the symbol of Kheru is dynamic.

This term (Maakheru) uses the glyph kheru is a rudder – oar (rowing), symbol of voice, meaning that purification occurs when the righteous movement of the word, when it is used (rowing-movement) to promote virtue, order, peace, harmony and truth. So Medu Neter is the potential word and Maa kheru is the perfected word.

The hieroglyphic texts (Medu Neter) become (Maakheru) useful in the process of religion when they are used as hekau - the Ancient Egyptian "Words of Power" when the word is Hesi, chanted and Shmai- sung and thereby one performs Dua or worship of the Divine. The divine word allows the speaker to control the gods and goddesses, i.e. the cosmic forces. This concept is really based on the idea that human beings are higher order beings if they learn about the nature of the universe and elevate themselves through virtue and wisdom.

CHAPTER 4: THE ANCIENT EGYPTIAN ORIGINS OF THE PRE-CLASSICAL PERIOD GREEK MYTHOLOGY AND ICONOGRAPHY

Ancient Egypt and Atlantis

In conjunction with Ancient Egypt, another ancient civilization, Atlantis, must be mentioned, as there is much speculation about Atlantis and Ancient Egypt. Atlantis, in the tradition of antiquity, was a mythical land and advanced civilization. It is credited by some as having existed prior to the Ancient Egyptian civilization, and also as giving rise to the Ancient Egyptian civilization. It is evident that there is more about history that is not known than is known. This is not to say that there can be no certainties, but that there can be no certain original dates. There may be several civilizations that existed prior to Ancient Egypt, and the Ancient Egyptians may very well be their descendants, so we must keep an open mind and eye for the evidences. History, therefore, should be studied with an open mind, and never be considered as an absolute end, since the winds of time have taken all evidences of many civilizations that existed in the past. The important point here is that Ancient Egyptian civilization emerged first out of the cataclysmic flood period, and resurrected an advanced society and religious systems in the distant past, which it then spread around the world in order to civilize it for the good of all humanity. This is why scholars from all countries were accepted in the Ancient Egyptian University Temples. Some Egyptian Pharaohs even sponsored and financed temples abroad which taught mystical philosophy as well as other disciplines. One such effort was put forth by the Ancient Egyptian king, Amasis, who financed the reconstruction of the famous Temple of Delphi in Greece, which was burnt down in 548 B.C.E.

As the evidence presented in this book shows, the history of Ancient Egypt goes back farther than most historians feel comfortable admitting. So in order to make this work complete, it is necessary to review the origins and history of the legend of Atlantis. To accomplish this task, we must have a working knowledge of ancient Greek history as well as the relationship between ancient Greek culture and the Ancient Egyptian culture. Through this review we will find intriguing correlations and answers.

The civilization of Atlantis supposedly existed prior to a "flood," or natural catastrophe. The landmass itself is said to have been engulfed by the ocean as the result of an earthquake. The first recorded accounts of Atlantis appear in two dialogues by Plato, known as the Timaeus and Critias. According to the account in Timaeus, the island was described to the Athenian statesman Solon by an Ancient Egyptian priest, who told him that Atlantis was larger in than Libya and Asia Minor combined. The priest also said that a highly advanced civilization existed on Atlantis at about the 10th millennium B.C.E. Further, the priest related that the nation of Atlantis had conquered all the peoples of the Mediterranean, except the Athenians. Solon and other Athenians had no knowledge of this ancient land.

Overview of Ancient Greek History

Ancient Greece was a civilization that flourished on the Greek Peninsula, in western Asia Minor (modern Turkey), and on the north coast of Africa (in the Alexandrian period).

1. In 3000 B.C.E., a culture known today as the Aegean civilization developed and was centered on the island of Crete. It is also known as the Minoan civilization. It was related

to the mainland population which was later know as the Mycenaean civilization at Peloponnesus. The Minoans built great palaces especially at their capital, Knossos, and developed maritime trade with African nations including the Kamitans. The name is derived from Minos, the legendary king of Crete. The civilization is divided into three main periods: early Minoan, about 3000–2200 B.C.E; middle Minoan, about 2200–1580 B.C.E; and late Minoan, about 1580–1100 B.C.E.[129]

2. This Bronze Age of Greek history is the period celebrated in the epic poems of Homer (Illiad and the Odyssey), who gives us some of the earliest records of the existence of the Minoans, besides those of the Kamitans.

3. The culture of Thera, another Aegean island Greek city-state[130], closely followed the Minoan civilization. The culture of the Mycenaeans roughly followed that of the Minoans whose civilization had deteriorated by about 1,400 B.C.E on Crete, due to a natural cataclysm (volcano eruption on Santorini), but the Mycenaeans on the mainland continued to prosper until the 12th century B.C.E.

4. About that time the Mycenaeans were conquered by the Dorians (creators of the famous Doric style architecture), who invaded from the north.

5. Hellenistic Period: The term 'Hellenism' refers to the culture of Classical Greece. It is most particularly associated with Athens during the 5th century B.C.E. This period saw the rise of Athens as the most powerful of the Greek city-states around the Aegean, epitomized by the creation of the Parthenon.

6. Macedonian Period: Philip II of Macedon (one of the Greek city-states), who ruled from 359-336 B.C.E, conquered Upper Macedon, Thrace, and Chalcidice.

7. Alexandrian Period: Philip's son, Alexander the Great, who ruled from 336-323 B.C.E, used his army to conquer the entire Greek world, Asia Minor, Western India and North East Africa (including Kamit) and placed them under his Macedonian Empire.

8. After Alexander died, the Greek city-states began infighting. This led to the deterioration of the Greek Empire. The rulership over the conquered territories fell to his generals. The general who took control of Kamit was Ptolemy. This began the Ptolemaic Pharaonic Dynasty of Kamit which lasted there from 332 B.C.E. to 30 B.C.E. In 146 B.C.E., what was left of the Greek cities fell under Roman control, and the ancient Greek world came to an end. Hellenism, as Greek culture had come to be called, retained its strength, however, and became the basis for the civilization of the Roman Empire.[131]

---

[129] Websters Copyright © 1995 Helicon Publishing Ltd
[130] Ancient Greece was a confederation of cities spread over the Aegean area of the Mediterranean sea that were united by common language and culture as well as ethnicity.
[131] Random House Encyclopedia Copyright (C) 1983,1990 by Random House Inc.

The Legend of Atlantis and the Ancient Minoans

Much work has been done by archeologists that reveals the Minoans as the mythical "Atlantians." This is evident in the writings of many archeologists, and it is accepted as the general view of Western historians as the following encyclopedia entry shows.

"Atlantis"

In Greek mythology, an island continent, said to have sunk following an earthquake. Although the Atlantic Ocean is probably named for it, the structure of the sea bottom rules out its ever having existed there. The Greek philosopher Plato created an imaginary early history for it and described it as a utopia.
Legends about the disappearance of Atlantis may have some connection with the volcanic eruption that devastated Santorini in the Cyclades islands, north of Crete, about 1500 BC. The ensuing earthquakes and tidal waves are believed to have been one cause of the collapse of the empire of Minoan Crete.

-Copyright © 1995 Webster's Helicon Publishing Ltd

Nevertheless, many fiction writers and New Age writers have seen fit to create speculative stories related to Atlantis and even suggest that it was an ideal country with enlightened peoples. This idealized version of this culture left no records or remains in Greek history, nor are there any records in the Greek history about a civilization that was lost or destroyed by a cataclysm except those related to Solon, a Greek legislator who visited Egypt in 590 B.C.E. Solon brought the legend of Atlantis to Greece, owing to the history of the Mediterranean that was kept by the Ancient Egyptians. The priests of Zau (Sais)[132] told Solon that the island city of Atlantis sunk into the ocean. In the year 395 B.C.E. Plato retold the story in his book *Timaeus and Critias*. Sometime later Plato himself consulted the Egyptian priests and was informed that there had been several great floods in history, and that the largest one had overcome Atlantis completely.

Don't you know that in your country had lived the most beautiful and the most noble race of men that ever lived? Race of which you and your town are the descendants, or a seed that survived.... But there were violent earthquakes and floodings, and in one day and one night of rain, all of your bellicose people, as one man, were buried under the ground, and the island of Atlantis, in the same manner, disappeared under the sea.... The result is that, in comparison to what was, there remain some small islets, nothing but the skeleton of a devastated body, all of the richest and the softest parts of the soil having been swallowed up, leaving only the skeleton of the country.... And this was unknown to you, because the survivors of this destruction have been dead for several generations without leaving any traces. *(Timaeus and Critias)*

The event supposedly took place 9,000 years before Solon (in 9,590 B.C.E.), who lived in 590 B.C.E., and was reported in the Egyptian texts 1000 years later (8,590 B.C.E.). The eminent scientist and scholar Cheikh Anta Diop suggested that if the dates given were to be

---

[132] Ancient Egyptian city of the goddess Net- Who was known to the Greeks as Athena; recall that Sais and Athens were later considered sister cities.

reduced by a factor of 10, the date falls on the devastating explosion of Santorini.[133] In most every way the known history and remains of the Minoan civilization on the island of Crete best fit the description of Atlantis. Artifacts confirming trade and contact with the Ancient Egyptians have been discovered on Crete up to the reign of Pharaoh Amenhotep III, which also confirms the date of 1400 B.C.E. (explosion at Santorini). In the Ancient Egyptian records, the Cretans are referred to as the *Keftiu*.

Above: Minoans offering tribute to the Egyptian king Djehutimes III (Thutmose 18th Dynasty). The Cretans are distinguishable by their clothing. (Norman de Garis Davies; Tomb of Rekh-mi-Ra at Thebes, vol. II, plates 19 and 18)

Above: Faience scarab from reign of Pharaoh Amenhotep III, found at Crete.

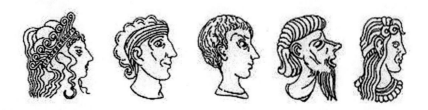

---

[133] Civilization or Barbarism pp 84-85

Above: The mixture of ethnic peoples in Crete is demonstrated by the different skull - types discovered in the excavations there. In general terms, however, the Minoans form part of the so - called "Mediterranean type." They were of medium height and had black curly hair and brown eyes. Essentially, they were a mixture of European (Greek), African, and Asiatic peoples, showing differences of ethnicity even from the city of Thera and Mycenae.

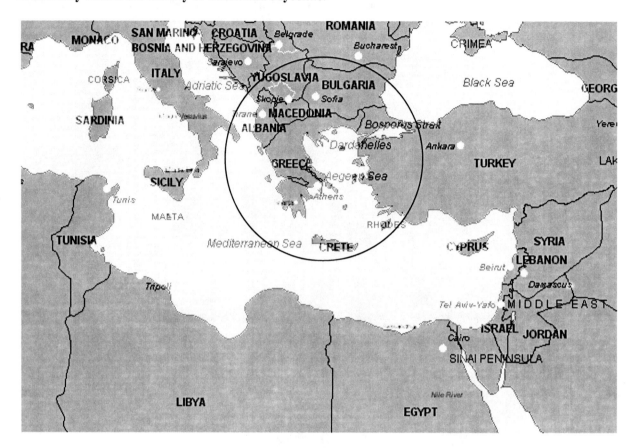

Above: Map of the Mediterranean with Crete, Greece and Egypt.

Figure 2: Below-left, Stele of Niptah - end of Middle Kingdom (Kamitan man in red, Kamitan woman in white with breasts exposed).

Figure 3: Below right- Minoan man in red and Minoan woman in white with breasts exposed. (1,400 B.C.E.).

The fresco above shows some important aspects of Minoan society which reveal similarities to the Ancient Egyptian culture. The men and women are depicted as going about bare-breasted. Also, like the Ancient Egyptian practice, the Minoans also depicted the men with a red color and the women with the white color.

Here we will explore some important correlations in the religious iconographies of the Ancient Egyptian New Kingdom period and the Greek archaic period. The images below are from goddesses of Ancient Kamit and Ancient Greece. They are included here to show the close matching in iconography, mythic symbolism and mystical philosophy.

(A)   (B)

(C)

Above: Left- Goddess Qadesh (Qdesh) (A) of Ancient Egypt, standing on a lion which is a symbol of the goddess Sekhemit (F- see below - lioness goddess) who is related to the leopard-cat goddess Mafdet (C) who are a forms of goddess Hetheru (G- see below) -Old Kingdom who are also snake goddesses. Above Right: Minoan snake goddess

(D)   (E)

(D) (1600-1400 B.C.E.) – Far right: closeup of the cat headdress of the Minoan goddess (E), relating her to the well known feline divinity, Bastet (B), of Ancient Egypt. Sekhmit and Bastet are related to Mafdet, the leopard goddess who kills evil snakes (the snakes the negative aspects of the personality that prevent the flow of the Serpent Power).

Qdesh is often depicted holding flowers, a mirror, or serpents. The Leopard Goddess Mafdet was associated with Sekhmet, the Eye of Ra and with Hetheru as well as the other feline forms of the Ancient Egyptian goddess. She is the embodiment of the destructive force that can be unleashed on the negative impetus, symbolized by the serpent demon Apep. Mafdet is also identified with the execution blade itself.

(F)   (G)

Above: Left- Ancient Egyptian goddess Sekhemit (F- a form of Hetheru) with the two serpents. Right: Ancient Egyptian Goddess Hetheru (G) Temple relief with the two serpents and the upward curled hair. (New Kingdom period)

Like Hetheru of Ancient Egypt, Qadesh was also known as the "mistress of the gods and goddesses, the eye of Ra, without a second." So the Minoan snake goddess, pictured in (D) above, exhibits all of the major aspects of the Ancient Egyptian goddess including having her skin painted white in the Egyptian fashion reserved for women.

The bull figures prominently in Minoan art and spirituality. One of the Minoan myths relates that there was a great Bull who lived in the underground labyrinths beneath the great palace; king Minos defeated it. The bull was called Minator. Another myth relates that it was to be given *seven virgins.* In Ancient Egyptian mythology, the bull is the symbol of Asar, one of the most important divinities. He is given seven cows, who in turn give rise to Creation.

Åsâr-Ḥâpi (Serapis).

Above left: The god Asar-Hapi, also known in later times as Serapis by the Greeks and Romans,
depicted as part bull and part human (mixed zoomorphic and anthropomorphic, respectively).
Above center: the Asar-Hapi bull in full zoomorphic form. Above right: Asar-Hapi (bottom tier) and the seven Hetheru cows.

Above: The Ancient Egyptian Bull (God Asar) and 7 Cow Goddesses (Hetheru)

Above left: the Minoan bull. Above right: a late period Minoan statue of a person wearing the bull horns with upraised arms.

Above: Ancient Egyptian *Sefer* (Griffin).

Note the almost identical features.

Below: Minoan Griffin (palace relief)

Above: Procession of red colored men and white colored women bringing offerings to the mummy of Any (Papyrus of Any 18th Dynasty-Ancient Egypt)

Above: Minoan sarcophagus with red colored men and white colored women bringing offerings to the dead personality.

CHAPTER 5: ANCIENT KAMITAN ORIGINS OF THE GREEK CLASSICAL PERIOD MYTHOLOGY

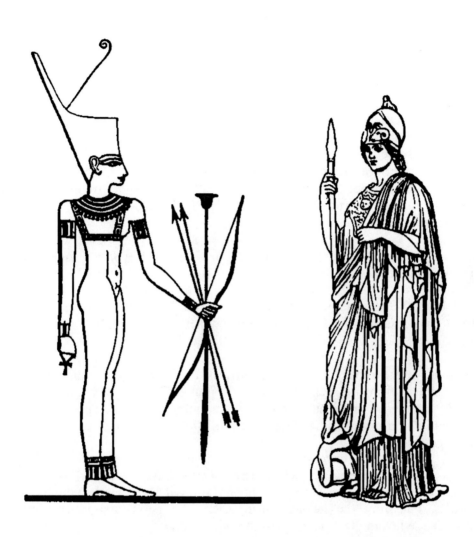

The Ancient Egyptian Origins of the Gods and Goddesses of Greece

Greek Mythology is a conglomeration of stories related to certain Divine personalities and their interactions with each other and with human beings. The main stories related to them are contained in the epics, Iliad and Odyssey written by Homer (whom the Greeks say traveled to Ancient Egypt). The main functions of the gods and goddesses and their mingling with human beings was outlined in these stories. The early Greeks also spoke of the origins of their gods and goddesses. It must be clearly understood that at the time when the early Greeks organized themselves sufficiently enough in order to take up the task of learning art and culture, they previously had very little in the way of culture and what was there was primitive. Through the contact with the Ancient Egyptians their culture flourished. Thus, the force of Ancient Egyptian culture created a strong impression but it was not the only impression, since the Greeks traveled to other lands and attempted to assimilate the teachings of others as well. This coupled with their own ideas caused a situation wherein they created a cultural synthesis and this synthesis is what should be recognized as early Greek culture and philosophy. In short, what is regarded as Greek was in reality a patchwork of differing ideas which had their strongest basis in Ancient Egyptian philosophy but which did not follow its precepts entirely. The following passages from the writings of Herodotus are instructive on the Ancient Egyptian origins of the Greek gods and goddesses. *(highlighted portions are by Ashby)*

35. **"Almost all the names of the gods came into Greece from Egypt. My inquiries prove that they were all derived from a foreign source, and my opinion is that Egypt furnished the greater number**. For with the exception of Neptune and the Dioscuri, whom I mentioned above, and Juno, Vesta, Themis, the Graces, and the Nereids, **the other gods have been known from time immemorial in Egypt**. This I assert on the authority of the Egyptians themselves."

36. "The gods, with whose names they profess themselves unacquainted, the Greeks received, I believe, from the Pelasgi, except Neptune. Of him they got their knowledge from the Libyans, by whom he has been always honored, and who were anciently the only people that had a god of the name. **The Egyptians differ from the Greeks also in paying no divine honors to heroes."**

37. "Besides these which have been here mentioned, there are many other practices whereof I shall speak hereafter, **which the Greeks have borrowed from Egypt. The peculiarity, however, which they observe in their statues of Mercury they did not derive from the Egyptians**, but from the Pelasgi; from them the Athenians first adopted it, and afterwards it passed from the Athenians to the other Greeks..."

38. "In early times the Pelasgi, as I know by information which I got at Dodona, offered sacrifices of all kinds, and prayed to the gods, but had no distinct names or appellations for them, since they had never heard of any. They called them gods (Theoi, disposers), because they disposed and arranged all things in such a beautiful order. **After a long lapse of time the names of the gods came to Greece from Egypt**, and the Pelasgi learnt them, only as yet they knew nothing of Bacchus, of whom they first heard at a much later date."

The Greek concept of the gods and goddesses was as follows. They believed that the gods and goddesses chose, as their home, an area known as Mount Olympus, which was in a region of Greece that was called Thessaly. There, they formed a kind of society and ranked themselves in terms of powers and authority. They roamed freely and became associated with three main realms or domains. These were the earth, the sky or heaven and the sea. The 12 leading gods and goddesses were called the "Olympians." Their names were Zeus, Hera, Hephaestus, Athena, Apollo, Artemis, Ares, Aphrodite, Hestia, Hermes, Demeter, and Poseidon.

Ancient Egyptian mythology held that there are three realms in creation, "Ta," the earth, "Pet," or the heavens, and "Duat," the Netherworld or Astral plane. The substitution of the Astral Plane for the sea points to the fact that the Greeks were primarily a seafaring nation and thus placed much importance on the sea. However, upon further study, it becomes clear that the Ancient Egyptians based their society on the Nile river and even named it after a god, but they never thought of it as a realm unto itself. The importance given to the sea points towards a worldly philosophy that is grounded in physical reality while the Astral Plane points to a reality that transcends the physical world and thus mortal life itself.

There is a danger in following divergent philosophies. This problem is most evident in mystical or religious settings. Spiritual philosophies may be thought of as roads. On these roads there are signs and these signs are the symbols and concepts of the philosophy which lead a person to the destination of the trip, in this case, self discovery and discovery of the Divine. The gods and goddesses are in reality the most important symbols and metaphors of a religion. Their struggles, myths and interactions between themselves, human beings and the world are the signposts, which lead a spiritual aspirant to enlightenment. Therefore, if the student of the philosophy does not follow the teaching properly he or she may not gain the proper insight into the deeper meaning. Even though it is possible to relate the deities of most religions this should be done only by highly advanced Sages and students of the philosophy. Plato put it very succinctly when he said: *None but the pure should approach the pure.*

Kamitan Terms and Ancient Greek Terms

It is important to understand that the names of the Ancient Egyptian divinities which have been used widely in Western literature and by Western scholars are actually Greek interpretations of the Kamitan (Ancient Egyptian) names. In keeping with the spirit of the culture of Kamitan spirituality, in this volume we will use the Kamitan names for the divinities through which we will bring forth the Philosophy of Neterianism (Ancient Egyptian religion and myth). Therefore, the Greek name Osiris will be converted back to the Kamitan (Ancient Egyptian) Asar (Asar), the Greek Isis to Aset (Auset), the Greek Nephthys to Nebthet, Anubis to Anpu or Apuat, Hathor to Hetheru, Thoth or Hermes to Djehuti, etc. (see the table below) Further, the term Ancient Egypt will be used interchangeably with "Kamit," or "Ta-Meri," as these were the terms used by the Ancient Egyptians to refer to their land and culture. The table below provides a listing of the corresponding names of the main Kamitan divinities.

135

Table 8: Kamitan Names of the main Gods and Goddesses of Ancient Egypt and the Greek translation in common use.

Ancient Kamitan Terms and Ancient Greek Terms

Kamitan (Ancient Egyptian) Names	Greek Names
Amun	Zeus
Ra	Helios
Ptah	Hephastos
Nut	Rhea
Geb	Kronos
Net	Athena
Khonsu, Heryshaf	Heracles
Set	Ares or Typhon
Bast	Artemis
Uadjit	Leto
Asar (Ausar), Asar-Hapi	Osiris or Hades
Asar	Dionysus
Aset (Auset)	Isis or Demeter
Nebthet	Nephthys
Anpu or Apuat	Anubis
Hetheru	Hathor (Aphrodite)
Heru	Horus or Apollo
Djehuti	Thoth or Hermes
Maat	Astraea or Themis
Nekhebit	Eileithyia

The following table shows basic correspondences between the functions of the Ancient Egyptian Gods and Goddesses and those of the later Greco-Roman period along with their metaphorical-religious function.

Table 9: Basic Correspondences Between Ancient Egyptian and the Greek/Roman Gods and Goddesses

ANCIENT EGYPTIAN	METAPHOR	GREEK	ROMAN
Amun-Ra	Supreme being	**Zeus** Ruler of the Gods	**Jupiter** Ruler of the Gods
Ra	Sun God and progenitor of the gods and goddesses	**Helios** Sun God	
Nut	Sky-heavens goddessMother Goddess	**Rhea** Mother Goddess wife/Kronos	Mother GoddessMother Goddess wife/Saturn
Geb	Earth god	**Kronos** God of the sky and the titans	**Saturn** God of agriculture
Aset (Aset)	Goddess of wisdom, motherhood, love and devotion	**Hera** Goddess of marriage, childbirth, Queen of the gods	**Juno** Goddess of marriage, childbirth, Queen of the gods
Asar (Osiris)	God of the afterlife, virtue, the soul	**Hades** God of the underworld, Lord of the dead	**Pluto** God of the underworld, Lord of the dead
Set	God of Disorder-violence-unrighteousness	**Typhon** God of Disorder-violence-unrighteousness	
Nebethet	Goddess of physicality, mortality and early life	**Hestia** Goddess of the home	**Vesta** Goddess of the home
Heru (Heru)	God of the sun, spiritual aspiration, kings, righteousness	**Apollo** God of prophecy, medicine, archery	**Apollo** God of the sun
The Seven Hathors	Seven powers of manifestation	The Fates (goddesses who determine future)	
Heru (Horus)	God of the sun, spiritual aspiration,	**Dyonysus** God of wine and vegetation	**Bacchus** God of wine and

	kings, righteousness		vegetation
Djehuti	God of writing and minister of Ra	HermesMessenger of the gods	MercuryMessenger of the gods
Maat	Goddess of justice, order, righteousness and truth	**Astraea** Goddess of divine justice **Themis** Goddess of divine justice	**Minerva** Goddess of wisdom
Hetheru (Hetheru)	Goddess of life force energy, love, sexuality and passion, enforcer of the divine law	**Aphrodite** Goddess of beauty and sexual desire	**Venus** Goddess of gardens and fields
Hetheru in aspect as Sefer (griffin), Sekhmet (lioness) or Art (right Eye of Ra)	Goddess of retribution against the sinful. No one can escape her power.	**Nemesis** Goddess of retribution against the sinful.	
Imhotep	Famous architect and doctor, deified in Ancient Egypt	**Asclepius** God of medicine	**Asclepius** God of medicine
Mut	Mother Earth	**Gaea** Mother Earth	**Terra** Mother Earth
Net	Goddess of protection	**Artemis** Goddess of the Hunt	**Diana** Goddess of the Moon
Asarian Resurrection	Passion and resurrection of Osiris	**Orphism** Passion and resurrection of Orpheus	
Bennu Mythology	Resurrection of the Solar Sunbird	**Phoenix** Resurrection of the Solar Sunbird	

The Main Ancient Egyptian Gods and Goddesses

Forms of Amun-Ra –Creator   Ra – Creator   Ptah – Creator   Atum – Demiurge

The Main Ancient Egyptian Gods and Goddesses

Khepri, the morning sun.   Rã, the noon-day sun.   Temu (Atem), the setting sun.

Rã, the god One or Only god, in his three chief aspects.

Shu – Air –Ether   Tefnut-Water   Geb – Earth   Nut – heavens   Djehuti – Intellect – Writing, words

Asar – Soul   Aset – Wisdom   Heru – Kingship, Spiritual Victory   Apuat – Discernment   Asar – King of the Dead

The Main Ancient Egyptian Gods and Goddesses Cont.

Sekhmet – Power of the sun

Hethor – Power of God

Mut – Great

Net – Decisive action, protection

Min – Generation, Sex Sublimation

Bes – Childbirth, merriment, war

Hapi – Nile – water

Saaa – Intelligence

Nebethet - Mortality

Set – Chaos

Sebek – Crocodile God Power of Nature

Arat – Serpent Power

The Forms of Maat

Selket – Power of Nature

The Main Ancient Greek Gods and Goddesses

36

37

38

39

40

41

42

141

43

44

45

46

47

48

49

Roman-Greek Gods and Goddesses

Fig. 36. JUPITER (Roman)-ZEUS *(Greek).* God of Heaven, Law, Thunder and Lightning

Fig. 37. VULCAN (Roman)-HFPHAESTUS *(Greek).* God of Fire and the Blacksmiths

Fig. 38. APOLLO *(Greek)-HELIOS (Roman).* God of the Sun, Science and Prophecy

Fig. 39. MINERVA (Roman)-ATHENE *(Greek).* Goddess of Wisdom and the Arts

Fig. 40. VENUS (Roman)-APHRODITE *(Greek).* Goddess of Love and Beauty

Fig. 41. DIANA (Roman)-ARTEMIS *(Greek).* Goddess of the Moon and the Hunt

Fig. 42. JUNO *(Roman)-HERA (Greek).* Goddess of Marriage and Birth

Fig. 43. HADES *(Greek)-PLUTO (Roman). God* of The Nether World

Fig. 44. HERCULES (Roman)-HERACLES *(Greek).* The Strength

Fig. 45. DEMETER (Greek)-CERES *(Roman).* Goddess of the Harvest

Fig. 46. HERMES (Greek)-MERCURIUS *(Roman).* God of Commerce, Transport and Thievery

Fig. 47. AESCULAPIUS (Roman)-ASCLEPIUS *(Greek).* Medicine and Health

Fig. 48. POSEIDON (Greek)-NEPTUNE *(Roman).* God of the Sea

Fig. 49. HEBE (Greek)-JUVENTAS *(Roman).* Goddess of Youth

Correspondences Between the Kamitan and Greek Divinities

In the TIMEUS, Plato confirms that the goddess Net of Ancient Egypt was the same divinity called Athena by the Greeks.

> He replied:-In the Egyptian Delta, at the head of which the river Nile divides, there is a certain district which is called the district of Sais, and the great city of the district is also called Sais, and is the city from which King Amasis came. The citizens have a deity for their foundress; she is called in the Egyptian tongue Neith, and is asserted by them to be the same whom the Hellenes call Athene; they are great lovers of the Athenians, and say that they are in some way related to them.[134]

Above left: Goddess Net (Neith) of Egypt. Right- Goddess Athena of Greece

---

[134] TIMAEUS by Plato 360 BC translated by Benjamin Jowett

Another correlation can be found between the goddess of righteousness and justice, Maat, of Egypt and the goddess of divine justice *Astraea* or *Themis* of Greece.

Above left: The goddess Maat presiding over the balance scales of justice.

Above: the goddess of Greece presiding over the balance scales of justice.

The Image of the Sphinx, the Quintessential Kamitan Symbol of Spiritual Enlightenment appears in Mesopotamian and Greek iconography

Left: Ancient Egyptian Winged Sphinx

Left: Assyrian Winged Sphinx. Right: Greek Winged Sphinx

Above Left: Ancient Egyptian Sefer (Griffin). Above Right: Griffin of Asian and Western myth

The Griffin is a mythical creature, originally thought to have originated in Asia Minor and Persia, the supposed guardian of hidden treasure, with the body, tail, and hind legs of a lion, and the head, forelegs, and wings of an eagle.[135] One of the most important Ancient Egyptian stories

---

[135] Copyright © 1995 Helicon Publishing Ltd

about the Sefer is the Myth of Hetheru and Djehuti.[136] The Ancient Egyptian god Djehuti (A) holds the caduceus. (from the Temple of Seti I-Abdu, Egypt). The caduceus is the symbol of the life force power wielded by the god, which sustains life and leads to spiritual enlightenment. The Greeks adopted the teaching of Djehuti and called him Hermes. (B)

(A)

(B)

---

[136] See the book *The Glorious Light* by Muata Ashby

The Ancient Egyptian Origins of Hercules and Ares

Hery-shaf-god of manliness, bravery, respect-he on his lake-his land"

Above: The Greek
God Hercules

Recognized as a form of Heru, as his name ⬭ 🝆 denotes, containing the *Her* ⬭ spelling, he was later identifiead with the Greek Heracles (Hercules) and the Ancient Egyptian town he came from was called Herakleopolis "town of Heracles." He is known in Neterian myth as the "Ba Asar" and "Ba Ra" or soul of Osiris and soul of Ra. He wears the Atef (Crown of Asar).

Anhur – "the one that leads back the distant one" is so named because in one myth he is said to have led the lioness goddess (Sekhmit) back to Egypt after being lost in foreign lands. Anhur is an anthropomorphic divinity usually seen holding a spear. So he is also known as "Lord of the lance." He was a worrior divinity compatible if not surpassing Muntju. He is a supporter of Heru and Ra and he is also known as "Son of Ra." The later Greeks knew him as *Onuris* and regarded him as *"Ares,"* the god of War. However, beyond the correlation of being divinities of war, the characters of the two are different, as Ares spent much time mischievously causing havok. Anhur is not known for those acts.

The Mystic Phoenix

The Benu (A) is a bird in Ancient Egyptian mythology that lived in the desert for 500 years and then consumed itself by fire, later to rise renewed from its ashes. It is associated with Khepri and Ra as the eternal renewal of the sun, which after burning itself out, rises from the ashes invigorated and renewed. This image and teaching was adopted by the Greeks (B) and other peoples of the ancient world.

(A)

(B)

The Correlations Between Ancient Egyptian and Greek Philosophy

Ancient Egyptian Philosophy	Greek Philosophy
A— Origins of gods and goddesses (c.30,000 B.C.E.) in the History of Manetho and Turin Papyrus and their mingling with human beings in the period of the Demigods. (c. 24,000 B.C.E.)	A— Origins of gods and goddesses and their mingling with human beings. (c. 9th century B.C.E.) According to Diodorus, **Homer** (c. 9th century B.C.E.) traveled to Egypt.
A1— The Ancient Egyptian Philosophy of the City of Anu based on the mythology of Ra stated that Creation began when Ra arose out of the Primeval Ocean or Nun.	A1— We have seen how **Thales** (c. 634-546 B.C.E.), studied in Ancient Egypt and then created the **Ionian School of Greek Philosophy**. This school was based on Thales' idea that all creation originates from water.
A2—From the earliest times the Cosmogony of Memphis stated that God is in his children who have taken form as the elements of creation.	A2—The Ionian School held that All things are full of God.
B— Ancient Egyptian Philosophy held that matter is in reality the ocean which has taken on the forms of creation and these forms are governed by Maat (Cosmic order) and maintained by neteru (Cosmic forces) sustained by Pa Neter "The God."	B— **Anaximander**, (611-547 B.C.E.) also from the Ionian School, refined the teaching of Thales and said that the constituent material of all matter a form of eternal substance which changes into the normally observable forms of creation in accordance with certain laws.
C— Ancient Egyptian Philosophy held that when Ra (sun-fire) emerged from the primeval ocean, he engendered creation and all the forms in it which arose out of his children whose principle represent pairs of opposites, in the forms of gods and goddesses (Shu and Tefnut, Geb and Nut).	C— **Heraclitus**, (536-470 B.C.E.) also from the Ionian School, believed that all matter arose from fire but that all objects are a combination of opposite principles.
C1— In the Creation cosmogony of Anu the understanding of the nature of change in the universe is given. Ra established order (Maat) and holds back chaos in order to maintain creation.	C1—**Heraclitus** also held that change is the governing factor of the universe.

C2—The Ancient Egyptian Conception of the Divine (creative) Word (*Medu Neter-Hekau)* comes from the creation stories of the major Ancient Egyptian Theologies. In the cosmology of Anu, Ra created the universe by act of emerging from the primeval waters and then controls creation through his mind (Logos) in the form of Djehuti (Greek Hermes), who is the god of divine words. In the creation story of Khepri, Khepri (God) creates the universe by uttering his own name. This mode of creation was also used by the Ancient Egyptian God Asar (Osiris) and by the Ancient Egyptian God Ptah. All of these cosmologies originated before 5,000 B.C.E. and were the basic teachings of the Ancient Egyptian temples-universities.

C2—**Heraclitus** (6th-century BCE) was the first Greek philosopher to use the term "Logos" in its metaphysical sense. He conceived of it as a divine force which produces order in nature. In Stoicism this idea developed into the concept of a rational divine power that directs and orders the universe which is semi-physical in nature and based on reason. In the 1st-century ACE the Jewish-Hellenistic philosopher, Philo Judaeus, used the term Logos when he tried to synthesize Platonism with Jewish tradition. The idea of the Logos became translated as the creative word which engendered creation: in the English Bible: "In the beginning was the Word, and the Word was with God, and the Word was God. . . . And the Word became flesh and dwelt among us . . ." (John 1:1-3, 14). Later in Christian philosophy the word became Jesus Christ himself ("word made flesh") as the vehicle for the creative force coming from the Father (God).

D— Ancient Egyptian Philosophy (in the mythology of Anu and of Waset (Thebes) and of Hetkaptah (Memphis)) held that mind is the subtlest form of energy and that it engenders creation of the physical world but that it is controlled by an even more subtle substance, that being the innermost Self or God.

D— **Anaxagoras** (500-428 B.C.E.), believed that "nous" or mind consists of extremely subtle particles of matter and that it permeates and controls very living object.

E—Ancient Egyptian Philosophy held that the soul is a separate entity from the body, eternal, subtle and transcendental, and that the body is transient and material. Hence the Ancient Egyptian proverb: "The soul belongs to heave and the body belongs to the earth."

"Ba ir pet Shat ir ta"

E—**Pythagoras** (580? BC-500? B.C.E.). He was of the Eleatic School, believed that understanding form is more important that understanding matter in the attempt to explain the structure of matter. Also, the Pythagoreans believed in the

"Soul is to heaven, body is to the earth"
From the Prt m Hru of the *Pyramid Texts*
(3,200-2,575 B.C.E.)

the body in explaining the nature of human existence. The body was seen as a temporary vessel of the soul, its "tomb."

E1—The teachings of vegetarianism as well as the practice of celibacy, abstaining from meat, alcohol were clearly stated in the temples of Ancient Egypt and all initiates were expected to keep these practices at all times. (see book Kemetic Diet for details)

E1—**Pythagoras** brought forth the teaching of vegetarianism as a means to purify the body and enable a person to practice the teachings that lead to understanding of the philosophy and ultimately to spiritual awakening.

E2— The teaching of the predicament of the soul and the cycle of births and deaths (reincarnation) was clearly stated in the Ancient Egyptian Books of Coming Forth By Day Chapter 125, as well as in many proverbs such as the ones below.
"Salvation is the freeing of the soul from its bodily fetters; becoming a God through knowledge and wisdom; controlling the forces of the cosmos instead of being a slave to them; subduing the lower nature and through awakening the higher self, ending the cycle of rebirth and dwelling with the Neters who direct and control the Great Plan."
"If a Soul on entering in the human body persists in its vice, it neither tastes deathlessness nor share in the Good; but speeding back again it turns into the path that leads to creeping things. This is the sentence of the vicious soul."

E2— **Pythagoras** held that the soul is contaminated with the body and when the body is purified the soul regains its pure nature. Otherwise it is caught up in a series of incarnations.

F—The Ancient Egyptian Philosophy of Anu (Heliopolis to the Ancient Greeks) held that matter is in reality the primeval ocean which has been given form by Ra through his emergence out of it. In Memphite Theology the God Ptah has given form to his own thoughts and these have become the objects of matter. At any time this sustaining force may be withdrawn and matter will revert to its true essence, unformed energy-consciousness, like a wave subsiding into the ocean and giving up its individuality and dissolving into its original state.

F—**Parmedides** (5th century B.C.E.), believed that while separate objects appeared to exist in creation, this is in reality an illusion or appearance.

F1—The teaching of the two paths is reflected in the teachings of Ancient Egypt throughout the temple schools. The following proverbs explain it further.
"On the journey to the truth, one must stay on the

F1—**Parmedides** held that there are two paths for human beings, the path of knowledge and the path of opinions of men (error and limitation).

151

path of love and enlightenment, the heart filled with greed and lust will be overcome by its selfishness."
"True knowledge comes from the upward path which leads to the eternal Fire; error, defeat and death result from following the lower path of worldly attachment."
"There are two roads traveled by humankind, those who seek to live MAAT and those who seek to satisfy their animal passions."

G— The main tenet of all branches of Ancient Egyptian Philosophy was that all of the answers to all questions lay in the discovery of one's true nature and identity. Therefore, they gave the injunction "Know thy heart" which they inscribed in various places and scriptures throughout Egypt. In Ancient Egyptian thought the heart is a metaphor of the deeper self. It is weighed in the balance at the time of death and one's character determines one's fate.

G—**Socrates** (470?-399 B.C.E.). taught that true knowledge it to be sought within oneself. Therefore he held that his purpose was "to fulfill the philosopher's mission of searching into myself and other men." Therefore, his method of promulgating the teachings was to give a philosophical proposition and then ask himself and others questions which ultimately lead to the root source answers within their own deepest self.

H—The Ancient Egyptian Philosophy of Waset (Thebes) held that creation is an effect of the transcendental Self, Neberdjer, which manifests in the form of the Trinity Amun-Ra-Ptah. The trinity symbolizes the three aspects of human perception (Awareness, senses and the physical objects) and the three realms of existence (Ta-Pet-Duat). The Self is regarded as the underlying reality behind Creation as stated in the following Ancient Egyptian Proverb: *"Knowledge derived from the senses is illusory, true knowledge can only come from the understanding of the union of opposites."*

H—**Plato** (427?-347? B.C.E) refined the ideas of Socrates into an organized philosophy. He held the objects of the world to be shadows or forms or ideas or reflections of a transcendental reality which is abiding. So the transcendental reality is the true object of knowledge because the phenomenal world is relative to the sense perceptions and therefore illusory.

H1—The Ancient Egyptian Philosophy of Maat contains over forty-two injunctions of righteous conduct (precepts of virtue) which when practiced will allow the practitioner to wade through the netherworld after-death stage and discover the inner shrine of the Divine Self in the form of Ra or Asar (Osiris).

H1—**Plato** also stated that the practice of virtue is the means by which the soul frees itself from the bondage to the physical nature.

I— While the teaching of the elements may be found in many Ancient Egyptian writings, nowhere is it more evident than in the Cosmogony of Gods and Goddesses of the school in the Ancient Egyptian city of Anu. The Ancient Egyptian Philosophy of the *Pautti* (Company of Gods and Goddesses) reveals the evolution of creation from the Supreme Being into the creation composed of the elements. From Nun (primeval undifferentiated consciousness) emerged Ra (sun-fire). From Ra emerge Shu (air) and Tefnut (water). From Shu and Tefnut emerge Geb (earth) and Nut (sky-heavens). Shu also assumes the role of Ether or the fifth element, space itself but Ra is the substratum or ultimate essence.

J— The Ancient Egyptian concept of God is monistic and this is where Xenophanes extracted the teaching of the nature of God. The following Ancient Egyptian proverbs illustrate the point.

"God is one and alone, none other existeth with Him, God is One."

"GOD is the father of beings." "There is only one God; ALL is IT; IT manifests itself in infinite forms and many Gods." (see also Hymns to Aton)

I—**Aristotle** (384-322 B.C.E.). proposed a teaching of universals. This teaching included a group of common properties which all real objects share but which are not independent of the objects. Aristotle held that the material universe consisted of four elements plus a fifth one that exists everywhere.

J—**Xenophanes** (6th? century B.C.E.) held that All is God and that all ears are God's ears, all eyes are God's eyes and all minds are Gods Minds.

The African Origins of The Greek God Dionysus

The ancient Greeks themselves documented that their main gods and goddesses came from Ancient Egypt. Asar was one of the most important gods of Ancient Egypt and similarly as well in ancient Greece under the name Dionysus. However, the mysteries of Asar, though including the concept of festivity, were exaggerated in the Greek adoption in the aspect of the god as being the god of wine, pleasure, etc.

The following image is of a Black figured vase. The Black figured vases are ancient Greek vases with black figures painted on reddish orange clay. In the Black figured vases the details within the silhouetted figures were incised before firing. The following image contains the god Dionysus and the Maenads.

137

The following description of the vase was given by Loggia Art:

This beautiful black figure vase painting by the Amasis Painter depicts Dionysos with a pair of attendant maenads. The image appears on a type of vessel that the ancient Greeks called an amphora. Amphorae (the plural form of the word amphora) were used to store such treasures as wine and oil.

The body of the vase is adorned with a gorgeous group of figures. Dionysos, the Greek god of wine and the theatre, stands on the left. The god is bearded and holds a kantharos (this kind of wine cup is often used as a symbol of Dionysos) in one of his hands. The right side of the vase features two women, who are often identified as maenads (female followers of Dionysos). These women are intertwined and clad in dark, intricately detailed garments. One of the maenads is holding a hare, while the other is carrying a deer. Each of the female figures is also grasping a sprig of stylized ivy. Notice how the skin of the male figure - Dionysos - is dark, while the female figures - the maenads - both have pale, buff colored skin. [1]

Notice that the top and bottom of the vase has classical

---

[137] http://www.usc.edu/dept/finearts/slide/pollini/Lecture6.html/250.html

lotus symbols of the ancient Egyptian Lotus. Further, the symbol of the hare is one of the primary signs of the Ancient Egyptian God Asar (Osiris). In fact, one of the main titles of Asar is "Unefer"

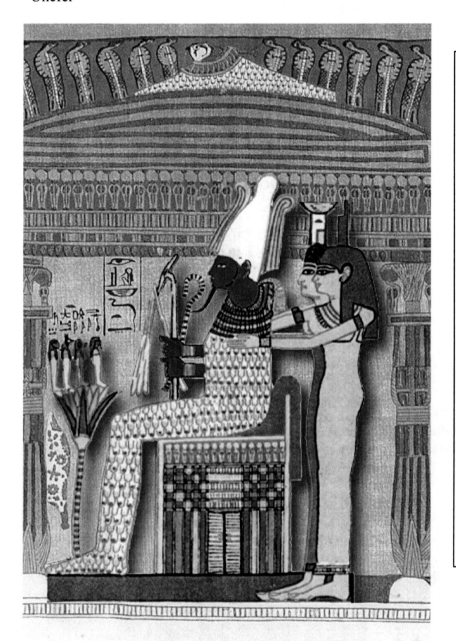

NOTE: the similarity in the black hue of Dionysus and his female companionship with white hue in the Greek iconography of Dionysus and that odf Asar (Osiris).

The Ancient Egyptian God Asar is usually depicted with green or black hue and he is usually accompanied by the two female divinities Aset "Isis" and Nebethet "Nephthys".

The "two Ladies" are usually depicted as yellow or as white.

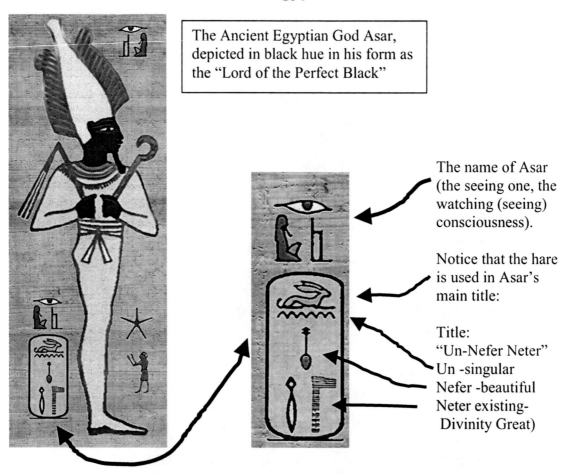

The Ancient Egyptian God Asar, depicted in black hue in his form as the "Lord of the Perfect Black"

The name of Asar (the seeing one, the watching (seeing) consciousness).

Notice that the hare is used in Asar's main title:

Title: "Un-Nefer Neter"
Un -singular
Nefer -beautiful
Neter existing-
Divinity Great)

The following excerpts from the book *History of Egypt* by Diodorus directly link the Ancient Egyptian god Asar (Osiris) with the Greek "Dionysus" as being one and the same. (Highlighted text by Ashby)

BOOK 1 II 1-5[138]

For when the names are translated into Greek Osiris means " many-eyed," and properly so; for in shedding his rays in every direction he surveys with many eyes, as it were, all land and sea. And the words of the poet I are also in agreement with this conception when he says:

The sun, who sees all things and hears all things.

And of the ancient Greek writers of mythology some give to Osiris the name Dionysus or, with a slight change in form, Sirius. One of them, Eumolpus, in his *Bacchic Hymn* speaks of Our Dionysus, shining like a star, With fiery eye in every ray; while Orpheus 2 Says:

NOTE: Greek mythology writers give the Greek name Dionysus to the Egyptian God Asar (Osiris) who is known as "firery eye." One of Asar's main symbols is the eye.

---

[138] *History of Egypt* by Diodorus

And this is why men call him Shining One And Dionysus.

BOOK 1. 12- 7-13. 2[139]

Now so far as the celestial gods are concerned whose genesis is from eternity, this is the account given by the Egyptians.

13. And besides these there are other gods, they say, who were terrestrial, having once been mortals, but who, by reason of their sagacity and the good services which they rendered to all men, attained immortality, some of them having even been kings in Egypt. Their names, when translated, are in some cases the same as those of the celestial gods, while others have a distinct appellation, such as

BOOK 1- 13. 2-14- 1

Helius, Cronus, and Rhea, and also the Zeus who is -alled Ammon by some, and besides these Hera and Hephaestus, also Hestia, and, finally, Hermes. Helius was the first king of the Egyptians, his name being the same as that of the heavenly star.' Some of the priests, however, say that Hephaestus was their first king, since he was the discoverer of fire and received the rule because of this service to mankind; for once, when a tree on the mountains had been struck by lightning and the forest near by was ablaze, Hephaestus went up to it, for it was winter-time and greatly enjoyed the beat; as the fire died down he kept adding fuel to it, and while keeping the fire going in this way he invited the rest of mankind to enjoy the advantage which came from it. Then Cronus became the ruler, and upon marrying his sister Rhea he begat Osiris and Isis, according to some writers of mythology, but, according to the majority, Zeus and Hera, whose high achievements gave them dominion over the entire universe. From these last were sprung five gods, one born on each of the five days which the Egyptians intercalate; 2 the names of these children were Osiris and Isis, and also Typhon, Apollo, and Aphrodite; and Osiris when translated is Dionysus, and Isis is more similar to Demeter than to any other goddess; and after Osiris married Isis and succeeded to the kingship he did many things of service to the social life of man.

> NOTE: The list of Divine rulers follows the same sequence as given in Anunian Theology of Ancient Egypt and the Ancient Egyptian account of Creation.

> "Osiris" translated is "Dionysus".

[139] *History of Egypt* by Diodorus

BOOK 1. 23. 1-5[140]

23. The number of years from Osiris and Isis, they say, to the reign of Alexander, who founded the city which bears his name in Egypt, is over ten thousand, but, according to other writers, a little less than twenty-three thousand. And those who say that the god 1 was born of Semele and Zeus in Boeotian Thebes are, according to the priests, simply inventing the tale. For they say that Orpheus, upon visiting Egypt and participating in the initiation and mysteries of Dionysus, adopted them and as a favour to the descendants of Cadmus, since he was kindly disposed to them and received honours at their hands, transferred the birth of the god to Thebes; and the common people, partly out of ignorance and partly out of their desire to have the god thought to be a Greek, eagerly accepted his initiatory rites and mysteries.

> Orpheus was initiatied into the mysteries of Dionysus ("Asar" – Osiris) and brought that religion to Greece where it was adopted. He then said that the god was born in Thebes (Greece) to facilitate people's acceptance of it.

---

[140] *History of Egypt* by Diodorus

CHAPTER 6: LATE PERIOD GREEK PHILOSOPHY AND MYTHOLOGY, JUDAISM AND CHRISTIANITY ORIGINATING IN ANCIENT EGYPT

"Humankind is the sole animal that is twofold. One part is simple: the human "essential", as say the Greeks, but which we call "the form of the divine similitude". Humankind is also fourfold: that which the Greeks call "hylic", which we call "cosmic."

-Ancient Kamitan Wisdom

159

Solon, Thales, Plato, Eudoxus and Pythagoras went to Egypt and consorted with the priests. Eudoxus they say, received instruction from Chonuphis of Memphis,* Solon from Sonchis of Sais,* and Pythagoras from Oeniphis of Heliopolis.*

–Plutarch (Greek historian c. 46-120 A.C.E.)

*(cities in Ancient Egypt)

Greek Philosophy has been equated with the origin of Western civilization. Ancient Greek philosophers such as Thales (c. 634-546 B.C.E.) and Pythagoras (582?-500? B.C.E.) are thought to have originated and innovated the sciences of mathematics, medicine, astronomy, philosophy of metaphysics, etc. These disciplines of the early Greek philosophers had a major impact on the development of Western culture and religion. The version of Christianity (primary western religion) which was practiced in the Western and Eastern empires was developed primarily in Alexandria (Greek city in late period Egypt) and Greece, alongside Greek culture and the Greek language. However, upon closer review, the ancient writings of contemporary historians (during the time of the development of early Christianity) point to different sources of Greek Philosophy and Christianity hence we are led to discover correlations in the earlier philosophy by tracing their origins to a common source in Ancient Egyptian religion.

There is evidence that shows how Ancient Egypt supported not only the education of the early Greek philosophers, who came to study in Egypt itself, but Egypt also supported the Egyptian Mystery Temples that were established in Greece. Some Egyptian pharaohs even sponsored or financed temples abroad which taught mystical philosophy as well as other disciplines. One such effort was put forth by the Ancient Egyptian King, Amasis, who is known to have financed the reconstruction of the famous Temple of Delphi in Greece, which was burnt down in 548 B.C.E. The oracle of Zeus at Dodona was the oldest; that at Delphi, the most famous with the teaching of "Know Thyself." Herodotus also records a Greek tradition which held that Dodona was founded from the Priesthood in Egyptian Thebes. Further, the oracle at Delos was founded by an Egyptian who became king of Athens in 1558 B.C.E. This would be one of the earliest suggested dates for the existence of civilization in Greece and it is being attributed here to an Ancient Egyptian origin by the Greeks themselves in their own mythology and folklore. The connection to and dependence on Ancient Egypt for the creation of Greek culture is unmistakable and undeniable.

Thales was the first Greek philosopher of whom there is any mention in Greek history and therefore, he is sometimes called the "Father of Greek philosophy." Thales was known to have traveled to and studied the wisdom of Ancient Egypt. After studying in Egypt with the Sages of the Ancient Egyptian temples he founded the Ionian school of natural philosophy which held that a single elementary matter, water, is the basis of all the transformations of nature. The similarity to the Ancient Egyptian Primeval Waters and the creation story in Genesis may be noted here. The ancient writings state that Thales visited Egypt and was initiated by the Egyptian priests into the Egyptian Mystery System and that during his time in Egypt he learned astronomy, surveying, engineering, and Egyptian Theology which would have certainly included the mystery teachings related to Asar (Osiris), Amun and Ptah. Pythagoras was a native of Samos who traveled often to Egypt on the advice of Thales and received education there. He was introduced to each of the Egyptian priests of the major theologies which comprised the whole of the Egyptian religious system based on the Trinity principle (*Amen-Ra-Ptah*). Each of these legs of the Trinity were based in three Egyptian cities. These were *Anu* (Heliopolis of the Greeks) -Priesthood of Ra, *Menefer* (Memphis of the Greeks) -Priesthood of Ptah and in Waset (Thebes of the Greeks) - Priesthood of Amen {Amun}) in Egypt.

Due to the immense impact which Pythagoras had on the whole of Ancient Greek religion and philosophy it is important to examine the writings about him. *Iamblichus* in the *Life of Pythagoras* writes *"Pythagoras met all the priests (Egyptian), learning from each what they knew ...and it is in these conditions that he passed twenty-two years in the temples of Egypt... He returned to Greece to teach in a way perfectly similar to the documents by which he had been instructed in Egypt."* Plutarch confirms this by saying: *"Most of the precepts he taught he copied from the Egyptian hieroglyphic texts."* Plutarch also reports that not only did Thales and Pythagoras study under the Egyptian philosophers but that Plato, Eudoxus, and Lycurgus did as well.

The Greek and Egyptian/Ethiopian Concepts of Supreme Divinity

The Ancient Egyptian Supreme Being in the form of Amun was identified with Zeus in Greek mythology and later with Jupiter by the Romans in Roman Mythology. The Greek philosophers acknowledged that the High God of Greek mythology, Zeus, along with the entire pantheon of Greek gods and goddesses which originated with him came from Ethiopia. One of the main titles of Zeus was *"Ethiops."* Ethiops means "burnt of skin" or "Black" and also the name of the country which is directly south of Egypt: Ethiopia. It is important to note here that the Ancient Egyptians also acknowledged their own origins in Ethiopia and that Kamit, the ancient name for the land of Egypt, also means "Black land or land of the blacks."

In Greek mythology Zeus, the king of the gods was also known as "Ethiops" and was thus associated with Ethiopia and even as having originally come from there. The reference to Ethiops is important because the ancient Greeks placed much importance on their association with Ethiopia as the early Ancient Egyptians did also. The following passage illustrates the early Greek fascination with Ethiopia and the Ethiopians.

> "They are the remotest of nations, most just of men, the favorite of the gods, the lofty inhabitants of Olympus journey to them to take part in their feasts. Their sacrifices are the most agreeable of all that mortals can offer them."
>
> -Homer, describing the Nubians

> Now Neptune had gone off to the Ethiopians, who are at the world's end, and lie in two halves, the one looking West and the other East.
>
> -Odyssey

> For Jove went yesterday to Oceanus, to a feast among the Ethiopians, and the other gods went with him.
>
> -Iliad

The main difference in the Greek and Roman interpretation of Zeus/Jupiter from the Ancient Egyptian Amun was in the emphasis on the anthropomorphic, personality and gender aspects of the God as well as the reduction in importance of the principles of immanence and panentheistic features of the Wasetian theology (Ancient Egyptian Religion of Amun). Also, the female aspect of Amun was not equally expressed in the European interpretations. Consequently, a more "male" oriented feeling was developed around the highest form of divinity which reflected the view of male superiority held generally within Western society. The idea of the transcendental aspect of Amun which goes beyond the name and form of the symbols was thus misunderstood. This misunderstanding gave rise to a phenomenal concept of a personal god which was believed to really exist, as a quasi super-human personality, separate from humanity instead of a symbol for the divinity which is the essence of all things. So moving away from mysticism, the popular religion of the Greeks developed into a philosophy wherein they did not look to a "Hidden" divinity within themselves but to a tangible personality whom they could call upon, seek out, converse with and pray to. This interpretation of divinity played an important role in the development of early Christianity since it was in the midst of Greek and Roman culture that Orthodox Christianity took form once it moved from Egypt to Palestine, Turkey, Greece and finally Rome.

Pythogora's theories of *Metempsychosis* or reincarnation and transmigration, the theory of communal living and poverty, the ideas of vegetarianism, his Asarian style funerary customs and his medical knowledge all point to his education in Ancient Egypt. These ideas and teachings were passed on into early Christianity through the Pythagorean schools which persisted into the Christian era as Neo-Pythagoreanism. Neo-Pythagoreanism was a philosophical movement begun in the 1st century B.C.E. which continued until it was diluted by the rise of Neo-Platonism in the 3rd century A.C.E. Neo-Pythagoreanism developed at the start of the Christian era and combined Hellenistic and Jewish elements with the more mystical and religious aspects of Pythagorean philosophy and was an influence on Neo-Platonism and the Jewish cult of the Essenes.

Neo-Platonism

Neo-Platonism, was a school of philosophy that came to prominence between the years 250 and 550 A.C.E. "Neo" means new, however this school of philosophy included more than just a new version of Platonic thought. It combined Stoic, Pythagorean, Aristotelian and Platonic ideas with portions from Egyptian, Jewish, Christian and Oriental religions. Thus, the newness does not refer to the introduction of new teachings but rather the consolidation of teachings and the revival of earlier teachings. Neo-Platonism tended to be mystical and poetic rather than philosophical. The formative leaders of the movement included two third century philosophers, Plotinus and Porphyry. When the Emperor Justinian closed the Neo-Platonic academies in 529 along with other cult systems such as that of the Egyptian Aset, Orthodox Christianity was closing the last links to the mystical traditions. Still, their influences on Christianity persisted through medieval times into the present because in order to be accepted, the Orthodox Church had to adopt many customs and symbols of other religions in order to convince the followers of other religions that Christianity had those symbols and customs previous to their "pagan" religion and therefore, that they should come to Christianity which is, according to the orthodox, the "true" and "original" religion.

Hellenism

The term 'Hellenism' refers to the culture of classical Greece. It is most particularly associated with Athens during the 5th century B.C.E. Thucydides and Herodotus exemplified the writing of history and Socrates (469-399 B.C.E.), followed by Plato (427-347 B.C.E.), his disciple, established standards for philosophy. It is notable that Hellenism followed a period in which the Greek historian Herodotus and the philosophers Plato, Pythagoras, Thales and others studied in Egypt and then brought back their learning to Greece. Hellenism represented a shift from the archaic period in such areas as art, music and philosophy.

Greek philosophy and mythology were inspired and carried on by Greek philosophers who had studied in Egypt and wished to enlighten their native country as many others who had also come to Egypt from elsewhere. Therefore, it is no surprise that reincarnation, transmigration, rebirth, or metempsychosis, the passage of the soul through successive bodies in a cycle of birth and death in order to gain varied experiences in order to grow spiritually, was a tenet of early Christianity. In the 6th century B.C.E. reincarnation was taught as a religious-philosophical doctrine in Ancient Egypt, Greece and India. This belief also appears in Hinduism, Buddhism, Jainism, and Sikhism. Herodotus informs us that this reincarnation and the immortality of the soul was understood and taught by the Egyptians before any other peoples.[64]

Alexander the Great emerged as a student of philosophy and world conqueror. When he took control of the Greek empire he tried to unite the entire civilized world under a single banner. He instinctively sought to conquer the major territories which were the sources of religious and philosophical strength of the ancient world which the Egyptian civilization had once covered.E31 Having achieved control over Greece itself by putting down all dissenting factions, he stretched forth southward and eastward into Egypt, Mesopotamia and India, thereby controlling these three centers of Art, Philosophy and religion of the then known world.

Alexander The Great and Alexandria

In reference to the Ionian school that Thales founded after his studies in Egypt, a student from that school became one of the most famous sage-philosophers. Socrates (470?-399? B.C.E.) was regarded as one of the most important philosophers of ancient Greece. He ended up spending most of his life in Athens, however, he was known to have studied under the Ionian philosophers. The Ionian school of Greek philosophy was founded by Thales (600 B.C.E.?) who as a direct student of the Ancient Egyptian sages. This establishes a direct link between Socrates and his teaching with Ancient Egypt. Socrates had a tremendous influence on many disciples. One of the most popular of these was Plato. Plato in turn taught others including Aristotle (384-322 B.C.E.) who was Plato's disciple for 19 years. After Plato's death, Aristotle opened a school of philosophy in Asia Minor. Aristotle educated Philip of Macedon's son Alexander (Alexander the Great) between the years 343 and 334 B.C.E. and then returned to Athens and opened a school in the Lyceum (the school near Athens where Aristotle lectured to his students). He urged Alexander on to his conquests since in the process, he, Aristotle, was able to gain in knowledge from the ancient writings of the conquered countries. After Alexander's conquest of Egypt, Aristotle became the author of over 1,000 books on philosophy. Building on Plato's theory of the Forms, Aristotle developed the theory of the *Unmoved Mover* which is a direct teaching from Memphite Theology in Ancient Egypt. Among his works are De Anima, Nicomachean Ethics and Metaphysics.

Alexander the Great represented a great military force which propelled Europeans for the first time out into the world. With the goal of uniting the known world under his realm, Alexander conquered Greece, Egypt and reached as far as India, where he and other Greek philosophers recognized that the Greek gods and goddesses corresponded to the Indian pantheon of Gods and goddesses of Hinduism and the gods and goddesses of Ancient Egypt. This *synchretic* view of religion was not held by the Jews. They would never say that Yahweh is equal to Shiva, Zeus or Osiris. Trade between the Mediterranean countries and the Far East was flourishing during the time following the conquests of Alexander the Great. Alexandria, his capital city in Egypt, became the center of the sciences, philosophy and Enlightenment in the ancient world. At the height of the Roman Empire, which had by that time succeeded the Greeks, European conquests encompassed North Africa, Europe, the Near East and Britain. Throughout this time the Roman empire used Persian soldiers and others who carried with them the varying religious beliefs

163

throughout all parts of the empire. The opportunity to study at Alexandria with it's great library was the ambition of all who wished to attain the heights of excellence in every field.

Alexandria, Greek Culture and Philosophy and their Impact on Christianity

When Alexander the Great conquered Egypt he founded the city of Alexandria and from this time on the interest that had been sparked by Greeks who had traveled to Egypt in previous years such as Thales, Pythagoras, Plato, Herodotus, etc., grew into a full incorporation of Kamitan religion and culture into the Greek and there was a melding with the Jews and non-Christian Gnostics as well as the Christian Gnostics.[141] Therefore, Alexandria is an important focal point in the final period of Ancient Egyptian religion as it played an important role in the formation of Greek religion and philosophy and the Judeo-Christian tradition. So it was transformed by the Greeks, Jews and Christians and its remnants remain with us to this day in those religions.

Alexandria, the city in Egypt founded by *Alexander the Great* upon his conquest of Egypt, became the center of scholarship and learning in the entire ancient world from 300 B.C.E. to 250 A.C.E. It was here that the doctrines of the Religion of Asar (Osiris) and Hermeticism from Ancient Egypt (5,500 B.C.E-300 B.C.E), the Buddhist missionaries from India, the cult of Christos from the Near East and the teachings of Zarathustra (Zoroaster) melded into an amalgam of several Jewish and Christian sects. *Dionysius the Areopagite* played an important role in bridging the gap between the mystical religious teachings, Judaism and Christianity. Up to this time the symbols associated with Gnosticism, Hermeticism and Christianity were known to be metaphors to describe the ultimate reality of the universe and man's relationship to it. It was not until the time of the Christians from the Byzantine throne, the Jewish leaders who followed Yahweh (a name for God used by the ancient Hebrews), and then later, the Muslims who followed a little known Arabian divinity named Allah (the supreme being in Islam), that the symbols and metaphors of religion began to be understood literally, as facts rather than as metaphors to explain the mystery of life and Creation. In those new religions (Judaism, Christianity, Islam) the idea of "God" became circumscribed by a particular doctrine, which was the exclusive property belonging to certain "chosen people." Thus, they began to see all other God-forms, other than their own, as idols or devils. All other religions were seen as heresies. Consequently, the followers of those forms were considered as pagans who must be subdued and converted or destroyed. This point is most strongly illustrated in the Bible itself in several passages.[142] This point is of great importance because the concept of a proprietary God is central to Western religions.

Thus, the Bible itself states that Moses (1200?-1000? B.C.E.), who is reputed to have written the laws and guidelines upon which Jewish, Christian and Islamic society are based, was knowledgeable in all of the "wisdom" and "words" of Egypt; i.e., he was an Ancient Egyptian priest. This is supported by the ancient historian Plutarch, Greek author (c. 46-120 A.C.E.), who called him, *"a priest of Aset, a Hierophant (high priest) of Heliopolis."* Philo of Alexandria (Gnostic Jewish philosopher c. 20 B.C.E. - c. A.C.E. 54) also made this point about Moses. They also say that his initiate name was *Osarisiph.* The similarity between the names Osarisiph and Osiris or Asar leads us to reflect further on the link between Ancient Egyptian and Old Testament mythologies and spiritual teachings. The Old Testament stories of Adam and Eve as well as Cain and Abel point us to the same conclusion. Adam and Eve beget Seth, which is the same name as the brother of Asar in Egypt (Seth, Set). Cain murders his brother Abel, just as Set had murdered his brother Asar in Egyptian Mythology.

---

[141] see the book Mystical Journey From Jesus to Christ by Muata Ashby
[142] See the book African Origins by Muata Ashby

There are other important links between Christianity and Ancient Egyptian religion. Ancient Egyptian Mythology holds that the first piece of land that was created by God was the Ancient Egyptian city of Anu. In the Ancient Egyptian city of Anu[143] there was a holy well. Egyptian tradition held that the God, Ra,, symbolized by the sun. Creator of the universe and father of Asar, had washed his face in its waters after rising for the first time on this earth out of the primeval ocean. The Christian tradition also holds that the Virgin Mary washed Jesus' clothes in the waters of this same well. The well is also known as the "Virgin's Well," and it is referred to as "Ain ash-shems" or "Well of the sun" by the Arabs.[110]

The following are additional quotes from ancient Greek authors which admit that Greek culture owes it existence to Ancient Egypt.

"The Sidonians, according to tradition, are skilled
   in many beautiful arts, as the poet also points out;
   and besides this they are philosophers in the sciences
   of astronomy and arithmetic, having begun their studies
   with practical calculations and with night-sailings;
   for each of these branches of knowledge concerns the
   merchant and ship-owner; as , for example, geometry was
   invented, it is said, from the measurement of lands which
   is made necessary by the Nile when it confounds the
   boundaries at the time of its overflows. **This science,
   then, is believed to have come to the Greeks (from the
   Egyptians**; astronomy and arithmetic from the Phoenicians;
   and at present the far the greatest store of knowledge
   in every other branch of philosophy is had from these
   cities. And if one must believe Poseidonius, the ancient
   dogma about atoms originated with Mochus, a Sidonian
      [Phoenician], born before the Trojan times." (Strabo,
   Geography, 16, 2, trans. by H. L. Jones)

"Hence when all the discoveries of this kind (practical)
   were fully developed, the sciences which relate neither
   to pleasure nor yet to the necessities of life were
   invented, and first in those places where men had leisure.
   **Thus the mathematical sciences originated in the
   neighborhood of Egypt**, because there the priestly class
   was allowed leisure." (Aristotle, _Metaphysics_ I.
   I. 15, 1, trans. by H. Tredennick)

"...Egyptians have not only been accepted by the present
   inhabitants but have aroused no little admiration among the
   Greeks; and for that reason those men who have won the
   **greatest repute in intellectual things have been eager
   to visit Egypt in order to acquaint themselves with its**

---

[143] "On" of the Bible and called "Heliopolis" by the Greeks.

laws and institutions, which they considered to be worthy of note. For despite the fact that for reasons mentioned
above strangers found it difficult in early times to
enter the country, it was nevertheless eagerly visited by
Orpheus and the poet Homer in the earliest times and
in later times by many others, such as **Pythagoras of Samos** and **Solon the lawgiver.**"
(Diodorus Siculus, Book I. 68)

"It was at this time, we are told, that Pythagoras, seeing
that the tyranny was growing in power, left the city and
went off to Egypt and Babylon, to satisfy his fondness for learning..." (Strabo, _Geography_
14. I. 16, trans. by H.L.
Jones)

And the people observed these initiatory rites,
partly through their ignorance, partly because
they were deceived through their ignorance, partly
because they were attracted to them by the
trustworthiness of Orpheus and his reputation is such
matters, and most of all because they were glad to receive
the god as a Greek, which, as has been said, is what he
was considered to be. Later, after the writers of myths and
poets had taken over this account of his ancestry, the theatres became filled with it and
among following generations faith in the story grew stubborn and immutable. **In general,
they say, the Greeks appropriate to themselves the most renowned of both Egyptian heroes and
gods, and also the colonies sent out by them.** (Diodorus, Book I. 23)

"They wear linen tunics with fringes hanging about the legs,
called "calasiris" and loose white woollen mantles over these.
But nothing of wool is brought into temples, or buried with
them; that is forbidden. In this they follow the same rule as
the ritual in **Orphic and Bacchic; but which is in truth Egyptian and Pythagorean;** for neither
may those initiated into these rites be buried in woolen wrappings. There is a sacred legend
about this." (Herodotus, Book II, 81)

"On this lake [in Sais] it is that the Egyptians
represent by night his [Osiris] sufferings whose name
I refrain from mentioning, and this representation
they call their Mysteries. I know well the whole course
of the proceedings in these ceremonies, but they shall
not pass my lips. So too, with regard the mysteries of
Ceres, which the Greeks term "the Thesmophoria," I
know them, but I shall not mention them, except so far
as may be done without impiety. **The daughters of Danaus brought these rites from Egypt,
and taught them to the Pelasgic women of the Peloponnese.**" (Herodotus, Book II,
171)

"He [Pythagoras] had three silver flagons made and took them
as **presents to each of the priests of Egypt**...While still

young, so eager was he for knowledge, he left his own country and had himself initiated into all the mysteries and rites
not only of Greece but also of foreign countries. Now he was in Egypt when Polycrates sent him a letter of introduction to
Amasis; **he learnt the Egyptian language,** so we learn from Antiphon in his book _On Men of Outstanding Merit, and he also journeyed among the Chaldaens and Magi." (Diogenes Laertius, VIII. 2-4)

"...Thales increased the reputation Pythagoras had already
acquired, by communicating to him such disciplines as he was able to impart: and, apologizing for his old age, and the
imbecility of his body, he **exhorted him to sail into Egypt,**
and associate with the Memphian and Diosolitan priests. For he confessed that his own
reputation for wisdom, was derived from the instructions of these priests; but that he was neither naturally, nor by exercise, endued with those excellent prerogatives, which were so visibly displayed in
the person of Pythagoras. Thales, therefore, gladly
announced to him, from all these circumstances, that he
would become the wisest and most divine of all men, if he
associated with these Egyptian priests." (Iamblichus,
_Life of Pythagoras, Chapter II)

"He (Thales) had no instructor, except he when to Egypt
and spent some time with the priests there...," (Diogenes
Laertius, I. 2-29)
'. . . **Thales of Milet made voyage to the priests and the astronomers of Egypt,** and according to his biographers, he seems to have **learned geometry from the Egyptians.** . .
Diogenes Lierce, Thales, 43 and 24

"If one were not determined to make haste, one might cite
many admirable instances of the piety of the Egyptians, that
piety which I am neither the first nor the only one to
have observed; on the contrary, many contemporaries and
predecessors have remarked it, of whom Pythagoras of Samos is one. **On a visit to Egypt he became a student of the**
religion of the people, and was first to bring to the Greeks all philosophy, and more conspicuously than others he seriously interested himself in sacrifices and in ceremonial purity, since he believed that even if should gain thereby no greater reward from the gods, among men, at any rate, his reputation would be greatly enhanced. (Isocrates, _Busiris_ 27-30)

FROM HERODOTUS, BK. II:

33. "Melampus, the son of Amytheon, cannot (I think) have been ignorant of this ceremony- nay, he must, I should conceive, have been well acquainted with it. He it was who introduced into Greece the name of Bacchus, the ceremonial of his worship, and the procession of the phallus. He did not, however, so completely apprehend the whole doctrine as to be able to communicate it entirely, but various sages since his time have carried out his teaching to greater perfection. Still it is

certain that Melampus introduced the phallus, and that the Greeks learnt from him the ceremonies which they now practice. I therefore maintain that Melampus, who was a wise man, and had acquired the art of divination, having become acquainted with the worship of Bacchus **through knowledge derived from Egypt, introduced it into Greece,** with a few slight changes, at the same time that he brought in various other practices."

34. " For I can by no means allow that it is by mere coincidence that the Bacchic ceremonies in Greece are so nearly the same as the Egyptian- they would then have been more Greek in their character, and less recent in their origin. **Much less can I admit that the Egyptians borrowed these customs, or any other, from the Greeks.** My belief is that Melampus got his knowledge of them from Cadmus the Tyrian, and the followers whom he brought from Phoenicia into the country which is now called Boeotia. "

41. "The **following tale is commonly told in Egypt** concerning the oracle of Dodona in Greece, and that of Ammon in Libya. My informants on the point were the priests of Jupiter at Thebes. They said `that two of the sacred women were once carried off from Thebes by the Phoenicians, and that the story went that one of them was sold into Libya, and the other into Greece, and these women were the first founders of the oracles in the two countries.' On my inquiring how they came to know so exactly what became of the women, they answered, `that diligent search had been made after them at the time, but that it had not been found possible to discover where they were; afterwards, however, they received the information which they had given me.'

42. "This was what I heard from the priests **at Thebes (Egypt)**; at Dodona, however, the women who deliver the oracles relate the matter as follows: `**Two black doves flew away from Egyptian Thebes,** and while one directed its flight to Libya, the other came to them. She alighted on an oak, and sitting there began to speak with a human voice, and told them that on the spot where she was, there should henceforth be an oracle of Jove. They understood the announcement to be from heaven, so they set to work at once and erected the shrine. The dove which flew to Libya bade the Libyans to establish there the oracle of Ammon.' This likewise is an oracle of Jupiter. The persons from whom I received these particulars were three priestesses of the Dodonaeans, the eldest Promeneia, the next Timarete, and the youngest Nicandra- what they said was confirmed by the other Dodonaeans who dwell around the temple.

45. "The Dodonaeans called the women doves because they were foreigners, and seemed to them to make a noise like birds. After a while the dove spoke with a human voice, because the woman, whose foreign talk had previously sounded to them like the chattering of a bird, acquired the power of speaking what they could understand. For how can it be conceived possible that a dove should really speak with the voice of a man? **Lastly, by calling the dove black the Dodonaeans indicated that the woman was an Egyptian.** And certainly the character of the oracles at Thebes and Dodona is very similar. **Besides this form of divination, the Greeks learnt also divination by means of victims from the Egyptians. "**
46. "The **Egyptians were also the first to introduce solemn assemblies, processions, and litanies to the gods; of all which the Greeks were taught the use by them. It**

seems to me a sufficient proof of this that in Egypt these practices have been established from remote antiquity, while in Greece they are only recently known. "

Plato records the words of an Egyptian priest to Solon, grandfather of Socrates:

Oh Solon, Solon, you Helienes are but children.... There is no old doctrine handed down among you by ancient tradition nor any science which is hoary with age, and I will tell you the reason behind this. There have been and will be again many destructions of mankind arising out of many causes, the greatest having been brought about by earth-fire and inundation. **Whatever happened either in your country or ours or in any other country of which we are informed, any action which is noble and great or in any other way remarkable which has taken place, all that has been inscribed long ago in our temple records, whereas you and other nations did not keep imperishable records.** And then, after a period of time, the usual inundation visits like a pestilence and leaves only those of you who are destitute of letters and education. And thus you have to begin over again as children and know nothing of what happened in ancient times either among us or among yourselves.

As for those genealogies of yours which you have related to us, they are no better than tales of children; for in the first place, you remember one deluge only, whereas there were a number of them. And in the next place there dwelt in your land, which you do not know, the fairest and noblest race of men that ever lived of which you are but a seed or remnant. And this was not known to you because for many generations the survivors of that destruction made no records.

Having been received by Amasis the king of Egypt M-525 B. C.1 he **(Pythagoras) obtained from them letters of recommendation from the priests of Heliopolis, . . .**

Porphyrius, Life of Pythagoras, 3

... frequenting all the sanctuaries of Egypt with great ardor ... he met all the priests, learning from each what he knew. And it is in these conditions that he passed twenty-two years in the temples of Egypt.

Iamblichus.- Life of Pythagoras, 4,18-19

On a visit to Egypt he (Pythagoras) became a student of the religion of the people, and was the first to bring to the Greeks all philosophy ...

Isocrates., Van Hook (Tr&DS.)Vol. 3

Pythagoras returned to Greece to teach 'in a way perfectly similar to the documents by which he had been instructed in Egypt.'

Iamblichus: Life Of Pythagoras,

'Most of the precepts which he taught he copied from Egyptian hieroglyphic texts.'

Plutarch. Moralis. Babbitt F.C.(Trans.)

'Still another wise men,, other Greek philosophers, came to learn in the Egyptian temples. Onenopidus, for example, learned several secrets from the priests and astronomers.

Diodorus., 1,199

Democritus, on his part, visited the priest (in Egypt) five years to learn things related to astronomy.'ll

Diogenes Laerce, Democritus, 3

".,for Eudoxus accompanied Plato this far: arrived at Heliopolis (Egypt), they established themselves here and both resided there thirteen years in the society of the priests: the fact is affirmed by several authors" Strabo (XVII,1,29)

"This is also confirmed by the most learned of Greeks such as Solon, Thales, Plato, Eudoxus, Pythagoras, and as some say, even Lycurgus going to Egypt and conversing with the priests; of whom they say Euxodus was a hearer of **Chonuphis of Memphis (city in Ancient Egypt)**, Solon of **Sonchis of Sais (city in Ancient Egypt)**, and Pythagoras of **Oenuphis of Heliopolis (city in Ancient Egypt)**. Wherefore the last named, being, as is probable, more than ordinarily admired by the men, and they also be him imitated their symbolic and mysterious way of talking; obscuring his sentiments with dark riddles. For the greatest part of Pythagoric precepts fall nothing short of those sacred writings they call hieroglyphical..." (Plutarch, _Morals_, 10)

CHAPTER 7: THE INFLUENCE OF ANCIENT EGYPTIAN MUSIC AND THEATER ON GREEK AND ROMAN THEATER

Historical Background of the Ancient Greek Theater

Definition and Origin of: "Theater"

> **A place or building in which dramatic performances for an audience take place; these include drama, dancing, music, mime, opera, ballet, and puppets.**
>
> **Theatre history can be traced to (Ancient) Egyptian religious ritualistic drama as long ago as 3200 BC. The first known European theaters were in Greece from about 600 BC.**
>
> -Copyright © 1995 Websters Encyclopedia
> Helicon Publishing Ltd.

Many people believe that the art of theater began with the ancient Greek theater. Thespis, the first actor-dramatist (about 560 B.C.E.), is considered to have been the first person to give the Greek drama its form; actors are still called "thespians." However, upon closer examination, it must be noted that just as Greek philosophers such as Thales and Pythagoras learned their wisdom from the Ancient Egyptians and then set up their schools of philosophy in Greece, it is likely that the first Greek actors and playwrights learned their profession from the Ancient Egyptian Sages when they came from Greece to learn the religion and the sciences.[144] Actually, a great debt is owed to the Greek writers of ancient times because their records attest to many details which the Ancient Egyptians did not record.

Ancient Greek theater had its origin in the mysteries of Dionysus. It is well known to scholars of Ancient Greece and Greek mythology that Orpheus is credited with introducing the cult of Dionysus to Greece along with its initiatory rites.

> Orpheus, king of the Ciconians, is counted among the ARGONAUTS. Orpheus practiced minstrelsy and by his songs moved stones and trees, holding also a spell over the wild beasts. He descended to the Underworld in order to fetch his dead wife, but had to return without her. Orpheus, whom Apollo taught to play the lyre, traveled to Egypt where he increased his knowledge about the gods and their initiatory rites, bringing from that country most of his mystic ceremonies, orgiastic rites, and his extraordinary account of his descent to the Underworld. Orpheus became famous because of his poems and his songs, excelling everyone in the beauty of his verse and music. He also reached a high degree of influence because he was believed to have discovered mysteries, purification from sins, cures of diseases, and means of averting divine wrath. Some say that Orpheus introduced a cult of Dionysus 2 that was very similar to the cult of Osiris, and that

---

[144] see the book "From Egypt to Greece" by Muata Ashby available through the Sema Institute and bookstores.

of Isis, which resembles the cult of Demeter. But others affirm that he praised all the gods except Dionysus 2.[145]

Upon cursory investigation it is discovered that Dionysus is the Greeks name for the god Asar (Osiris). The Greek writings attest to the fact the Dionysus was the same Osiris, brought into Greece from Egypt. The dates of the prominence of Dionysus coincide with the association of the first Greek philosophers of the Greek classical period with the Ancient Egyptian priests. The qualities of Dionysus are the same as those of the Egyptian Asar and the temple mysteries including vegetation, death and resurrection, were also the same. The enactment of those mysteries constitutes the Egyptian "Theater" which was adopted by the Greeks and which was later developed by the Greek playwrights into other themes.[146] (highlighted text by Ashby)

> Born of the union of Zeus and a mortal, Semele, **Dionysos rose to prominence around the 6th century B.C. under many names and forms.** The principles of life and generation, as well as the cyclical life of vegetation (death and rebirth), are central to the worship of Dionysos: lord of the vine, but also god of the tree. He is often considered in reference to the fig tree, ivy (undying life), and all blossoming things -- symbols of life and vitality. His celebration is marked by the joy of his epiphany in the Spring, and the sorrow of his death or descent in the Winter. Dionysos also appears as a bull god, long considered an important symbol of fertility in the Ancient World. Other symbols that are associated with him include snakes, goats, lightening bolts, as well as moistness, madness and the phallus. Dionysos is typically followed by satyrs and maenads who participate in the music, wine, and dancing which make up an integral aspect of his mystery. Satyrs, or primitive, goat-like men, usually lurk in the shadows of the more primary maenads, or mad women, which typified Dionysian worship. These maenads, "the frenzied sanctified women who are devoted to the worship of Dionysos."(Harrison -401), are 'nurses' who look after and follow the infant Dionysos-- likely referring to the largely female following he inspired and the great Mother goddess he came from.[147]

This section has been included to show the importance of theatrical-ritual in Neterian spirituality. It must be clear though that this form of art is reserved for the realm of spirituality and not for frivolous entertainment.

Early Greek Playwrights

The Influence of Ancient Egyptian Philosophy and Theater on Greek playwrights, and the Roman and Christian Theater began through the influence of early Greek philosophers who had studied philosophy and the Temple Mysteries of Ancient Egypt. Thespis, who lived in the mid-6th century B.C.E., was the first known Greek poet, who, according to tradition, is the founder of drama. He is also credited with instituting the use of masks to disguise the performers. None of

---

[145] *Greek Mythology Link*, created and maintained by Carlos Parada. Since 1997© 1993-2004 http://homepage.mac.com/cparada/GML/index.html
[146] Origin of the Greek Theater by B. H. Stricker, Journal of Egyptian Archeology
[147] *Greek Mythology Link*, created and maintained by Carlos Parada. Since 1997© 1993-2004 http://homepage.mac.com/cparada/GML/index.html

his works have survived. There are three important early Greek playwrights, many of whose works have survived and have influenced theater in Europe. Aeschylus (525-456 BC), Greek dramatist, was the earliest of the great tragic poets of Athens. He was the predecessor of Sophocles and Euripides and he called the father of Greek tragedy. From Herodotus, the best known historian of the time (484-425 B.C.E.), we learn of correspondences between the Ancient Egyptian gods and goddesses and the Greek gods and goddesses and also that Aeschylus drew from Ancient Egyptian myth and theater in his work.

The Egyptians tell the following story in connection with this island, to explain the way in which it first came to float:- "In former times, when the isle was still fixed and motionless, Latona, one of the eight gods of the first order, who dwelt in the city of Buto, where now she has her oracle, received Apollo as a sacred charge from Isis, and saved him by hiding him in what is now called the floating island. Typhon meanwhile was searching everywhere in hopes of finding the child of Osiris."

(According to the Egyptians, Apollo and Diana are the children of Bacchus and Isis, while Latona is their nurse and their preserver. They call Apollo, in their language, Horus; Ceres they call Isis. From this Egyptian tradition, and from no other, it must have been that Aeschylus, the son of Euphorion, took the idea, which is found in none of the earlier poets, of making Diana the daughter of Ceres.) The island, therefore, in consequence of this event, was first made to float. Such at least is the account which the Egyptians give.

—Herodotus: The Histories (484-425 B.C.E.)

Above: Mask of the goddess Hetheru as a lioness.
Below: Mask of the god Djehuti as a baboon.

Euripides (circa 480-406 B.C.E.), was a Greek dramatist, the third, with Aeschylus and Sophocles, of the great Attic tragic poets. His work, fairly popular in his own time, exerted great influence on Roman drama. In more recent times he has influenced English and German drama, and most conspicuously, such French dramatic poets as Pierre Corneille and Jean Baptiste Racine. Sophocles, born at about 496 B.C.E., was friends with the famed historian Herodotus, who traveled extensively throughout Ancient Egypt and wrote extensively on the mysteries (theater) of the Ancient Egyptian Temple.

African Masks

African masks are an integral part of African culture, art and spirituality. The mask tradition came to its height in Benin and Kamit. The following are examples of the Mask Art as it is used to relate humanity to the earth realm to the spiritual realm through ritual.

Above: Typical African Ritual Masks.

Below: Death of King Tutankhamun of Kamit

(c.1300 B.C.E.)

Above: Ancient Egyptian priest performs the rites of the dead while wearing a mask in the likeness of the god Anpu (center), the divinity of embalming.

Greek Tragedy Mask
(Classical Period)

There was no public theater in Ancient Egypt as the modern world knows theater at present. Theater in present day society is performed publicly for the main purpose of entertainment, but in Ancient Egypt the theatrical performances were reserved for the temple exclusively. This was because the performing arts, including music, were held to be powerful and sacred endeavors which were used to impart spiritual teachings and evoke spiritual feeling, and were not to be used as frivolous forms of entertainment. The Greek writer, Strabo, relates that multitudes of people would flock to festival centers (important cities and temples) where the scenes from myths about the gods and goddesses would be acted out.

Ancient Egyptian Theater

⬇

Greek Theater

⬇

Roman Theater

⬇

Christian Theater

⬇

Modern Western Theater

Sometimes the main episodes of the religious dramas were performed outside the temple, in the courtyard or between the pylons, of the "Paristyle Hall" or "Hypostyle Hall" areas and were the most important attraction of the festivals. The most esoteric (mystical) elements were performed in the interior portion of the temple for initiates, priests and priestesses only. The priests and priestesses took great care with costumes and the decorations (direction and set design). The spectators knew the myths that were being acted out but never stopped enjoying their annual performance, being a retelling of the divine stories, which bring purpose and meaning to life. Thus, the art of acting was set aside for spiritual purposes and was not to be used for mindless entertainment, which serves only to distract the mind from reality and truth. The spectators would take part by clapping, lamenting at sad parts, crying out with joy and celebrating when the ultimate triumph came. In this manner the spectators became part of the myth. As the myth is essentially about the life of the gods and goddesses, and it is their lives that not only sustain the world, but also leads to understanding the connection between the physical, material and spiritual worlds, the reenactment of these dramas serve to teach and reinforce in the general population, the spiritual values of the Kamitan culture. Further, the occasions were used as opportunities for enjoying life, though it was understood to be fleeting. Thus, the bridge between the mortal world and the eternal world was established, through mythological drama and the performing arts.

In the Ancient Egyptian view, life cannot be enjoyed without affirming the Divine, the Spirit. Further, theater, religion and mystical philosophy were considered to be aspects of the same discipline, known as "Shetaut Neter" or the "mysteries" or "Yoga Sciences." Every aspect of life in Ancient Egypt was permeated by the awareness and inclusion of spiritual philosophy. For example, lawyers and judges followed the precepts of Maat, and medical doctors followed and worshipped the teachings of the god Djehuti, who was adopted by the Greeks as the god Asclapius. This idea is also evident in the Ancient Egyptian manner of saying grace before meals even by ordinary householders. Prior to consuming food, the host of an ordinary household would invite the guests to view an image of a divinity, principally Asar (Osiris) the god of the afterlife, thereby reminding the guests that life is fleeting, even as they are about to enjoy a sumptuous meal. In this manner, a person is reminded of the ultimate fate and purpose of life and a reflective state of mind is engendered rather than an arrogant and egoistic state. This theme is present in every aspect of Ancient Egyptian culture at its height.

The Ancient Egyptian Sages instituted tight controls on theater and music because the indulgence in inappropriate entertainments was known to cause mental agitation and undesirable behaviors. The famous Greek Philosopher and student of the Ancient Egyptian Mysteries, Pythagoras, wrote that the Ancient Egyptians placed particular attention to the study of music. Another famous Greek Philosopher and student of the Ancient Egyptian Mysteries, Plato, states that they thought it was beneficial to the youths. Strabo confirms that music was taught to youths along with reading and writing, however, it was understood that music meant for entertainment alone was harmful to the mind, making it agitated and difficult to control oneself, and thus was strictly controlled by the state and the priests and priestesses. Like the sages of India, who instituted Nada Yoga, or the spiritual path of music, the Ancient Egyptians held that music was of Divine origin and as such was a sacred endeavor. The Greek writer, Athenaeus, informs us that the Greeks and barbarians from other countries learned music from the Ancient Egyptians. Music was so important in Ancient Egypt that professional musicians were contracted and kept on salaries at the temples. Music was considered important because it has the special power to carry the mind to either elevated (spiritual) states or (worldly) states. When there is overindulgence in music for entertainment and escapism (tendency to desire to escape from daily routine or reality by indulging in fantasy, daydreaming, or entertainment) or to promote other egoistic experiences (violence, hate, lust, greed, sentimentality, desire, etc.) the mind becomes filled with worldly impressions, cravings, lusting, and uncontrolled urges. In this state of mind, the capacity for right thinking and feeling are distorted or incapacitated. The advent of audio and visual recording technology and their combinations in movies and music videos, is more powerful because the visual element, coupled with music, and the ability to repeat with intensity of volume, acts to intoxicate the mind with illusory, egoistic and fantasy thoughts. The body is also affected in this process. The vibrations of the music and the feelings contained in it through the lyrics and sentiment of the performer evokes the production of certain psychological and corresponding bio-chemical processes in the mind and body, respectively. This capacity of music is evident in movies musicals, converts, audio recordings, etc., in their capacity to change a person's mood. Any and all messages given to the mind affect it, and therefore, great care should be taken to fill the mind with the right kinds of messages in the form of sublime ideas and feelings.

Those societies which produce and consume large quantities of audio and audio-visual entertainment for non-spiritual purposes will exhibit the greatest levels of cultural degradation which will express as mental agitation, violence, individual frustration, addiction, mental illness, physical illness, etc., no matter how materially prosperous or technologically advanced they may become. So true civilization and success of a society should not be judged by material prosperity or technological advancement, but rather by how successful it is in producing the inner fulfillment of its citizens. Being the creators of and foremost practitioners of Maat Philosophy (adherence to the principles of righteousness in all aspects of life[148]), the Ancient Egyptians created a culture which existed longer (at least 5,000 years) than any other known society and the construction methods of many of their monuments still defy explanation and cannot be duplicated. Therefore, the real measures of civilization and human evolution are to be discerned by the emphasis on and refinement of the performing and visual arts and spiritual[149] philosophy, for these endeavors serve to bring harmony to the individual and to society. It should be clearly understood that art should not become stagnant or rigid in its expression since this is the means

---

[148] See the book "The Wisdom of Maati" by Dr. Muata Ashby
[149] The word spiritual here implies any endeavor which seeks to bring understanding about the ultimate questions of life: Who am I? and What is life all about? So spirituality may or may not be related to organized religion.

by which it is renewed for the understanding of new generations. Rather, the principles contained in the arts should be kept intact in the performance of the rituals, paintings, sculptures, music, etc., since these reflect transcendental truths which are as effective today as they were 5,000 years ago in the Ancient Egyptian temple and will be effective until the end of time. The loss of these is the cause of disharmony in society, but societal dysfunction is in reality only a reflection of disharmony in the individual human heart which has lost its connection with the Higher Self within.

Dance was also an important part of Ancient Egyptian life. Dance, along with music, was used to worship the gods and goddesses, especially Asar and Hetheru. However, dance was also present in private dinner parties. Also, private parties were the scene for entertainments such as games (such as Senet-similar to modern day Parcheesi), juggling, mimes, music and limited theatrical performances. Men and women would dance together or alone and would improvise more than in the dances of the temples and special ceremonies. As is the custom in modern day India and Japan, the Ancient Egyptians would take off their shoes when entering a house or the temple as a sign of reverence for the host and a symbolic gesture of leaving the world outside when practicing higher endeavors.

Thus, the question of whether or not music and entertainment has an effect on youth and the mind of a person was resolved in ancient times. The Ancient Egyptians observed that the people from Greece and the Asiatic countries were more aggressive, and that their behavior was unstable.[150] They attributed these problems to their lifestyle, which was full of strife due to life in harsh geographical regions, meat eating and overindulgence in sense pleasures, and the inability to control the human urges and the consequent disconnection from the natural order of the universe as well as the spiritual inner self. These observations of the psychology and lifestyle of the foreigners prompted the Ancient Egyptian Sages to refer to the Greeks and Asiatics (Middle Easterners) as "children" and "miserable"..."barbarians." Their observations allowed the Ancient Egyptian Sages to create a philosophy of life and a psycho-spiritual environment wherein the Kamitan people could grow and thrive in physical, mental and spiritual health.

> *The Greek writer, Athenaeus, informs us that the Greeks and barbarians from other countries learned music from the Ancient Egyptians.*

From: The Republic – the Socrates character, in the book, asserts this.

> The Egyptians rated music highly, and Plato considered their music superior to the Greek, both for melody and energy. But harmony and rhythm were always subordinate to the words, and the subject matter was paramount. There were two sorts of Harmonies known to the old Egyptians, which the Greeks designated as "Dorian" and Phrygian" – the former, grave, slow and tranquil, the latter, a dithyrambic form, probably employed in these chants (Laments of Aset and Nebthet), which was forceful, appealing and energetic. [151]

> The Egyptians based their music on seven diatonics, which Demetrius of Phalerus attributes to the "seven vowels"; others say seven senses, or seven planets. Dion Cassius corroborates him, while Dionysos of Halicarnassus says: "Melody embraced an interval

---

[150] See the books Egyptian Yoga Vol. 1 and 2 and The 42 Laws of Maat and the Wisdom Texts
[151] The Republic – the Socrates character, in the book, asserts this.

of five-it never rose more than three and one-halftones towards high, and fell less towards bass." This probably was a result of the use of the three stringed lyre.[152]

In ancient Greece, theater became a practice which was open to the public, and later on in the Christian era it deteriorated into mindless entertainment or a corrupted endeavor of con artists. In present times it is a big business, a show business, wherein its participants are paid excessive and disproportionately high salaries for their entertainment skills; or otherwise said, their ability to sell merchandise. In modern times the almost unfettered creation and promotion of movies, videos, music and other forms of entertainment containing elements designed to promote sense pleasures and excitement, leads to mental agitation, but with little true satisfaction of the inner need of the heart. Thus, while the entertainments may cause excitation, they do not lead to abiding fulfillment and inner peace, but to more desires for more excitement in a never ending cycle which is impossible to fulfill. This process leads to mental confusion and stress which in turn lead to strife and conflict, internal frustration. Corresponding with the emergence of Western and Middle Eastern culture, with its negative lifestyle elements noted by the Ancient Egyptians, the world has also seen an increase in wars, violence against women, children, environmental destruction, enslavement and taking advantage of weaker human beings, drug abuse, crime, divorce, and overall personal dissatisfaction with life. In other words, the lack of restraints, in both individuals and in societies as a whole, has led to frustration with life, a kind of cultural depression and degradation, which has led to record numbers of people suffering from mental illnesses such as depression, schizophrenia, psychosis, as well as medical disorders of all kinds which were not present in ancient times due to self-control and the direction of life being guided by spiritual pursuits as opposed to egoistic pursuits. The Ancient Egyptian Mystery theater provides the means for allowing a human being to come into harmony with the spiritual reality (mental expansion and self-discovery) while frivolous entertainment serves to dull the intellectual capacity to discover and understand anything beyond the physical world and the physical sense pleasures of life (mental contraction and hardening of the ego). This inability to go beyond sense pleasures and experiences the world of human activity is what leads a person to mental stress, which in turn leads to mental illness and physical illness.

Therefore, understanding the message of Ancient Egyptian Theater is of paramount importance to human evolution. In Ancient Egypt, theater and music were used for spiritual education and to maintain harmony between the individual and the universe, the soul and the Divine. Thus, spiritual plays were acted by the priests and priestesses, initiates and sometimes by the relatives of the deceased (especially in the case of the Pert Em Heru Mysteries). The use of masks in theater did not originate in Greece. Their use already existed in Ancient Egypt. Unlike the Greek theater, which placed great importance on tragedy in life, masks, such as those presented in this volume were sometimes used by those playing the characters of the mystery in an effort to understand the mystery by becoming one with it, to embody the qualities of the divinity being portrayed and in so doing ultimately becoming one with the Divine. Also, the purpose was to promote the well being of others by directing one's mind and heart towards what is righteous, beautiful and good in the world and beyond. This was the motivation and source of strength which allowed Ancient Egyptian Culture, led by the priests and priestesses, to achieve a high degree of "civilization" and spiritual enlightenment.

Thus the earliest religious rituals in Egypt were performed as plays which were often part of festival periods. This tradition began with the early dynastic period and the Asarian Resurrection myth (5,000 B.C.E. or earlier), which surrounds the death and resurrection of the god Asar (Osiris). This was the main play that was performed universally in Kamit and then in Greece and

---

[152] BURDEN OF ASET by James Teackle Dennis 1910

Rome in later times after the Greeks came to Kamit to learn the arts, sciences, and spiritual philosophy upon which then established their civilization. In Ancient Egypt the story of Hetheru was revered so highly that an annual play and festivity was held in her honor which commemorated her saga, even down to the early Christian era. It was so popular that it was observed widely throughout the entire country of Egypt. Remnants of it and other Ancient Egyptian festivals, survive even today in the rituals of the Muslims who live in present day Egypt. Thus, theater emerged in ancient Africa and influenced Europe, and what would later develop into Greek and Christian theater. The practice of the mystery play was done for the purpose of worshipping the goddess, and also as a method of imparting some important mystical teachings. These have been presented at length in the gloss following the presentation of the play, which discusses the main themes of the myth of Hetheru. Therefore, anyone wishing to learn more about the teachings and practice of Ancient Egyptian philosophy can learn much from participating in the play and studying Ancient Egyptian Philosophy (Shetaut Neter-Smai Tawi-Ancient Egyptian or Kamitan Yoga).

CHAPTER 8: THE DEVIATION FROM THE ORIGINAL ANCIENT EGYPTIAN DOCTRINE

"The Greek tongue is a noise of words, a language of argument and confusion."

-Ancient Egyptian Proverb

In ancient times the Greeks were open about admitting the origins of their philosophy and mythology in Ancient Egypt. However, another important theme emerges from these same descriptions. That is the deviation from the teachings they originally learned from the Ancient Egyptians.

The Egyptian Priests are supreme in the science of the sky (astronomy). Mysterious and reluctant to communicate, they eventually let themselves be persuaded, after much soliciting, to impart some of their precepts; although they conceal the greater part. They revealed to the Greeks the secrets of the full year, **whom the latter ignored as with many other things...**" (Strabo 64 B.C.E.-25 A.C.E.)

An important theme emerges from the quote above. It states that even those early Greeks, who after much effort and determination, were allowed into the temples of Egypt to study the wisdom there they actually "ignored" some of the teachings that they were given. Any college student knows that when they attend a class the information given by the professor is not all of a teaching but that it is the essential part of the teaching which is given orally with the expectation that they may read the books and then be able to understand their contents. Therefore, if the information imparted in the classroom is ignored, the student does so at the risk of misunderstanding the teachings in their advanced stage, just as a mathematics student cannot hope to understand calculus unless they successfully attend the class on algebra which is itself preceded by arithmetic. Thus, a flaw emerges in the beginning of Greek Philosophy and it will have important implications later on in Greek history and subsequently in the development of western culture. For what modern western culture hails as the dawn of western culture and even presents as required reading in western colleges and universities, including epics such as the Iliad and the Odyssey or the philosophical writings of Plato, in reality have their origins in Ancient Egypt but it is clear, from the writings of the Greeks themselves that the teachings were not learned and followed in their entirety. Therefore, the true, deeper meaning of the Ancient Egyptian teachings was not fully transmitted by the Greek philosophers. So what modern western culture claims as the dawn of western culture and sometimes even as the dawn of culture itself as the emergence of Greek philosophy, is in reality only a partial reflection of Ancient Egyptian wisdom which was misunderstood. The problems of Western culture reveal its distance from the ideal of Ancient Egyptian culture and the incapacity of Western culture to govern itself and relate with other nations of the world with justice and in peace. The ancients never advocated sexism, racism, government by special interest groups veiled by the illusion of democratic votes, or capitalism.

In ancient times, the practice of the teachings deteriorated as it came down from the original Greek students of the Egyptians (Pythagoras, Plato, Thales, etc.) to their descendants. In later times their successors (those who uphold western culture) indulged in philosophy as a means for debating and thus became lost in the philosophy without understanding its meaning. One example of the divergence from the original teachings is evident from the Greek text below.

> 36. "The gods, with whose names they profess themselves unacquainted, the
> Greeks received, I believe, from the Pelasgi, except Neptune. Of him they got
> their knowledge from the Libyans, by whom he has been always honored,
> and who were anciently the only people that had a god of the name. **The Egyptians
> differ from the Greeks also in paying no divine honors to heroes.**"

Ancient Egyptian Religion pays homage to the philosophy as well as the Divinity and not to individuals because this aggrandizes the status of the human ego beyond its normal bounds. This leads a person to intensify their illusions of life and the frustrations and confusions which they lead to. The preference towards revering charismatic individuals and deifying them is in reality a primitive and base human tendency and this form of culture is intensified almost every time that a movie is produced or advertising is aired wherein heroism in the form of individuals saving others or leading others are promoted. This exaltation of the ego and the promotion of materialism along with its attending detrimental aspects for society are expressly denounced by the scriptures of Shetaut Neter (Ancient Egyptian Religion). See below:

"If your fields prosper, do not boast to your NEIGHBOR; there is great respect for the silent person. A person of character is a person of wealth."

"Do not multiply your speech overmuch."

"Do not behave with arrogance."

"Do not magnify your condition beyond what is fitting or increase your wealth, except with such things as are (justly) your own possessions."

-Ancient Egyptian Proverbs

Another example of the deviation from Ancient Egyptian standards is included below.

37. "Besides these which have been here mentioned, there are many other practices whereof I shall speak hereafter, **which the Greeks have borrowed from Egypt. The peculiarity, however, which they observe in their statues of Mercury they did not derive from the Egyptians**, but from the Pelasgi; from them the Athenians first adopted it, and afterwards it passed from the Athenians to the other Greeks..."

Upon comparison, while the basic aspects are alike many of the iconographies of the Greek gods and goddesses are different from that of the Ancient Egyptians, although some symbols and their mythical symbolic meanings have been retained. If a teaching is not maintained in an uncorrupted form and if it is not passed on by someone who truly understands the symbolism the meaning will be lost and the effectiveness of the teaching will also be diminished or even lost. Much of what people believe they understand about Greek mythology, therefore, is relegated to egoism unrelated to the deeper or original meaning. A person may feel cultured because they have read Plato's work but do they understand it and do they practice its wisdom in day to day life? In modern times most knowledge about the Ancient Greeks is used as a status symbol. People use it to feel that they are above others just as most Christians learn the Ten Commandments but then do not practice them or even remember them in the course of their lives.

In order for the philosophy of Ancient Egypt to be understood it cannot stay in the realm of philosophy because this is the realm of the mind. The mind, being imperfect, cannot gain a complete understanding of the sublime concepts of spiritual enlightenment presented in Shetaut Neter. The early Greek Philosophers came by this understanding through years of study, reflection and meditation upon them. It must be clearly understood that there are two forms of knowledge, indirect and direct. Indirect knowledge is intellectual knowledge, academic knowledge, and it is gained by studying the teachings and listening to lectures. This occurs in the realm of the mind. Direct knowledge is gained when a person transcends the mind entirely and discovers intuitional realization of the wisdom contained in the knowledge. For example, studying about Africa is not the same as traveling there. When you travel there you are transcending the studies and you are experiencing the object of the studies itself, yet the studies prepared you for the actual visit. In the same way the studies of the philosophy are to prepare you to discover a higher form of spiritual experience. If a person stays at the level of mental philosophizing then the knowledge leads to confusion and argument because philosophy cannot be used to prove philosophy absolutely. For this transcendence of philosophy into the realm of intuitional realization is needed. This is why an authentic teacher is necessary in philosophy just as a college student needs a professor to learn to be an engineer, lawyer, doctor, etc. This understanding is reflected in the following Ancient Egyptian proverbs included below.

"Keep this teaching from translation in order that such mighty Mysteries might not come to the Greeks and to the disdainful speech of Greece, with all its looseness and its surface beauty, taking all the strength out of the solemn and the strong - the energetic speech of Names."

"Unto those who come across these words, their composition will seem most simple and clear; but on the contrary, as this is unclear, and has the true meaning of its words concealed, it will be still unclear, when, afterwards, the Greeks will want to turn our tongue into their own - for this will be a very great distorting and obscuring of even what has heretofore been written. Turned into our own native tongue, the teachings keepeth clear the meaning of the words. For that its very quality of sound, the very power of Egyptian names, have in themselves the bringing into act of what is said."

Ancient Egyptian Architecture and Greek Architecture

(A)

(B)

Pictures A and B: Doric Columns from Egypt

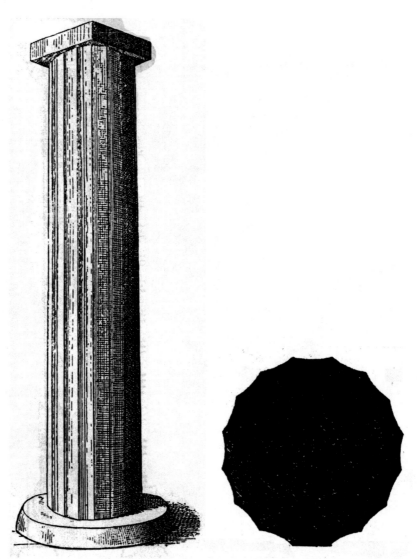

Above left: Proto-Doric column from Ancient Egypt (Beni Hassan-Middle Kingdom Period).
Above right: Horizontal section showing the grooves of the Doric style column.

Many people do not realize that Doric style columns existed in Ancient Egyptian temples long before they were used in ancient Greece. The Ancient Egyptian columns did not make use of a *cramp and socket* system to secure the drum sections as the Greeks did. Some archeologists (such as J. Garner Wilkinson) have suggested that this shows a lack of precision on the part of the Ancient Egyptians. However, they have discounted the fact that Greece is frequently troubled by earthquakes and the additional securing of the drums is necessary in Greece while this was not a problem in Egypt.

(C)

(D)

The Doric style of column architecture is one of the five types of column in early Greek classical architecture. Picture (A) shows the same columns already being used in Ancient Egyptian temples (Djozer-4,500 B.C.E.) and (B- Hatshepsut-Amun) 1,850 B.C.E. long before the Greek use. The Parthenon (C), or temple of the goddess Athena (aspect of the Ancient Egyptian goddess Neith), was erected in 447-432 B.C.E. by Pericles on the Acropolis in Athens and follows the Doric order.

The Ionic Column ((D) the Temple of Pallas Athena-Priene Turkey) style was more common on the coast of Asia Minor, as in the temples of Miletus, and the Corinthian was only used extensively after the masterpieces of the Athenian empire had been built.[153]

Slavery and Racism in the Ancient World

From the Tomb of Ramses III: The four branches of mankind, according to the Egyptians: A- Egyptian as seen by himself, B- Indo-European, C- Other Africans, D- Semites (Middle Easterners). (Discovered by Cheikh Anta Diop)

In more recent times some western Egyptologists have mistakenly or intentionally characterized images such as the one above as not just evidence of a recognition by the Ancient Egyptians of an ethnic difference between the Ancient Egyptians and Nubians but as a "racial" discrimination. In fact the Ancient Egyptians did recognize an ethnic difference or rather a cultural/geographical difference between themselves and the Nubians. There is no evidence of racial typing, discrimination or slavery such as that which has been known in India (under the Caste system) or in Europe and the United States of America (African Slave Trade). In order to mark this cultural/geographical they instituted a standardized but not rigid system of iconographical features for each group.

It should be understood that the modern concept of slavery such was and is imposed in countries such as the US, Europe, Middle East, Africa and Asia, was not present in Ancient Egypt. People were imprisoned for crimes or if they were captured by enemy armies but these were naturalized (incorporated into the population) and their children were full citizens. This means that the racist, ethnic or religious segregation, or animosity of modern times was not present.

We do not find statements that are denigrative, demonizing, debasing or racist in Ancient Egyptian texts. Statements such as those people are evil, monsters, devils, snakes, cowards, etc. These kinds of statements are meant to demonize and dehumanize other people and they lead the people who do the demonizing to not think of the other group as people at all and this makes it easier to hurt them, make war against them and set out to destroy them. These kinds of statements are used by modern day by some political leaders as they were used for example

---

[153] Random House Encyclopedia Copyright (C) 1983,1990 by Random House Inc.

190

against Africans during the slave trade Holocaust and the Jews during the Holocaust to excuse the subhuman treatment since they have now been characterized as "less than human."

The Ancient Egyptians were the first people to recognize that there is only one human race who, due to different climactic and regional exposure, changed to a point where there seemed to be different "types" of people. Differences were noted with respect to skin color, hair texture, customs, languages, and with respect to the essential nature (psychological and emotional makeup) due to the experiences each group had to face and overcome in order to survive.

The following passages from the most important Kamitan texts directly and succinctly contradict any notion of racism, sexism and racial discrimination. Therefore, the concept that the Ancient Egyptians were racist or biased towards other groups is unfounded and misleading.

> **"Thou makest the color of the skin of one race to be different from that of another, but however many may be the varieties of mankind, it is thou that makes them all to live."**
> —Ancient Egyptian Proverb from *The Hymns of Amun*

> **"Souls, Heru, son, are of the self-same nature, since they came from the same place where the Creator modeled them; nor male nor female are they. Sex is a thing of bodies not of Souls."**
> —Ancient Egyptian Proverb from *The teachings of Aset to Heru*

> **"Thou settest every person in his place. Thou providest their daily food, every man having the portion allotted to him; [thou] dost compute the duration of his life. Their tongues are different in speech, their characteristics (or forms), and likewise their skins (in color), giving distinguishing marks to the dwellers in foreign lands... Thou makest the life of all remote lands."**
> —Ancient Egyptian *Hymns to Aton* by Akhenaton

The last statement by the Sage/King Akhenaton is especially important in understanding the Kamitan view of humanity. God has <u>created all peoples</u>, all nations and countries and has appointed each person's country of residence, language and even their ethnicity and physical appearance or features. So there is a recognition that all people of Africa and including those of foreign lands, have the same Creator and owe their continued existence to the same Divine Being.

Slavery in Ancient Egypt, among the Hebrews, Greeks, and Muslims and Race Relations in Ancient TImes

The earliest record of the Hebrew people comes from an Ancient Egyptian Temple inscription (at Karnak) which describes them as a tribe of nomadic peoples in one of the subject territories of the Ancient Egyptian realm (Canaan). However, they are not referred to as slaves, but as one of the many groups which the Egyptians had conquered in the area. This misconception about the slavery of the Jews in Egypt has been promulgated throughout history based on the writings of the Bible. Yet there is no evidence that the Hebrews were ever slaves of the Ancient Egyptians, except in the writings of the Bible itself. Further, there is no evidence that the Hebrews were used as slave laborers to construct the Great Pyramids at Giza. In fact, their construction occurred long before the reputed birth date of Abraham, who is supposed to be the first Jew. While there is no factual evidence to support it, biblical scholars believe that Abraham may have lived around 2,100 B.C.E. According to the most conservative dating by modern Egyptologists, the pyramids were constructed in the Old Kingdom Period (2,575-2,134 B.C.E.). In any case, discoveries by Egyptologists in the late 20th century, such as burial tombs for the those who worked to build the Pyramids, have shown that the labor that went into the Ancient Egyptian projects came from <u>free</u> Ancient Egyptian laborers, artisans, builders and architects. The ancient Hebrews also used slaves, but they were required by religious law to free slaves of their own nationality at certain fixed times.[154]

In Ancient Egypt and Nubia slavery did exist, but not as a dominant institution[155] and not in the form that people have come to know in the period of Greek and Roman domination or in modern times (European Slave trade, Indian caste system). In Ancient Africa, people could find themselves in the position of slavery if defeated in war, or if they had committed some violation against society. In Greek classical times, the commercial North African state of Carthage as well as the Greek states and Rome all relied on slave labor in ship galleys and in agriculture, and acquired some of their slaves through trade with sub-Saharan Africa.

Ancient Athens (Greece), the supposed birthplace of "democracy" presents a sobering look at the nature of the prosperity of the Greeks in the classical period and the illusoriness of the democratic process that was developed there which led to the formation of the most powerful city-state of its time. Firstly, a very large part of the population were slaves, and the historical record shows that the Athenian state was based economically on a foundation of slavery. Two fifths (some researchers say the figure was closer to four fifths) of the population was composed of slaves. As in the United States of America and the European countries that partook in the African slavery, slave labor in ancient Greece produced most of the wealth of the country and this allowed the citizens of Athens to take time and have sufficient financial resources to pursue art and learning. When cities were conquered by the Greeks, their inhabitants were often sold as slaves. Kidnapping boys and men in "barbarian" (non-Greek) lands and even in other Greek states was also practiced by the Greeks.[156]

Furthermore, in Ancient Egypt women were full participants of the social order, having equal rights under the law. In ancient Athens and Rome, as in the more recent European governments, including the United States of America, up to the 20th century, women were not allowed to participate in any decisions of the state. Greek male citizens alone decided upon these decisions by majority vote. There was no participation by anyone else and no input or debate by anyone outside that group. So this cannot be considered a democracy or even its genesis just as the

---

[154] "Slavery," Microsoft (R) Encarta. Copyright (c) 1994 Microsoft Corporation. Copyright (c) 1994 Funk & Wagnall's Corporation.

[155] "Slavery in Africa," *Microsoft® Encarta® Africana.* ©1999 Microsoft Corporation. All rights reserved.

[156] Excerpted from *Compton's Interactive Encyclopedia.* Copyright (c) 1994, 1995 Compton's NewMedia, Inc. All Rights Reserved

governments of the present day which advertise themselves as democracies cannot be considered as such either for the same reasons.

A true democracy would have decentralized power, something which is antithetical to the very concept of capitalism, the basis of Western economic systems, and the power structure of governments, i.e. Presidents, Vice-presidents, Prime ministers, etc. would also be decentralized so that people could really control their lives. In western countries those who have the most wealth can control the legal system, who is elected in government and the social order. The standard here is not ethics or merit but greed and power.

While there are several examples of cohabitation, social interaction, trade, participating in religious rituals together and supporting each other's Temples, etc., between Ancient Egypt and Ancient Greece, one example of a statement attributed to Alexander the Great, denotes a tone which may be considered as a prototype for the modern concept of racism. Also, let us not forget that Alexander had by this time conquered India and had no doubt discovered and experienced the caste system that was at this time transforming from a system of social order to becoming a system of organized racism based on skin color. It is also possible to surmise from the tone of the letter that he despised the Nubians for having something that he did not, which also allowed them to elude his grasp. So in view of the overall relationship between Ancient Egypt and Greece, the isolated statement may be seen as a manifestation of jealousy and frustration and not necessarily racism. However, racism can be born out of such sentiments, especially when there is an ulterior political or economic motive, i.e. the desire to conquer someone (steal their possessions, enslave them, etc.). An early biographer of Alexander the Great records that the queen of Nubia responded to an inquisitive letter from him in the following manner:

> "Do not despise us for the color of our skin. In our souls we are brighter than the whitest of your people."[157]

It should be understood that the modern concept of slavery such as was imposed by countries such as the U.S.A., Europe, and continues to be imposed by countries in the Middle East and Asia, was not present in Ancient Egypt. People were imprisoned for crimes or made into slaves if they were captured by Egyptian armies, but the captured "slaves" were naturalized (incorporated into the population) and their children were made full citizens. This means that the racist, ethnic or religious segregation, or animosity of modern times that is designed to keep people segregated permanently and to create a concept of difference between them as if they were different species of animals was not present in Ancient Egypt.

In Ancient Egyptian texts we do not find statements that are designative, demonizing, debasing or racist. Statements such as "those people are evil," "monsters," "devils," "snakes," "cowards," "animals," etc. as can be found in the rhetoric of modern governments and people within those societies whose purpose is to engender hatred and fear among peoples of varied ethnicities or religious affiliations. These kinds of statements are meant to demonize and dehumanize other people in the minds of the masses of the population of the people who are doing the demonizing. The social environment created by the statements and their attendant

---

[157] Smithsonian Magazine issue June 1993

rituals, (burning of effigies, grotesque cartoons of the people being demonized, etc.) lead the people of the country that does the demonizing to not think of the other group as people at all. This makes it easier to hurt the people who are being demonized, make war against them, enslave them and set out to destroy them. These kinds of statements are still used by some modern day political leaders, much in the same manner that they were used against Africans during the African (slave trade) Holocaust, and the Jews during the World War II Holocaust, to excuse the subhuman treatment and exploitation of these peoples, having now characterized them as "less than human." This is a dangerous trend and habit that many continues adopt any time other cultures act in ways that are viewed as being in contradiction to one group's policies or political desires. It is wrong, and against the philosophy of righteousness of mystical religions. The Ancient Egyptian philosophy of righteousness (Maat) would call this "evil speech."

There are however, some irate, deploring statements expressing dissatisfaction or resentment, that can be found in Ancient Egyptian writings relating to certain foreigners ('wretched,' 'the disgust of Ra,' or 'the miserable enemy,' etc.). The context in which these words are used do not relate to dehumanizing others, but to understanding their aggressive, contrary, or desolate living conditions and consequently dull state of mind that leads to them to experience misery that causes them to go around attacking others (usually the Ancient Egyptians) due to anger, hatred, greed and lust. The Nubians are sometimes refered to as "wretched" as they are kinfolk to the Kamitans and vied with them in certain periods in history for rulership of all northeast Africa.

These statements and or behaviors are seen as vices in the Ancient Egyptian mind and are therefore repugnant to the Divine, and thus all the Kamitan divinities are said to, in one way or another, repudiate such behavior because it does not allow one to enter into the Divine presence which requires purity through virtuous living. What we see in Ancient Egyptian culture and philosophy, in such texts as the "Wisdom of Merikara," which explains the "Asiatic" mentality of violence versus the Kamitan mentality of peace, cannot be in any way compared with modern day examples of racism and its attendant deprecatory statements and actions. At the times when Ancient Egypt and Nubia were contending with each other for supremacy in the ancient world they were doing so as competing cultures who saw each other as human beings and not the way modern racist-supremacists who portray others as lower forms of life that are to be derided, exploited and enslaved either physically or economically. Just as family members have disputes, so too the Ancient Egyptians and Nubians contended.

The Kamitan Origins of Greek Culture and Religion

The picture below (mural found at Herculaneum – 1st century A.C.E.) clearly shows Greek and African practitioners of the mysteries of Isis (Egyptian Aset) conducting a ritual together. This pictorial evidence along with the writings of the Greeks themselves indicates that the Greeks had no conception of racism or racial supremacy even though they did acknowledge the ethnic differences which included skin color. The modern conceptualization of race in western culture is therefore a separate development in history, removed and disconnected from the Ancient Cultures.

Alexandria and the Degradation of The Ancient Culture

The Divine Chile Pointing to the Mouth

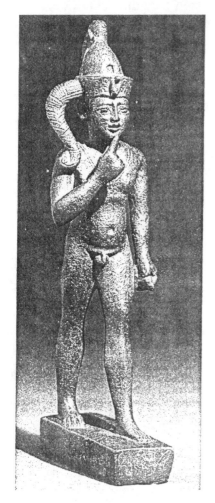
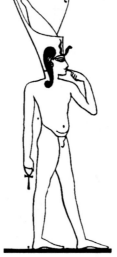

Above Center and far left: Harpocrates (Heru-papkhart, Heru the child)- as the Divine solar Child of Creation Photograph-British Museum. Far right: the Greek version of the Divine solar Child of Creation (Alexandria Museum – Alexandria, Egypt)

Heru pointing to the mouth is one of the oldest and most important motifs in Kamitan spirituality. It relates to the concept of name and the concept of expansion in consciousness. The Ancient Egyptian word Ren means "name." The name is an essential attribute to the personification of a being. You cannot exist without a name. Everything that comes into existence receives a name. The Divinity thereby brings existence into being by "calling" its' name, which produces a vibration in the ocean of time and space and polarizes undifferentiated matter and causes it to take form as a physical object.[158]

---

[158] For a detailed examination of the principles embodied in the neteru or cosmic forces of the company of gods and goddesses, the reader is referred to the books *Memphite Theology, Resurrecting Osiris* and *Anunian Theology* by Dr. Muata Ashby.

The God Anpu-Wepwawet is the Embalmer of Gods and Men

In the painting below (from a Pre-Greek-Roman influenced Ancient Egyptian Tomb) Anpu can be seen preparing the body of the Asar for the afterlife.

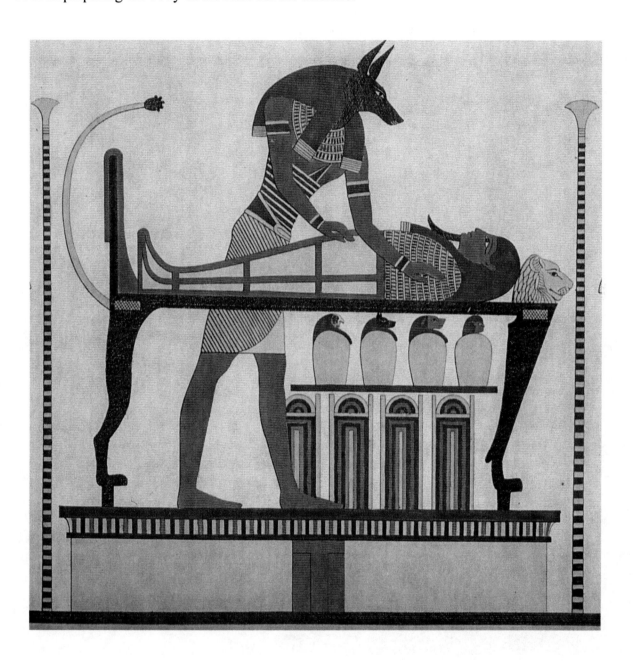

Relief from the Catacombs of Alexandria

In the scene below (Catacombs of Alexandria– Alexandria, Egypt) the god Anpu is embalming the Asar (Osiris), assisted by the god Heru (left) and Djehuti (right). This depiction appears to follow the ancient iconography fairly closely and indicates the adoption by the Greeks of much of the Ancient Egyptian ritual and religious imagery.

Painting from the catacombs of Alexandria

In the scene below (Catacombs of Alexandria– Alexandria, Egypt) the god Anpu is embalming the Asar (Osiris). The goddess Aset is at the far right. This depiction appears to follow the ancient tradition but there is one important deviation.

When the scene is examined closely (see below) it becomes clear that the person being embalmed is not a person but a horse; it is the horse of one of the Roman emperors. This application of the embalming scene is entirely unprecedented and therefore represents a departure from the original Ancient Egyptian-African teaching.

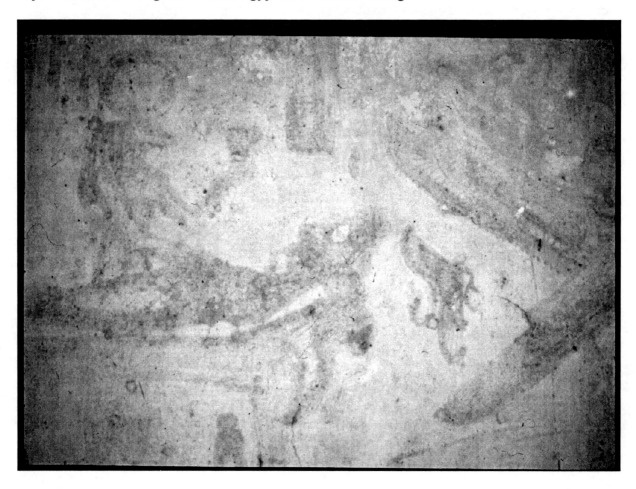

Deviations in Sexual Norms

Ancient Greek culture openly advocated the practice of sexual intercourse between minors with adult men. The Ancient Egyptian 42 Laws of Maat (basis of Ancient Egyptian culture) contained specific injunctions against adultery and homosexuality. Also, Greek culture placed heavy emphasis on sexuality as evinced from the large number of images of sexual intercourse that have survived. Further, unlike Ancient Egyptian culture, the Greek culture allowed sexual intercourse with animals, orgies[159] and advocated sodomy as well as sex between adult men and boys.[160] There is clear evidence of these practices in Greek art and writings. However, there is no evidence of sexual intercourse with animals, orgies, sodomy or pederasty practices in Ancient Egyptian culture prior to its being invaded and conquered by the Greeks and Romans. Also it is notable that the sexual imagery of Ancient Egypt is almost exclusively metaphorical, tantric[161] in nature and philosophical, related to the characters of Ancient Egyptian religion and their spiritual teachings, as opposed to representations of ordinary people engaging in sex for pleasure or entertainment as occurs in Greco-Roman culture.

Above: Greek illustration of sex with animals. (Agora excavations)

Above: Greek sex orgy - Pottery - Louvre Museum

---

[159] A secret rite in the cults of ancient Greek or Roman deities, typically involving frenzied singing, dancing, drinking, and sexual activity.(American Heritage Dictionary)

[160] *Love, Sex and Mariage in Ancient Greece*, by Nikolaos A. Vrissimtzis

[161] *Egyptian Tantra Yoga* by Muata Ashby

In Tantrism, sexual symbolism is used frequently because these are the most powerful images denoting the opposites of Creation and the urge to unify and become whole, for sexuality is the urge for unity and self-discovery albeit limited to physical intercourse by most people. If this force is understood, harnessed and sublimated it will lead to unity of the highest order that is unity with the Divine Self.

Figure 4: Above- the Kamitan God Geb and the Kamitan Goddess Nut separate after the sexual union that gave birth to the gods and goddesses and Creation. Below: three depictions of the god Asar in tantric union with Aset.

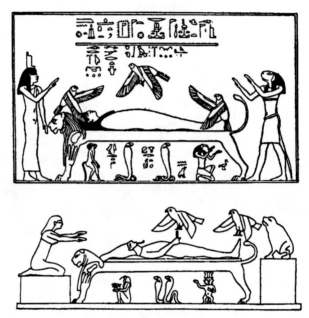

Figure 5: Above-The virgin birth of Heru (The resurrection of Asar - higher, Heru consciousness). Isis in the winged form hovers over the reconstructed penis of dead Asar. Note: Asar uses right hand.

Figure 6: Drawing found in an Ancient Egyptian Building of The Conception of Heru[162]

Isis (representing the physical body-creation) and the dead body of Asar (representing the spirit, that essence which vivifies matter) are shown in symbolic immaculate union (compare to the "Kali Position" on the following page) begetting Heru, symbolizing to the virgin birth which takes place at the birth of the spiritual life in every human: the birth of the soul (Ba) in a human is the birth of Heru.

-From a Stele at the British Museum 1372. 13th Dyn.

---

[162] *Sexual Life in Ancient Egypt* by Lise Manniche

CHAPTER 9: THE MISREPRESENTATION OF MODERN WESTERN CULTURE AS AN EVOLUTION OF ANCIENT GREEK AND ANCIENT EGYPTIAN CULTURE

The History of Fraternities and Sororities

Fraternities and Sororities, associations, mainly of college and university students in the United States, established to further the social, scholastic, and professional interests of the members. Because they are almost always designated by letters of the Greek alphabet, they are frequently called Greek-letter societies.

Social fraternities and sororities are organized primarily for social purposes. Membership in these associations is by invitation. Kappa Alpha Society, the oldest social fraternity in continuous existence, was founded in 1825; Alpha Delta Pi, the oldest sorority was established in 1851. Professional fraternities and sororities invite the membership of students and faculty involved in a specific professional or vocational field, for example, journalism, law, medicine, or music. One of the oldest professional societies is Phi Delta Phi, a legal fraternity founded in 1869.

Honor societies are composed mostly of students who achieve distinction in scholarship and meet with the standards of character and other requirements established by the societies. A number of honor societies are limited to those fulfilling high standards of scholarship in a single field of study, for example, engineering, or to those who display outstanding qualities of leadership. The oldest, largest, and most distinguished of such honor societies is Phi Beta Kappa, the oldest association of college students in the country, which was founded as a social fraternity in 1776 and reorganized as an honor society in 1883. The second oldest honor society is Tau Beta Phi, established in 1885 for students who achieve distinction in the study of engineering.[1]

Thus, it is clear to see that the modern concept of fraternities and sororities is based on the idea that the Greek philosophers were the first to pursue wisdom and excellence in academia. The following section will be a brief overview of Greek mythology and philosophy that will show how the earliest Greek philosophers received extensive training in Ancient Egypt.

In the context of the evidences presented in this small book it is amusing to travel and visit the universities around the world and to see students as they proudly associate themselves with fraternities and sororities, thinking that they are part of an ancient tradition of culture and advancement which began with the ancient Greeks, not realizing that they owed their culture to the Ancient Egyptians. This is important because while paying homage to the Greeks modern society is revering an incomplete story which has many gaps and which is deficient. The deviations from the Kamitan teachings have led western culture down a road of self-indulgence, egocentricity and greed that is destroying the resources of the world as well as the moral fabric of humanity.

After the early Christian Orthodox Church of Rome began closing mystery schools and temples, Greek culture and the rest of western culture developed a paradigm that diverged from that which was set by the Ancient Egyptians as well as their students the Greek philosophers and mystics. The mysteries were repudiated in favor of orthodox dogmas. The symbols of the mystery schools were co-opted while the mystical philosophy was outlawed. Therefore, the ill-conceived reverence for ancient Greek culture has led to the development of Masonic orders which also follow the teachings of mystical spirituality in name only and thus lead followers to a misunderstood notion of what culture and social norms should be. So while western governments have adopted Greek architecture and language for use in the legal system or the medical profession, the traditions of Ancient Egypt or even the Greek students of the Ancient Egyptians, are not followed or even studied. They are using the terms and icons of the ancient culture but do not follow its precepts. They are actually following their own ideal while dressing it up in the look and feel of ancient traditions. This is called "co-optation."

What the Kamitan Mysteries Are Not

When studying or following the culture, history and philosophy of ancient Africa it is necessary to distinguish between what has been presented in modern times as Kamitan culture through modern day organizations which purport to follow the Kamitan teachings and may even claim to be descendants of the original teachers and the actual history and teachings of Ancient Kamit. It is important to understand that the Egyptian Mysteries (Shetaut Neter) are not teachings originated by or controlled by organizations which in modern times refer to themselves as *fraternal orders, lodges, masons, freemasons, illuminati, Odd Fellows, Shriners, new world orders, Satanists, occultists,* or *psychics.* In fact, the organizations just mentioned have their origins in Western countries and not in Africa although the original Grand Temples of the Mystery teachings of Kamit influenced them.

Aspirants should be careful when examining the use of Kamitan symbols by modern organizations. For example, the use of the pyramid on the reverse of the seal of the United States would seem to mean that the founding fathers of the United States had the idea of invoking the principles of the Kamitan tradition in the founding of the new country (United States). It was explained by the occultist and reputed expert in Masonic lore, Manly Hall, that many of the U.S. founding fathers were masons and that they received assistance from masons in Europe to establish the United States for *"a peculiar and particular purpose known only to the initiated few."* Hall said that the seal was the signature of the masons and that the unfinished pyramid symbolizes the task that the government has to accomplish. The eagle is a representation of the phoenix, which is the ancient Greek reinterpretation of the Kamitan (ancient African) Benu bird (symbol of the god Ra and rebirth).

Another Kamitan symbol used to represent the United States is the Washington Monument, which is a copy of the Ancient Egyptian Obelisk. The Lincoln memorial and Mount Rushmore, two of the most important icons of the United States were admittedly (by their creators) inspired by the Temple of Rameses II at Abu Simbel.

So the question may be asked, if the founding fathers of the United States intended to use Kamitan representation which essentially means that they are wishing to adopt their meaning and symbolism, why then did the founding fathers allow a government to be set up that is in almost complete contradiction with Kamitan principles? Some of the more obvious contradictions are listed below.

Differences between Ancient Kamit and The United States (Western Culture)

Kamitan Culture	Western Culture
1. In Kamit the equality of men and women was a standard.	1. In the West women continue to be second class citizens. In the United States women were relegated to the position of servitude to men with no voting rights
2. Ancient Egypt did not engage in racism or racial slavery which dehumanizes people.	2. Modern western culture was founded on racism and racial slavery which dehumanizes people. In the United States slavery was an economic boon and the country would not have developed into a superpower without it.
3. In Ancient Egypt religion was an integral part of the government and when a separation occurred the degradation of culture and the downfall of society occurred.	3. Western Culture is based on a separation of government and church. In the United States there is a philosophy of separation of church and state which has led to corruption in government and business since the moral aspect of culture is actively detached from day to day life.
4. The initiatic principles of the pyramid related to a mystical spiritual awakening.	4. The pyramid is used as a symbol of prestige and not as an initiatic symbol. Mysticism is actively shunned in the United States and other western countries though practiced in rudimentary forms. The pyramid is seen as an architectural monument rather than a mystical symbol.
5. The obelisk is a tantric symbol relating to the union of the opposites in	5. The Washington monument is a symbol of the power of the government of the United States. The obelisk as a mystical tantric symbol in the United

Creation – using sexual symbolism it represents the penis of the god Geb. The union symbolizes a completeness of the soul with spirit. (Above and below).	States is unknown. It is a symbol of power in the United States and therefore it is a projection of the sexual energy of western culture into technology, economics and politics to control the world as opposed to a spiritual mystical goal.
6. The Temple of Abu Simbel contains monumental sculptures of the gods of Ancient Egypt and therefore is a spiritual monument.	6. In the United States Mount Rushmore is a monumental sculpture dedicated to presidents, political leaders.
7. The Benu bird is the symbol of spiritual awakening and resurrection.	7. The Eagle is a symbol of political and military power.

Above: Obelisk at Karnak Temple (Egypt)

While the Ancient Egyptian Obelisk is a monument to the God Geb and the Goddess Nut, the western obelisk is a monument to western culture.

Below: Washington Monument (replica of the Ancient Egyptian obelisk)

Below: Lincoln Memorial, using ancient Greek architecture. (1922 A.C.E.)

Below: Parthenon Temple of Athena in Greece. C. 447 and 432 B.C.E..

Below: Temple of Queen Hatshepsut of Ancient Egypt (c. 1503)

Abu Simbel of Ramases ll and Mt. Rushmore and Lincoln Memorial

Below: Lincoln Memorial, using Ancient Kamitan (Egyptian) architecture for the posture of Lincoln.

The Lincoln memorial and Mount Rushmore, two of the most important icons of the United States were admittedly inspired by the Massive Temple of Rameses II at Abu Simbel.

Below: Front of the Temple of Abu Simbel by Rameses, dedicated to Amun-Ra and Ptah (c. 1279 B.C.E.)

Mount Rushmore (United States of America)

Further, any of the organizations mentioned above that profess to be the originators, descendants or authentic custodians of the Kamitan Mysteries have much to prove since it is well established that those organizations have a recent origin by comparison. This is demonstrated easily by the records of modern encyclopedias which are themselves produced by the same culture (Western) in question. Also, the regulations against the admittance of women that are endemic in most of the organizations mentioned above are a modern convention instituted by the impetus within the male dominated Western culture to exclude females from the pursuit of spiritual enlightenment and social empowerment. These injunctions were foreign to the mystery systems of Ancient Africa in which women participate as equal partners and sometimes even in positions that would today be referred to as "Grand Masters," or "Pontifs."

The Order of the Hospital of St. John of Jerusalem, or the Knights of Malta, for instance, originated as a crusading order in 1070. The first Grand Lodge of Freemasonry, probably the best known of the secret orders, was founded in London in 1717.

Lodges and other secret orders are primarily men's organizations. Women may not join the Masons, Odd Fellows, or Shriners. There are, nevertheless, a number of women's societies associated with individual lodges. Perhaps the best known is the Order of the Eastern Star, founded in 1876. Its rituals are devised by Masons, and the organization is presided over by Masons. Men are allowed to join the Eastern Star.

The secret orders have a great deal of ritual at their meetings. It is used to initiate members and to promote fellowship and religious and moral values. One may not simply join a society such as the Masons but must be elected to membership. Once initiated, a member may advance within the society in a series of stages called degrees. In one rite of Freemasonry, there are 32 degrees. Some lodges have eased their rules.

The Sons of Norway, for instance, was founded in 1895 as a fraternal society to provide aid to members who were ill or who had lost someone through death. Like the secret orders, the Sons of Norway had membership requirements and secret rituals.

A similar society, the Aid Association for Lutherans, was founded by Germans at Appleton, Wis., in 1899. [1]

We have already presented evidence in this book of the existence of Kamitan civilization, culture, religion and philosophy at the very remote date of 10,000 B.C.E. Moreover, there was no system of "degrees" in ancient times. This again is a modern invention, as an attempt to qualify philosophical attainment. This concept is again a product of logical thinking as opposed to mystical thinking, a feature that characterizes western philosophy. How can one qualify what is beyond qualification? The realization of spiritual knowledge cannot be recorded on a ledger and quantified (computed) like a machine, nor can the quality of that knowledge be assessed except by the review of Spiritual Masters. The attainment of spiritual knowledge is evident in your way of living, as opposed to your acquisition of a grade, score or ranking. These methods may work in a classroom, an academic setting, where the student is expected to amass information, but true philosophy means understanding the principle behind the information. This is the difference between people who have intellectual knowledge and those who have wisdom. The priests and priestesses were accorded rankings in accordance with their years of service and their understanding of the wisdom they were initiated into. So they were ranked in positions of relative authority thereby.

"The many do confound philosophy with multifarious reasoning... by mixing it, by means of subtle expositions, with diverse sciences not easy to be grasped-such as arithmetic, and music, and geometry. But pure philosophy, which doth depend on Godly piety alone, should only so far occupy itself with other arts, that it may appreciate the working out in numbers of the fore-appointed stations of the stars when they return, and of the course of their procession...know how to appreciate the Earth's dimensions, qualities and quantities, the Water's depths, the strength of Fire, and the effect and nature of all these...give worship and give praise unto the Art and Mind of God."
-Ancient Egyptian Proverb

The Mysteries are not "hit and miss" or "trial and error" secret knowledge that has been lost and must be attained through experiments with drugs, unnatural medical operations, or any means that are outside nature. Actually the mysteries are scientific teachings to develop superhuman capacities that are only beyond the grasp of ordinary human beings because of their ignorance and immaturity. From the perspective of elevated personalities, the degraded human beings are so because they have, through ignorance and egoism, allowed themselves to believe that normal human existence means being weak, limited, ignorant and worldly. Actually, all human beings have the potential to discover their true nature which is supernormal, transcendental, enlightened, eternal and unlimited.

"Men and women are to become God-like through a life of virtue and the cultivation of the spirit through scientific knowledge, practice and bodily discipline."
-Ancient Egyptian Proverb

The idea of the mysteries as being secret knowledge for the privileged or elite of society is also a modern invention. In ancient times the mysteries were of two levels, that of the masses which was practiced outside the temple walls referred to as the "lower," i.e. the public rituals and festivals (in other words, religion), and that of the initiates which was considered the "higher" and practiced within the temple walls, i.e. the higher mystical philosophy, meditation, cultivation of the Life Force and transcendental consciousness, in other words, mysticism. The practices of the masses were led by the priests and priestesses so that they would be eventually led to initiation into the higher mysteries.

"Gods are immortal men, and men are mortal Gods."

"True knowledge comes from the upward path which leads to the eternal Fire; error, defeat and death result from following the lower path of worldly attachment."

-Ancient Egyptian Proverbs

The higher teachings were kept from the masses because the mystical wisdom must be introduced properly so as not to unbalance the aspirant. Otherwise we might expect exactly what we have in modern times, people running around espousing many teachings, but understanding little, making a mess of their lives and that of others, i.e. leading themselves and others astray, to ignorance and adversity. The world religions, while having a legitimate purpose, are the abode of many well meaning but ignorant people who would like to believe that they are the purveyors of "absolute truths" or the "word of God," but in fact are promoting a misconceived notion of what Creation and the Divine actually are. Thus, their followers cannot attain a true spiritually enlightened state. Instead, critical thinking and reflective reasoning are replaced with dogmatism and intolerance born of impatience, greed, and ignorance. This is partly why there are so many supposedly "religious" people who commit crimes in ordinary society, or engage in wars and promote a society of greed, lust, jealousy, envy and other maladies which are considered a "normal" part of human existence. There are many "faithful" who appear not to be involved with the negative behaviors of others, and yet by their acquiescence or omission of action in challenging the unrighteousness, are actually accomplices to the degradation of society and the moral character of humanity.

During the ninth dynasty, 3000 B.C.E., before the first Eurasian invasion of Egypt by the Hyksos, a Pharaoh passed on to his heir the following wisdom:

"Lo the miserable Asiatic, he is wretched because of the place he's in, short of water, bare of wood. Its paths are many and painful because of mountains. He does not dwell in one place. Food propels his legs. He fights since the time of Horus."

The Kamitan Masters knew that those people with agitated minds, minds that are not cultivated and balanced, due to miserable living conditions, are prone to reinterpret the teachings in an erroneous manner. They misunderstand the teaching because they are internally disordered and impure, bent on worldly enjoyments. The desire-filled mind has a way of twisting the teaching, remaking it in its own image. Then the teaching is changed from its original meaning and its effectiveness becomes weakened or neutralized altogether. Therefore, the Kamitan masters enjoined that such personalities should not be given any teaching.

"The Greek tongue is a noise of words, a language of argument and confusion."

"Keep this teaching from translation in order that such mighty Mysteries might not come to the Greeks and to the disdainful speech of Greece, with all its looseness and its surface beauty, taking all the strength out of the solemn and the strong - the energetic speech of Names."

The Kamitan Origins of Greek Culture and Religion

-Ancient Egyptian Proverbs

Authentic practitioners of the mysteries do not look to oracles for guidance, or to mother ships to carry them away from their troubles to discover higher planes of existence. Nor do they look to messianic leaders who will save them or to cults that ask them to give up their possessions or their very lives to satisfy a leader. This would be like an elephant searching for and relying upon an ant for his prosperity and spiritual enlightenment. Kamitan spirituality is the orderly guidance of individuals as well as society as a whole, to order, peace and spiritual enlightenment. Authentic mystics have elevated themselves without dependency on spaceships, special technologies or other worldly crutches. Further, they are not dependant on worldly enjoyments or pleasures and are therefore not bound by these fetters. They have purified themselves so as to at will traverse the entire universe and its infinite dimensions. They have discovered that all which is in the universe is an emanation from the Divine Self, who is the very essential nature that is their very own Self. Thus, with this realization, the Supreme Knowledge, they need no sustenance or supports from the world. They are supremely peaceful and content. They have attained what is worth, attaining and they look at the world and all its fancy as a child looks at a toy. In this manner, without resentment, fear, jealousy or greed, they can truly lead others not just to tolerance but to genuine understanding and universal love, which leads to real peace and prosperity among peoples.

"They who know self, good and pious are, and still while on earth, divine. They will not say much nor lend their ear too much. For those who spend time in arguing and hearing arguments, doth shadow fight. God is not to be obtained by speech or hearing."

-Ancient Egyptian Proverb

How to Know Who is an Authentic Teachers?

The authentic masters and true leaders of humanity are not the ones that subject others or enslave others or keep others ignorant purposely. If you want to know who is authentic just look at their productions. Do they promote life and that which supports health or that which leads to disease and death, conflict and unrest? Do they promote peace and purity or war and self-righteousness? If they promote the culture of pleasure seeking and promiscuity, again, this is specifically prohibited by the Kamitan scriptures. Do they promote harmony and the welfare of all? Do they have the good of humanity at heart or is it a social club with exclusive membership bent on world domination? Do they provide higher knowledge and guidance to understand and use it wisely or is it a hodgepodge of theories, conjectures and invented or synthesized pseudo-religious schemes? Do they promote elevation of the initiates or rituals and blind faith? Do they promote understanding and clarity or do they try to control by fear, intimidation and withholding information? Do they promote unity of the human family or discord, racism, sexism and economic disparity? Many people claim to follow the Kamitan Mysteries or other authentic Eastern or Western religious paths and yet they smoke, eat meat and engage in other acts that are specifically prohibited by the Kamitan scriptures as well as their own religious injunctions. Authentic personalities espouse teachings that promote the <u>natural order</u> (teachings and practices in harmony with nature – life, balance, peace, truth) and they FOLLOW these teachings in their own lives as well as an example to others.

"Morals are judged by deeds."

215

-Ancient Egyptian Proverb

The final point here to understand about what the Kamitan Mysteries are not is that they are not a creation of people from outside of Africa. Also, the modern day inhabitants of Egypt who are historically known to have come into the country from Asia Minor around the 6th to the 10th centuries A.C.E.[163] cannot be considered as descendants of the Ancient Egyptians. The Ancient Egyptians were Africans in every sense of the word. They looked like modern day Nubians, i.e. they were dark skinned people. The idea that they were from Asia Minor or were descendants of the Asiatics is a modern interpretation of fabricated evidence.[164] The Ancient Egyptians refer to themselves as being the descendants of the Nubians, people who in modern times still look like their ancestors whom the Ancient Egyptians represented on reliefs. Further, the early Greek explorers and historians who visited Ancient Egypt attested to the "Blackness" and "Africanness" of the Ancient Egyptians even describing them as being "black."

The specific statements by the Greek classical writers are:

Still the Egyptians said that they believed the Colchians to be descended from the army of Sesostris (Egyptian Pharaoh Senusert[2]). *My own conjectures were founded, first, on the fact that they are black-skinned and have woolly hair.*

-History of Herodotus (Greek historian 484 B.C.E.)

"Egyptians settled Ethiopia and Colchis."
-*Geography,* Strabo c. 64 B.C.E., (Greek historian and geographer)

"And upon his return to Greece, they gathered around and asked, "tell us about this great land of the Blacks called Ethiopia." And Herodotus said, "There are two great Ethiopian nations, one in Sind (India) and the other in Egypt."
-*Diodorus* (Greek historian 100 B.C.)

"From Ethiopia, he (Osiris)[3] passed through Arabia, bordering upon the Red Sea to as far as India, and the remotest inhabited coasts; he built likewise many cities in India, one of which he called Nysa, willing to have remembrance of that (Nysa) in Egypt where he was brought up. At this Nysa in India he planted Ivy, which continues to grow there, but nowhere else in India or around it. He left likewise many other marks of his being in those parts, by which the latter inhabitants are induced, and do affirm, that this God was born in India. He likewise addicted himself to the hunting of elephants, and took care to have statues of himself in every place, as lasting monuments of his expedition."
-*Diodorus* (Greek historian 100 B.C.)

"They also say that the Egyptians are colonists sent out by the Ethiopians, Osiris having been the leader of the colony. For, speaking generally, what is now Egypt, they maintain, was not land, but sea, when in the beginning the universe was being formed; afterwards, however, as the Nile during the times of its inundation carried down the mud from Ethiopia, land was gradually built up from the deposit...And the larger parts of the

[163] *African Origins of Civilization, Religion and Yoga* by Muata Ashby
[164] *Black Athena : The Afroasiatic Roots of Classical Civilization (The Fabrication of Ancient Greece 1785-1985,* by Martin Bernal, by Muata Ashby

customs of the Egyptians are, they hold, Ethiopian, the colonists still preserving their ancient manners. For instance, the belief that their kings are Gods, the very special attention which they pay to their burials, and many other matters of a similar nature, are Ethiopian practices, while the shapes of their statues and the forms of their letters are Ethiopian; for of the two kinds of writing which the Egyptians have, that which is known as popular (demotic) *is learned by everyone, while that which is called sacred* (hieratic), *is understood only by the priests of the Egyptians, who learnt it from their Fathers as one of the things which are not divulged, but among the Ethiopians, everyone uses these forms of letters. Furthermore, the orders of the priests, they maintain, have much the same position among both peoples; for all are clean who are engaged in the service of the gods, keeping themselves shaven, like the Ethiopian priests, and having the same dress and form of staff, which is shaped like a plough and is carried by their kings who wear high felt hats which end in a knob in the top and are circled by the serpents which they call asps; and this symbol appears to carry the thought that it will be the lot of those who shall dare to attack the king to encounter death-carrying stings. Many other things are told by them concerning their own antiquity and the colony which they sent out that became the Egyptians, but about this there is no special need of our writing anything."*

-Recorded by *Diodorus* (Greek historian 100 B.C.)

Lastly, the Ancient Egyptians depict themselves as looking like the Nubians and Ethiopians. Therefore, the idea that the Ancient Egyptians were something other than African people is fallacious at best, and misleading at worst. It is important to acknowledge the ethnicity of the Ancient Egyptians not only because it is a matter of upholding and living by truth and become free from the modern day misrepresentations, but because it is necessary to understand Kamitan Culture in order to understand Kamitan Philosophy (The Mysteries). Those who practice the mysteries while living a culture other than the Kamitan will have much difficulty in understanding it. People who dabble or otherwise play at practicing the Kamitan Mysteries do themselves and others a disservice. Actually, what they are doing is superimposing their own culture on the mystery teaching and transforming it to fit that culture. No wonder their result is a distorted vision of mystical philosophy that allows impiety and sensual pleasures to coexist with mysticism even though in reality they are as oil and water. In order to succeed in mysticism one must be free from impiety and sensual pleasures. This is called purity of heart, the goal of Maat Philosophy.

The earliest Ancient Egyptians originated in Nubia, migrated north and there later mixed with Asiatics and Indians to form what later became a multi-ethnic society which was centered on the Kamitan Mysteries. Much later, other societies drew from the Kamitan model and developed mystery schools elsewhere (Greece, Rome, Asia Minor, India, etc.). Thus, the Kamitan teachers are owed a great debt by all the cultures of the ancient world and their descendants. However this debt has not been paid, as the teaching has been distorted and forgotten by them while at the same time misappropriated and misrepresented. Therefore, it is extremely important to set the record right and dispel the ignorance related to the people who originated the first mysteries in history. In this manner, the modern righteous practitioners will have a honorable model to follow, and thereby the mysteries will be restored to their rightful place as the means to promote social harmony, and spiritual enlightenment.

CONCLUSION

From this brief overview of history, mythology and religious philosophy it has been shown that Ancient Egypt was the primary source which inspired the sages of ancient Greece to record and teach the ancient mystical philosophy which later became the basis of western culture. The study of Ancient Egypt and the deviations from the teachings given there are therefore of paramount importance in understanding modern culture as well as social and religious problems in modern times. This study will allow the aspirant or researcher to discern the original teaching and implement such in order to improve the practice of the teachings in their lives and in society at large. This will lead to the revitalization of the mysteries, the reestablishment of social order and justice as well as harmony between all peoples and between people and nature. This endeavor will also lead to the revival of African culture as the mysteries formed the basis of ancient African culture, which was the first civilization in human history. Today, Africa is in dire need of cultural uplifment. Philosophy and spirituality are cornerstones of culture and a righteous culture leads to peace, prosperity and spiritual enlightenment.

The following book series has been designed for the in depth study of Ancient Egyptian mythology and mystical philosophy. When the original teaching of Ancient Africa is redeemed, then it will truly be a positive and elevating movement of wisdom from Egypt to Greece.

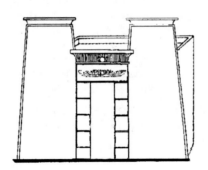 

INDEX

The Kamitan Origins of Greek Culture and Religion

OTHER BOOKS BY MUATA ASHBY

P.O.Box 570459
Miami, Florida, 33257
(305) 378-6253 Fax: (305) 378-6253

This book is part of a series on the study and practice of Ancient Egyptian Yoga and Mystical Spirituality based on the writings of Dr. Muata Abhaya Ashby. They are also part of the Egyptian Yoga Course provided by the Sema Institute of Yoga. Below you will find a listing of the other books in this series. For more information send for the Egyptian Yoga Book-Audio-Video Catalog or the Egyptian Yoga Course Catalog.

Now you can study the teachings of Egyptian and Indian Yoga wisdom and Spirituality with the Egyptian Yoga Mystical Spirituality Series. The Egyptian Yoga Series takes you through the Initiation process and lead you to understand the mysteries of the soul and the Divine and to attain the highest goal of life: ENLIGHTENMENT. The *Egyptian Yoga Series*, takes you on an in depth study of Ancient Egyptian mythology and their inner mystical meaning. Each Book is prepared for the serious student of the mystical sciences and provides a study of the teachings along with exercises, assignments and projects to make the teachings understood and effective in real life. The Series is part of the Egyptian Yoga course but may be purchased even if you are not taking the course. The series is ideal for study groups.

Prices subject to change.

Prices subject to change.

1. EGYPTIAN YOGA: THE PHILOSOPHY OF ENLIGHTENMENT An original, fully illustrated work, including hieroglyphs, detailing the meaning of the Egyptian mysteries, tantric yoga, psycho-spiritual and physical exercises. Egyptian Yoga is a guide to the practice of the highest spiritual philosophy which leads to absolute freedom from human misery and to immortality. It is well known by scholars that Egyptian philosophy is the basis of Western and Middle Eastern religious philosophies such as *Christianity, Islam, Judaism,* the *Kabala*, and Greek philosophy, but what about Indian philosophy, Yoga and Taoism? What were the original teachings? How can they be practiced today? What is the source of pain and suffering in the world and what is the solution? Discover the deepest mysteries of the mind and universe within and outside of your self. 8.5" X 11" ISBN: 1-884564-01-1 Soft $19.95

2. EGYPTIAN YOGA II: The Supreme Wisdom of Enlightenment by Dr. Muata Ashby ISBN 1-884564-39-9 $23.95 U.S. In this long awaited sequel to *Egyptian Yoga: The Philosophy of Enlightenment* you will take a fascinating and enlightening journey back in time and discover the teachings which constituted the epitome of Ancient Egyptian spiritual wisdom. What are the disciplines which lead to the fulfillment of all desires? Delve into the three states of consciousness (waking, dream and deep sleep) and the fourth state which transcends them all, Neberdjer, "The Absolute." These teachings of the city of Waset (Thebes) were the crowning achievement of the Sages of Ancient Egypt. They establish the standard mystical keys for understanding the profound mystical symbolism of the Triad of human consciousness.

3. THE KEMETIC DIET: GUIDE TO HEALTH, DIET AND FASTING Health issues have always been important to human beings since the beginning of time. The earliest records of history show that the art of healing was held in high esteem since the time of Ancient Egypt. In the early 20th century, medical doctors had almost attained the status of sainthood by the promotion of the idea that they alone were "scientists" while other healing modalities and traditional healers who did not follow the "scientific method' were nothing but superstitious, ignorant charlatans who at best would take the money of their clients and at worst kill them with the unscientific "snake oils" and "irrational theories". In the late 20th century, the failure of the modern medical establishment's ability to lead the general public to good health, promoted the move by many in society towards "alternative medicine". Alternative medicine disciplines are those healing modalities which do not adhere to the philosophy of allopathic medicine. Allopathic medicine is what medical doctors practice by an large. It is the theory that disease is caused by agencies outside the body such as bacteria, viruses or physical means which affect the body. These can therefore be treated by medicines and therapies The natural healing method began in the absence of extensive technologies with the idea that all the answers for health may be found in nature or rather, the deviation from nature. Therefore, the health of the body can be restored by correcting the aberration and thereby restoring balance. This is the area that will be covered in this volume. Allopathic techniques have their place in the art of healing. However, we should not forget that the body is a grand achievement of the spirit and built into it is the capacity to maintain itself and heal itself. Ashby, Muata ISBN: 1-884564-49-6 $28.95

4. INITIATION INTO EGYPTIAN YOGA Shedy: Spiritual discipline or program, to go deeply into the mysteries, to study the mystery teachings and literature profoundly, to penetrate the mysteries. You will learn about the mysteries of initiation into the teachings and practice of Yoga and how to become an Initiate of the mystical sciences. This insightful manual is the first in a series which introduces you to the goals of daily spiritual and yoga practices: Meditation, Diet, Words of Power and the ancient wisdom teachings. 8.5" X 11" ISBN 1-884564-02-X   Soft Cover $24.95 U.S.

5. *THE AFRICAN ORIGINS OF CIVILIZATION, MYSTICAL RELIGION AND YOGA PHILOSOPHY* HARD COVER EDITION ISBN: 1-884564-50-X $80.00 U.S.   81/2" X 11"   Part 1, Part 2, Part 3 in one volume 683 Pages Hard Cover First Edition Three volumes in one. Over the past several years I have been asked to put together in one volume the most important evidences showing the correlations and common teachings between Kamitan (Ancient Egyptian) culture and religion and that of India. The questions of the history of Ancient Egypt, and the latest archeological evidences showing civilization and culture in Ancient Egypt and its spread to other countries, has intrigued many scholars as well as mystics over the years. Also, the possibility that Ancient Egyptian Priests and Priestesses migrated to Greece, India and other countries to carry on the traditions of the Ancient Egyptian Mysteries, has been speculated over the years as well. In

chapter 1 of the book *Egyptian Yoga The Philosophy of Enlightenment,* 1995, I first introduced the deepest comparison between Ancient Egypt and India that had been brought forth up to that time. Now, in the year 2001 this new book, *THE AFRICAN ORIGINS OF CIVILIZATION, MYSTICAL RELIGION AND YOGA PHILOSOPHY,* more fully explores the motifs, symbols and philosophical correlations between Ancient Egyptian and Indian mysticism and clearly shows not only that Ancient Egypt and India were connected culturally but also spiritually. How does this knowledge help the spiritual aspirant? This discovery has great importance for the Yogis and mystics who follow the philosophy of Ancient Egypt and the mysticism of India. It means that India has a longer history and heritage than was previously understood. It shows that the mysteries of Ancient Egypt were essentially a yoga tradition which did not die but rather developed into the modern day systems of Yoga technology of India. It further shows that African culture developed Yoga Mysticism earlier than any other civilization in history. All of this expands our understanding of the unity of culture and the deep legacy of Yoga, which stretches into the distant past, beyond the Indus Valley civilization, the earliest known high culture in India as well as the Vedic tradition of Aryan culture. Therefore, Yoga culture and mysticism is the oldest known tradition of spiritual development and Indian mysticism is an extension of the Ancient Egyptian mysticism. By understanding the legacy which Ancient Egypt gave to India the mysticism of India is better understood and by comprehending the heritage of Indian Yoga, which is rooted in Ancient Egypt the Mysticism of Ancient Egypt is also better understood. This expanded understanding allows us to prove the underlying kinship of humanity, through the common symbols, motifs and philosophies which are not disparate and confusing teachings but in reality expressions of the same study of truth through metaphysics and mystical realization of Self. (HARD COVER)

6. AFRICAN ORIGINS BOOK 1 PART 1 African Origins of African Civilization, Religion, Yoga Mysticism and Ethics Philosophy-Soft Cover $24.95 ISBN: 1-884564-55-0

7. AFRICAN ORIGINS BOOK 2 PART 2 African Origins of Western Civilization, Religion and Philosophy(Soft) -Soft Cover $24.95 ISBN: 1-884564-56-9

8. EGYPT AND INDIA (African Origins Book 3 Part 3) African Origins of Eastern Civilization, Religion, Yoga Mysticism and Philosophy-Soft Cover $29.95 (Soft) ISBN: 1-884564-57-7

9. THE MYSTERIES OF ISIS: **The Ancient Egyptian Philosophy of Self-Realization** - There are several paths to discover the Divine and the mysteries of the higher Self. This volume details the mystery teachings of the goddess Aset (Isis) from Ancient Egypt- the path of wisdom. It includes the teachings of her temple and the disciplines that are enjoined for the initiates of the temple of Aset as they were given in ancient times. Also, this book includes the teachings of the main myths of Aset that lead a human being to spiritual enlightenment and immortality. Through the study of ancient myth and the illumination of initiatic understanding the idea of God is expanded from the mythological comprehension to the metaphysical. Then this metaphysical understanding is related to you, the student, so as to begin understanding your true divine nature. ISBN 1-884564-24-0 $22.99

10. EGYPTIAN PROVERBS: TEMT TCHAAS *Temt Tchaas* means: collection of ——Ancient Egyptian Proverbs How to live according to MAAT Philosophy. Beginning Meditation. All proverbs are indexed for easy searches. For the first time in one volume, ——Ancient Egyptian Proverbs, wisdom teachings and meditations, fully illustrated with hieroglyphic text and symbols. EGYPTIAN PROVERBS is a unique collection of knowledge and wisdom which you can put into practice today and transform your life. 5.5"x 8.5" $14.95 U.S   ISBN: 1-884564-00-3

11. THE PATH OF DIVINE LOVE The Process of Mystical Transformation and The Path of Divine Love This Volume focuses on the ancient wisdom teachings of "Neter Merri" –the Ancient Egyptian philosophy of Divine Love and how to use them in a scientific process for self-transformation. Love is one of the most powerful human emotions. It is also the source of Divine feeling that unifies God and the individual human being. When love is fragmented and diminished by egoism the Divine connection is lost. The Ancient tradition of Neter Merri leads human beings back to their Divine connection, allowing them to discover their innate glorious self that is actually Divine and immortal. This volume will detail the process of transformation from ordinary consciousness to cosmic consciousness through the integrated practice of the teachings and the path of Devotional Love toward the Divine. 5.5"x 8.5" ISBN 1-884564-11-9 $22.99

12.   INTRODUCTION TO MAAT PHILOSOPHY: Spiritual Enlightenment Through the Path of Virtue Known as Karma Yoga in India, the teachings of MAAT for living virtuously and with orderly wisdom are explained and the student is to begin practicing the precepts of Maat in daily life so as to promote the process of purification of the heart in preparation for the judgment of the soul. This judgment will be understood not as an event that will occur at the time of death but as an event that occurs continuously, at every moment in the life of the individual. The student will learn how to become allied with the forces of the Higher Self and to thereby begin cleansing the mind (heart) of impurities so as to attain a higher vision of reality. ISBN 1-884564-20-8 $22.99

13.   MEDITATION The Ancient Egyptian Path to Enlightenment   Many people do not know about the rich history of meditation practice in Ancient Egypt. This volume outlines the theory of meditation and presents the Ancient Egyptian Hieroglyphic text which give instruction as to the nature of the mind and its three modes of expression. It also presents the texts which give instruction on the practice of meditation for spiritual Enlightenment and unity with the Divine. This volume allows the reader to begin practicing meditation by explaining, in easy to understand terms, the simplest form of meditation and working up to the most advanced form which was practiced in ancient times and which is still practiced by yogis around the world in modern times. ISBN 1-884564-27-7 $24.99

14.   THE GLORIOUS LIGHT MEDITATION TECHNIQUE OF ANCIENT EGYPT ISBN: 1-884564-15-1 $14.95 (PB) New for the year 2000. This volume is based on the earliest known instruction in history given for the practice of formal meditation. Discovered by Dr. Muata Ashby, it is inscribed on the walls of the Tomb of Seti I in Thebes Egypt. This volume details the philosophy and practice of this unique system of meditation originated in Ancient Egypt and the earliest practice of meditation known in the world which occurred in the most advanced African Culture.

15.   THE SERPENT POWER: The Ancient Egyptian Mystical Wisdom of the Inner Life Force.   This Volume specifically deals with the latent life Force energy of the universe and in the human body, its control and sublimation. How to develop the Life Force energy of the subtle body. This Volume will introduce the esoteric wisdom of the science of how virtuous living acts in a subtle and mysterious way to cleanse the latent psychic energy conduits and vortices of the spiritual body. ISBN 1-884564-19-4 $22.95

16.   EGYPTIAN YOGA *The Postures of The Gods and Goddesses* Discover the physical postures and exercises practiced thousands of years ago in Ancient Egypt which are today known as Yoga exercises. This work is based on the pictures and teachings from the Creation story of Ra, The Asarian Resurrection Myth and the carvings and reliefs from various Temples in Ancient Egypt 8.5" X 11" ISBN 1-884564-10-0 Soft Cover $21.95   Exercise video $20

17.   EGYPTIAN TANTRA YOGA: The Art of Sex Sublimation and Universal Consciousness This Volume will expand on the male and female principles within the human body and in the universe and further detail the sublimation of sexual energy into spiritual energy. The student will study the deities Min and Hathor, Asar and Aset, Geb and Nut and discover the mystical implications for a practical spiritual discipline. This Volume will also focus on the Tantric aspects of Ancient Egyptian and Indian mysticism, the purpose of sex and the mystical teachings of sexual sublimation which lead to self-knowledge and Enlightenment. 5.5"x 8.5" ISBN 1-884564-03-8 $24.95

18.   ASARIAN RELIGION: RESURRECTING OSIRIS The path of Mystical Awakening and the Keys to Immortality NEW REVISED AND EXPANDED EDITION! The Ancient Sages created stories based on human and superhuman beings whose struggles, aspirations, needs and desires ultimately lead them to discover their true Self. The myth of Aset, Asar and Heru is no exception in this area. While there is no one source where the entire story may be found, pieces of it are inscribed in various ancient Temples walls, tombs, steles and papyri. For the first time available, the complete myth of Asar, Aset and Heru has been compiled from original Ancient Egyptian, Greek and Coptic Texts. This epic myth has been richly illustrated with reliefs from the Temple of Heru at Edfu, the Temple of Aset at Philae, the Temple of Asar at Abydos, the Temple of Hathor at Denderah and various papyri, inscriptions and reliefs.   Discover the

myth which inspired the teachings of the *Shetaut Neter* (Egyptian Mystery System - Egyptian Yoga) and the Egyptian Book of Coming Forth By Day. Also, discover the three levels of Ancient Egyptian Religion, how to understand the mysteries of the Duat or Astral World and how to discover the abode of the Supreme in the Amenta, *The Other World*   The ancient religion of Asar, Aset and Heru, if properly understood, contains all of the elements necessary to lead the sincere aspirant to attain immortality through inner self-discovery. This volume presents the entire myth and explores the main mystical themes and rituals associated with the myth for understating human existence, creation and the way to achieve spiritual emancipation - *Resurrection.* The Asarian myth is so powerful that it influenced and is still having an effect on the major world religions. Discover the origins and mystical meaning of the Christian Trinity, the Eucharist ritual and the ancient origin of the birthday of Jesus Christ. Soft Cover ISBN: 1-884564-27-5 $24.95

19. THE EGYPTIAN BOOK OF THE DEAD MYSTICISM OF THE PERT EM HERU $28.95   ISBN# 1-884564-28-3 Size: 8½" X 11" I Know myself, I know myself, I am One With God!–From the Pert Em Heru "The Ru Pert em Heru" or "Ancient Egyptian Book of The Dead," or "Book of Coming Forth By Day" as it is more popularly known, has fascinated the world since the successful translation of Ancient Egyptian hieroglyphic scripture over 150 years ago. The astonishing writings in it reveal that the Ancient Egyptians believed in life after death and in an ultimate destiny to discover the Divine. The elegance and aesthetic beauty of the hieroglyphic text itself has inspired many see it as an art form in and of itself. But is there more to it than that? Did the Ancient Egyptian wisdom contain more than just aphorisms and hopes of eternal life beyond death? In this volume Dr. Muata Ashby, the author of over 25 books on Ancient Egyptian Yoga Philosophy has produced a new translation of the original texts which uncovers a mystical teaching underlying the sayings and rituals instituted by the Ancient Egyptian Sages and Saints. "Once the philosophy of Ancient Egypt is understood as a mystical tradition instead of as a religion or primitive mythology, it reveals its secrets which if practiced today will lead anyone to discover the glory of spiritual self-discovery. The Pert em Heru is in every way comparable to the Indian Upanishads or the Tibetan Book of the Dead." Muata Abhaya Ashby

20. ANUNIAN THEOLOGY THE MYSTERIES OF RA The Philosophy of Anu and The Mystical Teachings of The Ancient Egyptian Creation Myth Discover the mystical teachings contained in the Creation Myth and the gods and goddesses who brought creation and human beings into existence. The Creation Myth holds the key to understanding the universe and for attaining spiritual Enlightenment. ISBN: 1-884564-38-0 40 pages $14.95

21. MYSTERIES OF MIND Mystical Psychology & Mental Health for Enlightenment and Immortality based on the Ancient Egyptian Philosophy of Menefer -Mysticism of Ptah, Egyptian Physics and Yoga Metaphysics and the Hidden properties of Matter.   This volume uncovers the mystical psychology of the Ancient Egyptian wisdom teachings centering on the philosophy of the Ancient Egyptian city of Menefer (Memphite Theology). How to understand the mind and how to control the senses and lead the mind to health, clarity and mystical self-discovery. This Volume will also go deeper into the philosophy of God as creation and will explore the concepts of modern science and how they correlate with ancient teachings. This Volume will lay the ground work for the understanding of the philosophy of universal consciousness and the initiatic/yogic insight into who or what is God? ISBN 1-884564-07-0 $22.95

22. THE GODDESS AND THE EGYPTIAN MYSTERIESTHE PATH OF THE GODDESS THE GODDESS PATH The Secret Forms of the Goddess and the Rituals of Resurrection The Supreme Being may be worshipped as father or as mother. *Ushet Rekhat* or *Mother Worship*, is the spiritual process of worshipping the Divine in the form of the Divine Goddess. It celebrates the most important forms of the Goddess including *Nathor, Maat, Aset, Arat, Amentet and Hathor* and explores their mystical meaning as well as the rising of *Sirius,* the star of Aset (Aset) and the new birth of Hor (Heru). The end of the year is a time of reckoning, reflection and engendering a new or renewed positive movement toward attaining spiritual Enlightenment. The Mother Worship devotional meditation ritual, performed on five days during the month of December and on New Year's Eve, is based on the Ushet Rekhit. During the ceremony, the cosmic forces, symbolized by Sirius - and the constellation of Orion ---, are harnessed through the understanding and devotional attitude of the participant. This propitiation draws the light of wisdom and health to all those who share in the ritual, leading to prosperity and wisdom. $14.95 ISBN 1-884564-18-6

23. *THE MYSTICAL JOURNEY FROM JESUS TO CHRIST* $24.95   ISBN# 1-884564-05-4 size: 8½" X 11" Discover the ancient Egyptian origins of Christianity before the Catholic Church and learn the mystical teachings given by Jesus to assist all humanity in becoming Christlike. Discover the secret meaning of the Gospels that were discovered in Egypt. Also discover how and why so many Christian churches came into being. Discover that the Bible still holds the keys to mystical realization even though its original writings were changed by the church. Discover how to practice the original teachings of Christianity which leads to the Kingdom of Heaven.

24. THE STORY OF ASAR, ASET AND HERU: An Ancient Egyptian Legend (For Children)   Now for the first time, the most ancient myth of Ancient Egypt comes alive for children. Inspired by the books *The Asarian Resurrection: The Ancient Egyptian Bible* and *The Mystical Teachings of The Asarian Resurrection, The Story of Asar, Aset and Heru* is an easy to understand and thrilling tale which inspired the children of Ancient Egypt to aspire to greatness and righteousness. If you and your child have enjoyed stories like *The Lion King* and *Star Wars you will love The Story of Asar, Aset and Heru.* Also, if you know the story of Jesus and Krishna you will discover than Ancient Egypt had a similar myth and that this myth carries important spiritual teachings for living a fruitful and fulfilling life. This book may be used along with *The Parents Guide To The Asarian Resurrection Myth: How to Teach Yourself and Your Child the Principles of Universal Mystical Religion.* The guide provides some background to the Asarian Resurrection myth and it also gives insight into the mystical teachings contained in it which you may introduce to your child. It is designed for parents who wish to grow spiritually with their children and it serves as an introduction for those who would like to study the Asarian Resurrection Myth in depth and to practice its teachings. 41 pages 8.5" X 11"   ISBN: 1-884564-31-3 $12.95

25. THE PARENTS GUIDE TO THE AUSARIAN RESURRECTION MYTH: How to Teach Yourself and Your Child the Principles of Universal Mystical Religion.   This insightful manual brings for the timeless wisdom of the ancient through the Ancient Egyptian myth of Asar, Aset and Heru and the mystical teachings contained in it for parents who want to guide their children to understand and practice the teachings of mystical spirituality. This manual may be used with the children's storybook *The Story of Asar, Aset and Heru* by Dr. Muata Abhaya Ashby. 5.5"x 8.5"   ISBN: 1-884564-30-5 $14.95

26. HEALING THE CRIMINAL HEART BOOK 1 Introduction to Maat Philosophy, Yoga and Spiritual Redemption Through the Path of Virtue   Who is a criminal? Is there such a thing as a criminal heart? What is the source of evil and sinfulness and is there any way to rise above it? Is there redemption for those who have committed sins, even the worst crimes?   Ancient Egyptian mystical psychology holds important answers to these questions. Over ten thousand years ago mystical psychologists, the Sages of Ancient Egypt, studied and charted the human mind and spirit and laid out a path which will lead to spiritual redemption, prosperity and Enlightenment.   This introductory volume brings forth the teachings of the Asarian Resurrection, the most important myth of Ancient Egypt, with relation to the faults of human existence: anger, hatred, greed, lust, animosity, discontent, ignorance, egoism jealousy, bitterness, and a myriad of psycho-spiritual ailments which keep a human being in a state of negativity and adversity. 5.5"x 8.5"   ISBN: 1-884564-17-8 $15.95

27. THEATER & DRAMA OF THE ANCIENT EGYPTIAN MYSTERIES: Featuring the Ancient Egyptian stage play-"The Enlightenment of Hathor' Based on an Ancient Egyptian Drama, The original Theater -Mysticism of the Temple of Hetheru $14.95 By Dr. Muata Ashby

28.   GUIDE TO PRINT ON DEMAND: SELF-PUBLISH FOR PROFIT, SPIRITUAL FULFILLMENT AND SERVICE TO HUMANITY Everyone asks us how we produced so many books in such a short time. Here are the secrets to writing and producing books that uplift humanity and how to get them printed for a fraction of the regular cost. Anyone can become an author even if they have limited funds. All that is necessary is the willingness to learn how the printing and book business work and the desire to follow the special instructions given here for preparing your manuscript format. Then you take your work directly to the non-traditional companies who can produce your books for less than the traditional book printer can. ISBN: 1-884564-40-2 $16.95 U. S.

29.   Egyptian Mysteries: Vol. 1, Shetaut Neter ISBN: 1-884564-41-0 $19.99 What are the Mysteries? For thousands of years the spiritual tradition of Ancient Egypt, *Shetaut Neter,* "The Egyptian Mysteries," "The Secret Teachings," have fascinated, tantalized and amazed the world. At one time exalted and recognized as the highest culture of the world, by Africans, Europeans, Asiatics, Hindus, Buddhists and other cultures of the ancient world, in time it was shunned by the emerging orthodox world religions. Its temples desecrated, its philosophy maligned, its tradition spurned, its philosophy dormant in the mystical *Medu Neter*, the mysterious hieroglyphic texts which hold the secret symbolic meaning that has scarcely been discerned up to now. What are the secrets of *Nehast* {spiritual awakening and emancipation, resurrection}. More than just a literal translation, this volume is for awakening to the secret code *Shetitu* of the teaching which was not deciphered by Egyptologists, nor could be understood by ordinary spiritualists. This book is a reinstatement of the original science made available for our times, to the reincarnated followers of Ancient Egyptian culture and the prospect of spiritual freedom to break the bonds of *Khemn*, "ignorance," and slavery to evil forces: *Såaa* .

30.   EGYPTIAN MYSTERIES VOL 2: Dictionary of Gods and Goddesses ISBN: 1-884564-23-2 $21.95 This book is about the mystery of neteru, the gods and goddesses of Ancient Egypt (Kamit, Kemet). Neteru means "Gods and Goddesses." But the Neterian teaching of Neteru represents more than the usual limited modern day concept of "divinities" or "spirits." The Neteru of Kamit are also metaphors, cosmic principles and vehicles for the enlightening teachings of Shetaut Neter (Ancient Egyptian-African Religion). Actually they are the elements for one of the most advanced systems of spirituality ever conceived in human history. Understanding the concept of neteru provides a firm basis for spiritual evolution and the pathway for viable culture, peace on earth and a healthy human society.   Why is it important to have gods and goddesses in our lives? In order for spiritual evolution to be possible, once a human being has accepted that there is existence after death and there is a transcendental being who exists beyond time and space knowledge, human beings need a connection to that which transcends the ordinary experience of human life in time and space and a means to understand the transcendental reality beyond the mundane reality.

31.   EGYPTIAN MYSTERIES VOL. 3 The Priests and Priestesses of Ancient Egypt ISBN: 1-884564-53-4 $22.95 This volume details the path of Neterian priesthood, the joys, challenges and rewards of advanced Neterian life, the teachings that allowed the priests and priestesses to manage the most long lived civilization in human history and how that path can be adopted today; for those who want to tread the path of the Clergy of Shetaut Neter.

32.   THE KING OF EGYPT: The Struggle of Good and Evil for Control of the World and The Human Soul ISBN 1-8840564-44-5 $18.95 This volume contains a novelized version of the Asarian Resurrection myth that is based on the actual scriptures presented in the Book Asarian Religion (old name –Resurrecting Osiris). This volume is prepared in the form of a screenplay and can be easily adapted to be used as a stage play. Spiritual seeking is a mythic journey that has many emotional highs and lows, ecstasies and depressions, victories and frustrations. This is the War of Life that is played out in the myth as the struggle of Heru and Set and those are mythic characters that represent the human Higher and Lower self. How to understand the war and emerge victorious in the journey o life? The ultimate victory and fulfillment can be experienced, which is not changeable or lost in time. The purpose of myth is to convey the wisdom of life through the story of divinities who show the way to overcome the challenges and foibles of life. In this volume the feelings and emotions of the characters of the myth have been highlighted to show the deeply rich texture of the Ancient Egyptian myth. This myth contains deep spiritual teachings and insights into the nature of self, of God and the mysteries of life and the means to discover the true meaning of life and thereby achieve the true purpose of life. To become victorious in the battle of life means to become the King (or Queen) of Egypt.Have you seen movies like The Lion King, Hamlet, The Odyssey, or The Little Buddha? These have been some of the most popular movies in modern times. The Sema Institute of Yoga is dedicated to researching and presenting the wisdom and culture of ancient Africa. The Script is designed to be produced as a motion picture but may be addapted for the theater as well. $19.95   copyright 1998 By Dr. Muata Ashby

33.   FROM EGYPT TO GREECE: The Kamitan Origins of Greek Culture and Religion ISBN: 1-884564-47-X $22.95 U.S. FROM EGYPT TO GREECE   This insightful manual is a quick reference to Ancient Egyptian

mythology and philosophy and its correlation to what later became known as Greek and Rome mythology and philosophy. It outlines the basic tenets of the mythologies and shoes the ancient origins of Greek culture in Ancient Egypt. This volume also acts as a resource for Colleges students who would like to set up fraternities and sororities based on the original Ancient Egyptian principles of Sheti and Maat philosophy. ISBN: 1-884564-47-X $22.95 U.S.

34.   THE FORTY TWO PRECEPTS OF MAAT, THE PHILOSOPHY OF RIGHTEOUS ACTION AND THE ANCIENT EGYPTIAN WISDOM TEXTS ADVANCED STUDIES This manual is designed for use with the 1998 Maat Philosophy Class conducted by Dr. Muata Ashby. This is a detailed study of Maat Philosophy. It contains a compilation of the 42 laws or precepts of Maat and the corresponding principles which they represent along with the teachings of the ancient Egyptian Sages relating to each. Maat philosophy was the basis of Ancient Egyptian society and government as well as the heart of Ancient Egyptian myth and spirituality. Maat is at once a goddess, a cosmic force and a living social doctrine, which promotes social harmony and thereby paves the way for spiritual evolution in all levels of society. ISBN: 1-884564-48-8 $16.95 U.S.

MUSIC BASED ON THE PRT M HRU AND OTHER KEMETIC TEXTS

Available on Compact Disc $14.99 and Audio Cassette $9.99

Adorations to the Goddess

Music for Worship of the Goddess

NEW Egyptian Yoga Music CD
by Sehu Maa
Ancient Egyptian Music CD
Instrumental Music played on reproductions of Ancient Egyptian Instruments– Ideal for
<u>meditation</u> and
reflection on the Divine and for the practice of spiritual programs and <u>Yoga exercise sessions.</u>

©1999 By Muata Ashby
CD $14.99 –

MERIT'S INSPIRATION
NEW Egyptian Yoga Music CD
by Sehu Maa
Ancient Egyptian Music CD
Instrumental Music played on
reproductions of Ancient Egyptian Instruments– Ideal for <u>meditation</u> and
reflection on the Divine and for the practice of spiritual programs and <u>Yoga exercise sessions.</u>
©1999 By
Muata Ashby

CD $14.99 –
UPC# 761527100429

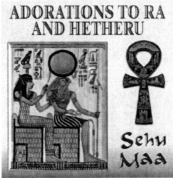

ANORATIONS TO RA AND HETHERU
NEW Egyptian Yoga Music CD
By Sehu Maa (Muata Ashby)
Based on the Words of Power of Ra and HetHeru
played on reproductions of Ancient Egyptian Instruments **Ancient Egyptian Instruments used: Voice, Clapping, Nefer Lute, Tar Drum, Sistrums, Cymbals** – The Chants, Devotions, Rhythms and Festive Songs Of the Neteru – Ideal for meditation, and devotional singing and dancing.

©1999 By Muata Ashby
CD $14.99 –
UPC# 761527100221

SONGS TO ASAR ASET AND HERU
NEW
Egyptian Yoga Music CD
By Sehu Maa
played on reproductions of Ancient Egyptian Instruments– The Chants, Devotions, Rhythms and Festive Songs Of the Neteru - Ideal for meditation, and devotional singing and dancing.
Based on the Words of Power of Asar (Asar), Aset (Aset) and Heru (Heru) Om Asar Aset Heru is the third in a series of musical explorations of the Kemetic (Ancient Egyptian) tradition of music. Its ideas are based on the Ancient Egyptian Religion of Asar, Aset and Heru and it is designed for listening, meditation and worship. ©1999 By Muata Ashby
CD $14.99 –
UPC# 761527100122

GLORIES OF THE DIVINE MOTHER
Based on the hieroglyphic text of the worship of Goddess Net.
The Glories of The Great Mother
©2000 Muata Ashby
CD $14.99 UPC# 761527101129`

Order Form

Telephone orders: Call Toll Free: 1(305) 378-6253. Have your AMEX, Optima, Visa or MasterCard ready.

    Fax orders: 1-(305) 378-6253   E-MAIL ADDRESS: Semayoga@aol.com

Postal Orders: Sema Institute of Yoga, P.O. Box 570459, Miami, Fl. 33257. USA.

Please send the following books and / or tapes.

ITEM

_____Cost $_____

_____Cost $_____

_____Cost $_____

_____Cost $_____

_____Cost $_____

Total $_____

Name:_____

Physical Address:_____

City:_____ State:_____ Zip:_____

Sales tax: Please add 6.5% for books shipped to Florida addresses

_____Shipping: $6.50 for first book and .50¢ for each additional

_____Shipping: Outside US $5.00 for first book and $3.00 for each additional

_____Payment:_____

_____Check -Include Driver License #:

    _____

_____Credit card: _____ Visa, _____ MasterCard, _____ Optima,

_____ AMEX.

Card number:_____

Name on card:_____ Exp. date:_____/_____

Copyright 1995-2005 Dr. R. Muata Abhaya Ashby
Sema Institute of Yoga
P.O.Box 570459, Miami, Florida, 33257
(305) 378-6253 Fax: (305) 378-6253

2469218